Talha MYTH (BANGLADE

15/06/2024

CLASSICS IN THEORY

General Editors

Brooke A. Holmes
Miriam Leonard
Tim Whitmarsh

CLASSICS IN THEORY

Classics in Theory explores the new directions for classical scholarship opened up by critical theory. Inherently interdisciplinary, the series creates a forum for the exchange of ideas between classics, anthropology, modern literature, philosophy, psychoanalysis, politics, and other related fields. Invigorating and agenda-setting volumes analyse the cross-fertilizations between theory and classical scholarship and set out a vision for future work on the productive intersections between the ancient world and contemporary thought.

Biopolitics and Ancient Thought

Edited by
Jussi Backman and Antonio Cimino

OXFORD
UNIVERSITY PRESS

Great Clarendon Street, Oxford, OX2 6DP,
United Kingdom

Oxford University Press is a department of the University of Oxford.
It furthers the University's objective of excellence in research, scholarship,
and education by publishing worldwide. Oxford is a registered trade mark of
Oxford University Press in the UK and in certain other countries

Published in the United States of America by Oxford University Press
198 Madison Avenue, New York, NY 10016, United States of America

British Library Cataloguing in Publication Data
Data available

Library of Congress Control Number: 2021950144

ISBN 978–0–19–284710–2

DOI: 10.1093/oso/9780192847102.001.0001

Printed and bound in the UK by
TJ Books Limited

Acknowledgments

For valuable and smooth collaboration, assistance, and guidance in the production of this volume, we are deeply thankful to the editors of the *Classics in Theory* series, Brooke A. Holmes, Miriam Leonard, and Tim Whitmarsh, and the editorial team at Oxford University Press, Dharuman Bheeman, Henry Clarke, Imogene Haslam, Charlotte Loveridge, and Kalpana Sagayanathan. For high-quality copyediting, we are indebted to Juliet Gardner. We were honored with detailed commentaries on the manuscript by two anonymous external readers who provided decisive insights for individual chapters and for the framing of the volume as a whole. For financial support, we thank the Academy of Finland (project *Creation, Genius, Innovation: Towards a Conceptual Genealogy of Western Creativity*, decision number 317276). For the content and substance of the volume, we are, of course, entirely in debt to our marvelous contributors and their patience, flexibility, and openness to feedback—and, above all, their incomparable scholarship. All those involved deserve a very particular mention for working under the trying circumstances of a global pandemic.

Contents

List of Contributors

Jussi Backman is Academy of Finland Research Fellow in philosophy at the University of Jyväskylä, Finland. His work has involved contemporary continental thought, ancient philosophy, political theory, and philosophy of religion; his ongoing project is related to the conceptual history of creation and creativity. Backman is the author of *Complicated Presence: Heidegger and the Postmetaphysical Unity of Being* (State University of New York Press, 2015), *Omaisuus ja elämä: Heidegger ja Aristoteles kreikkalaisen ontologian rajalla* (Eurooppalaisen filosofian seura, 2005), and nearly fifty academic articles and book chapters.

Sara Brill is Professor of Philosophy at Fairfield University, USA. She works on the psychology, politics, and ethics of Plato and Aristotle as well as broader questions of embodiment, life, and power as points of intersection between ancient Greek philosophy and literature and contemporary critical theory. She is the author of *Aristotle on the Concept of Shared Life* (Oxford University Press, 2020) and *Plato on the Limits of Human Life* (Indiana University Press, 2013), coeditor of *Antiquities beyond Humanism* (with Emanuela Bianchi and Brooke Holmes; Oxford University Press, 2019) and of the forthcoming *Routledge Handbook on Women and Ancient Greek Philosophy* (with Catherine McKeen), and has also published numerous articles on Plato, Aristotle, Greek tragedy, and the Hippocratic corpus.

Antonio Cimino is Assistant Professor in history of philosophy at the Center for the History of Philosophy and Science, Radboud University, Nijmegen, the Netherlands. His books include *Enactment, Politics, and Truth: Pauline Themes in Agamben, Badiou, and Heidegger* (Bloomsbury, 2018) and *Phänomenologie und Vollzug: Heideggers performative Philosophie des faktischen Lebens* (Klostermann, 2013). His main fields of research are the history of contemporary European thought and the reception of ancient philosophy in modern and contemporary thought.

Kathy L. Gaca is Associate Professor of Classics and Associate Member of the Divinity School at Vanderbilt University, USA. Her research explores aspects of sexual and social injustice against women and girls and the sustainability of civil society that are rooted in antiquity, remain problematic in the modern day, and need a clearer ethical and historical understanding. She is the author of *The Making of Fornication: Eros, Ethics, and Political Reform in Greek Philosophy and Early Christianity* (University of California Press, 2003; winner of the CAMWS 2006 Outstanding Publication Award) and numerous articles. She is currently finalizing her next book, *Rape and Enslave or Kill: Men, Women, and the Religion of Sexual Warfare and Colonialism from Antiquity to Modernity*.

Kalliopi Nikolopoulou teaches comparative literature at the University at Buffalo, focusing on the relationship between philosophy and tragedy, and between ancients and moderns. She is the author of *Tragically Speaking: On the Use and Abuse of Theory for Life* (University of Nebraska Press, 2012) as well as of numerous articles on tragedy, Homer, Plato, Aristotle, Romanticism, the modern lyric, and modern aesthetics. Currently, she is completing a manuscript on Aeschylus's cosmological view of justice.

Mika Ojakangas is Professor of Political Thought, Rhetoric and Culture at the Department of Social Sciences and Philosophy at the University of Jyväskylä, Finland. He is the author of seven books, including *On the Greek Origins of Biopolitics: A Reinterpretation of the History of Biopower* (Routledge, 2016) and *The Voice of Conscience: A Political Genealogy of Western Ethical Experience* (Bloomsbury, 2013). His research interests include history of political thought, political theory, and political theology.

Sergei Prozorov is Professor of Political Science at the Department of Social Sciences and Philosophy at the University of Jyväskylä, Finland. He is the author of nine books, including *Biopolitics after Truth* (2021), *Democratic Biopolitics* (2019), and *The Biopolitics of Stalinism* (2016), all published by Edinburgh University Press. He has published more than thirty articles in major international journals. His research interests include political philosophy, theories of democracy and totalitarianism, biopolitics, and governance. His current research develops a biopolitical approach to post-truth politics.

Ville Suuronen recently defended his doctoral dissertation *Thinking through the Twentieth Century with Carl Schmitt and Hannah Arendt: Essays on Politics, Law, and Technology* at the Centre of Excellence in Law, Identity, and the European Narratives, located at the University of Helsinki, Finland. Suuronen has published broadly on twentieth-century political theory in English, Italian, and Finnish, including peer-reviewed articles in *Political Theory, History of European Ideas, Contemporary Political Theory, New German Critique,* and *Alternatives: Global, Local, Political.*

Adriel M. Trott is Chair and Associate Professor of Philosophy at Wabash College. She has authored two books on Aristotle—*Aristotle on the Matter of Form: A Feminist Metaphysics of Generation* (Edinburgh University Press, 2019) and *Aristotle on the Nature of Community* (Cambridge University Press, 2014)—and numerous articles joining ancient resources to contemporary social and political concerns, specifically around the concepts of nature, gender, and politics, including on contemporary figures such as Hannah Arendt, Luce Irigaray, Jacques Rancière, and Alain Badiou. She is the editor of the Women in Philosophy series at the APA Blog.

Abbreviations of Classical Works

The abbreviations for classical authors and works used in this volume are the ones found in *The Oxford Classical Dictionary*, 4th ed., edited by Simon Hornblower, Antony Spawforth, and Esther Eidinow (Oxford: Oxford University Press, 2012), xxvi–liii, https://doi.org/10.1093/acref/9780199545568.001.0001.

Aelian	(Claudius Aelianus)
VH	*Varia historia*
Andocides	
Andoc.	Andocides
Appian	
Mith.	*The Mithridatic Wars* (*Mithridateios*)
Aristotle	
Cael.	*On the Heavens* (*De caelo*)
De an.	*On the Soul* (*De anima*)
Eth. Eud.	*Eudemian Ethics* (*Ethica Eudemia*)
Eth. Nic.	*Nicomachean Ethics* (*Ethica Nicomachea*)
Hist. an.	*History of Animals* (*Historia animalium*)
Metaph.	*Metaphysics* (*Metaphysica*)
Pol.	*Politics* (*Politica*)
Athenaeus	
Ath.	Athenaeus
Caesar	
BGall.	*Gallic War* (*Bellum Gallicum*)
Diels-Kranz	
DK	Diels, Hermann, and Walther Kranz, eds. 1951–2. *Die Fragmente der Vorsokratiker: Griechisch und deutsch*. 3 vols. 6th edition. Berlin: Weidmann.
Dio Chrysostom	
Dio Chrys. *Or.*	Dio Chrysostom, *Discourses* (*Orationes*)
Diodorus Siculus	
Diod. Sic.	Diodorus Siculus
Euripides	
Tro.	*Trojan Women* (*Troades*)
Fragmente der griechischen Historiker	
FGrH	Jacoby, Felix, ed. 1923–. *Die Fragmente der griechischen Historiker*. Berlin: Weidmann; Leiden: Brill.
Herodotus	
Hdt.	Herodotus

Homer
Il. Iliad (*Ilias*)
Isaeus
Isae. Isaeus
Nicolaus of Damascus
Nic. Dam. Nicolaus Damascenus
Oxyrhynchus Papyri
POxy. Oxyrhynchus Papyri
Pausanias
Paus. Pausanias
Plato
Grg. Gorgias
Leg. Laws (*Leges*)
Plt. Statesman (*Politicus*)
Prt. Protagoras
Resp. Republic (*Respublica*)
Soph. Sophist (*Sophista*)
Tht. Theaetetus
Ti. Timaeus
Plutarch
Alex. Life of Alexander
De mul. vir. On the Virtues of Women (*De mulierum virtutibus*)
Mor. Moralia
Tim. Life of Timoleon
Vit. Parallel Lives (*Vitae parallelae*)
Polybius
Polyb. Polybius
Sextus Empiricus
Math. Against the Mathematicians (*Adversus mathematicos*)
Sophocles
Ant. Antigone
OT Oedipus Tyrannus
Stoicorum veterum fragmenta
SVF Arnim, Hans von, ed. 1903–5. *Stoicorum veterum fragmenta*. 3 vols. Leipzig: Teubner.
Tacitus
Hist. Histories (*Historiae*)
Theopompus
Theopomp. Theopompus Historicus
Thucydides
Thuc. Thucydides
Xenophon
An. Anabasis
[Ath. pol.] [Constitution of the Athenians (*Respublica Atheniensium*)]
Cyr. Cyropaedia
Mem. Memorabilia

Introduction

Jussi Backman and Antonio Cimino

Biopolitics has in recent decades become a seminal concept—a theoretical "buzzword," as Thomas Lemke (2011, 1) puts it—within philosophy, the social sciences, and the humanities, and in several other disciplines and interdisciplinary approaches belonging to the wider human sciences. In a recent anthology, Jeffrey R. Di Leo and Peter Hitchcock (2020b, 1) characterize biopolitics as "one of the most influential critical paradigms in the human sciences and the humanities today." There has been talk of a "biopolitical turn" in the social sciences and humanities (see, for example, Minca 2015), and Carlos Gómez Camarena (2014, 164) goes so far as to claim that, "[a]t the beginning of the twenty-first century, the concept of biopolitics has almost totally monopolized philosophical debates about politics, thus marking a new stage in political philosophy."[1]

While the concept of biopolitics has had such a notable influence, its success goes hand in hand with a certain amount of inherent ambiguity on both the conceptual and the terminological level; the more the term has gained in popularity, the more denotations and connotations it has accrued. "Biopolitics" as a term was introduced by political theorists of the early twentieth century as a designation for political theories, metaphors, discourses, or practices informed by biology and vitalism; it was first coined by the Swedish political scientist Rudolf Kjellén (1905, 24; see also 1916; 1920, 92–4) in the context of his study of the state as a "form of life."[2] The term was given its most influential contemporary definition in the 1970s by Michel Foucault, who uses it in his Collège de France lecture courses (Foucault 1997,

---

[1] For the most important general scholarly volumes on the topic of biopolitics, see Fehér and Heller 1994; Heller and Puntscher Riekmann 1996; Van den Daele 2005; Rose 2007; Lemke 2007, 2011; Clough and Willse 2011; Campbell and Sitze 2013; Lemm and Vatter 2014; Prozorov and Rentea 2017; Mills 2018; Di Leo and Hitchcock 2020a.

[2] Organistic and vitalistic approaches to politics, similar to that of Kjellén, were also developed by such German theorists as Karl Binding (1920), Eberhard Dennert (1920), and Jakob von Uexküll (1920). An early example of a use of the term in a sense similar to the later Foucauldian approach is a 1911 diatribe by G. W. Harris in the British weekly review *The New Age*, calling for "bio-politics" in the sense of a policy taking into consideration the quantity and the quality of the population. On the conceptual history of biopolitics, see Esposito 2008, 16–24.

Jussi Backman and Antonio Cimino, *Introduction* In: *Biopolitics and Ancient Thought*. Edited by: Jussi Backman and Antonio Cimino, Oxford University Press. © Oxford University Press 2022. DOI: 10.1093/oso/9780192847102.003.0001

213–35; 2003, 239–64; 2004a; 2004b, 3–118; 2008; 2009, 1–114) and in the first volume of *The History of Sexuality* (Foucault 1976, 177–91; 1978, 135–45) to describe the discourses and practices through which human beings in modern societies are increasingly categorized and controlled as members of a species, as biological populations.[3] Biopolitics, for Foucault, is based on the exercise of *biopower*, defined as the "set of mechanisms through which the basic biological features of the human species became the object of a political strategy" (Foucault 2004b, 3; 2009, 1)—that is, governmental and administrative technologies and interventions aimed at sexuality, reproduction, heredity, health and disease, hygiene, natality, and mortality, as well as (in certain notorious cases) eugenicist considerations. For Foucault himself, "biopolitics" and "biopower" are highly versatile and polyvalent concepts, initially applied especially to the racist and racialist ideas and strategies inherent in Nazism as well as modern socialism (Foucault 1997, 213–35; 2003, 239–64), but later also situated within the general framework of liberalism (Foucault 2004a, 24n; 2008, 22n).

The term and the topic have since been expanded and developed by theorists such as Giorgio Agamben (1995, 1998), Michael Hardt and Antonio Negri (2000, 2004, 2009), and Roberto Esposito (1998, 2002, 2004, 2008, 2010, 2011). In these subsequent redeployments of the Foucauldian theory of biopolitics and its predecessors, new approaches to the concept and redefinitions proliferate. Agamben has reframed the concepts of biopower and biopolitics by introducing the notion of "bare life," which has resulted in a controversial account of Europe's political history. Hardt and Negri have instead proposed a terminological distinction between biopower and biopolitics, defining the former as "power over life" and the latter as "the power of life to resist and determine an alternative production of subjectivity" (Hardt and Negri 2009, 57). Yet another approach has been put forward by Esposito, who discusses the possibility and necessity of an "affirmative biopolitics" (2004, 211–5; 2008, 191–4; on this, see also chapter 8 by Sergei Prozorov in this volume). In view of this semantic diversity of "biopolitics" and "biopower," this volume takes these concepts and terms as inherently problematic starting points. One of its central aims is to map out and explore their multiple meanings and facets with a particular focus on ancient thought and its modern reappropriations.

The terminological and conceptual ambiguities of biopolitics go hand in hand with different—at times, widely diverging and even opposing—narratives about its history. According to Foucault's genealogy, biopolitics is

---

[3] Foucault's earliest attested use of the term "biopolitics" is in his 1974 lectures on "social medicine" in Rio de Janeiro (Foucault 2000, 137; 2001, 210).

primarily a modern phenomenon that gains predominance as the sovereign power of the early modern rulers over life and death evolves, starting in the seventeenth century, into a disciplinary "anatomo-politics"—the administration of the individual bodies of subjects—and a "bio-politics of the population" (Foucault 1976, 177–91; 1978, 135–45). The rise of biopolitics coincides with the emergence, since the late eighteenth century, of the new biological and social sciences and the development of industrial capitalism, and is centered around the modern concept of population; Foucault mentions Jean-Baptiste Moheau (1745–94), author of one of the earliest treatises on demography (Moheau 1778), as the "first great theorist" of biopolitics (Foucault 2004b, 23–4; 2009, 22). We should note that, as Di Leo and Hitchcock (2020b, 1) point out, "biopolitics in various theoretical forms precedes its name" in the sense that several thinkers prior to Foucault provide strikingly similar accounts of the origins of modern political thought. Foucault's analysis resonates particularly well with Hannah Arendt's account of the transformation of the human being in industrial society into a "laboring animal" (*animal laborans*) for whom biological life and its subjective quality constitute the "greatest good" (see Arendt 1998, 305–25). Arendt, without using the term itself, outlines a version of the history of biopower emphasizing the modernity of the phenomenon but also its ancient roots (on this, see chapters 6 and 7 by Jussi Backman and Ville Suuronen in this volume). Following Foucault and Arendt, Agamben has insisted on the link between modernity and biopolitics, but at the same time, he has tried to locate the ancient origins of biopower and biopolitics; accordingly, his genealogy of biopolitical phenomena has often resulted in, or is based on, thought-provoking interpretations of ancient philosophical, juridical, medical, and literary sources. However, as pointed out especially in chapters 4 and 9 by Kalliopi Nikolopoulou and Antonio Cimino, a number of Agamben's relevant concepts—notably his notion of "bare life"—have not gone uncontested.

One may thus wonder whether, and to what extent, the thesis of the exclusively modern origin of biopolitics is tenable. Recent studies have indeed started questioning that thesis.[4] Mika Ojakangas (2016) has argued that biopolitical discourses on population control, eugenics, and public health and hygiene are, in fact, a fundamental keystone of Platonic and Aristotelian theories of politics and the art of government. While Foucault traces the roots of biopolitical "governmentality" to the Christian idea of the pastoral power of

---

[4] For previous studies on the topic of biopolitics and antiquity, see Arnhart 1988; Forti 2006; Milbank 2008; Finlayson 2010; Lemke 2010; Frías Urrea 2013; Ojakangas 2013, 2016, 2017; Almeida 2014; Jobe 2015; Skornicki 2015; Hawkins 2018.

the church, Ojakangas, by contrast, sees Christianity as interrupting the bio-political theories and practices of classical antiquity, which were then gradu-ally resumed by secularized modern government. In chapter 2 of this volume, Ojakangas develops this thesis by way of a reading of Plato. Other, modified senses and contexts in which biopolitics can be attributed to antiquity are suggested in chapters 1 and 3 by Sara Brill and Kathy L. Gaca. Critical eval-uations of different aspects of such an attribution can be found in chapters 4, 5, and 6 by Kalliopi Nikolopoulou, Adriel M. Trott, and Jussi Backman.

By studying the complex relationship between classical antiquity and bio-politics from different perspectives, this volume seeks to introduce new lines of research that aim at problematizing and rearticulating the concepts, terms, and histories of biopolitics and biopower by elaborating the extent and sense of their applicability to the ancient context. The contributions comprised in the volume explore and utilize these concepts as tools for explicating the dif-ferences and continuities between antiquity and modernity and for narrating Western intellectual and political history in general. Without committing itself to any particular thesis or approach, the volume evaluates both the rel-evance of ancient thought for the contemporary understanding of "biopoli-tics" and the relevance of biopolitical theories for the study of ancient thought. Biopolitics may turn out to provide a novel reference point for articulating the relationship between modernity and antiquity from various possible perspectives. It can be used for looking, in the famous words of Bernard of Chartres, at the moderns as dwarves standing on the shoulders of the ancient giants: even in the field of biopolitical theory, it is perhaps only through the support of the monumental intellectual achievements of antiq-uity that we are able to see (marginally) farther.[5] On the other hand, biopoli-tics can offer yet another vantage point for regarding, with J. G. Herder (1796, 5–6), classical antiquity as the irretrievably lost youth of Western cul-ture, a state of (pre-biopolitical) conceptual and theoretical innocence to which there is no return; for seeking, like the early Martin Heidegger (1975, 157; 1988, 111), to "understand the Greeks better than they understood themselves"—that is, to articulate their thinking with the help of concepts and notions that were unavailable to them (such as biopolitics); or for attempting, with Foucault, to construct a historical genealogy of modernity, a "critical ontology of ourselves" (Foucault 1984, 47; 2001, 1396), in which antiquity is used as a narrative point of reference and comparison, as a "mir-ror" of modernity differentiated from and contrasted with it with the help of concepts like biopolitics and governmentality.

---

[5] Quoted by John of Salisbury ca. 1159 in *Metalogicon* 3.4.

The volume consists of nine contributed chapters by leading scholars in the field. The contributions in part I ("Biopolitics in Ancient Thought") study different senses in which instances of biopolitical discourse can be detected in ancient thought. Chapter 1 by Sara Brill, "Biopolitics and the 'Boundless People': An Iliadic Model," discusses the extent to which the concept of "population," which plays a defining role in Foucault's narrative of biopower, is present in ancient Greek thought. On the one hand, Brill argues that the notion of population as such cannot be unequivocally identified in antiquity. On the other, excavating the conception of political power and human collective action that undergirds the Aristotelian understanding of the formation of a political multitude, Brill traces its roots to the ways in which the Homeric *Iliad* uses animal imagery to figure human sociality, politics, and collective action.

In chapter 2, "Plato and the Biopolitical Purge of the City-State," Mika Ojakangas questions Agamben's interpretation of the nonviolent character of Plato's understanding of the law and argues that from Plato's point of view, violence is an integral part of political management and beneficial to the well-being of the city-state. In accordance with the theses developed in his seminal book on the history of biopower, Ojakangas maintains that this violence is essentially biopolitical in nature, and puts great emphasis on the intersection of politics and medicine in Plato. In so doing, he also shows the extent to which Plato's "biopolitical state racism" aims at both enhancing the physical and mental well-being of the population and eliminating those who are incurable.

Chapter 3, "Sovereign Power and Social Justice: Plato and Aristotle on Justice and Its Biopolitical Basis in Heterosexual Copulation, Procreation, and Upbringing" by Kathy L. Gaca, discusses the biopolitical substance of Plato's and Aristotle's views on the significance of sexual and procreative customs for social justice. Gaca's argument is that the Platonic and Aristotelian accounts of justice promote a more equitable approach to heterosexual relations and moral upbringing and that, conversely, Plato and Aristotle also maintain that equitable sexual relations and upbringing enhance the attainment of a genuinely inclusive social justice. This biopolitical project helped Aristotle and his Peripatetic followers to highlight, in their studies on Greek polities, the dangers of ravaging warfare and martial sexual violence as an extreme example of sovereign biopower in the form of militarized aggression leading to precipitous social injustice and disadvantaged upbringing. Further, the Peripatetics' new discursive stance of openly discussing the practice of martial rape in ravaging warfare influenced later ancient authors likewise to be more frank in discussing this sexual aggression and its adverse social effects.

Part II ("Ancient Thought beyond Biopolitics") focuses on dimensions of ancient thought that elude, transcend, contrast with, or are alternative to different aspects of biopolitics. Chapter 4 by Kalliopi Nikolopoulou, "Otherwise than (Bio)politics: Nature and the Sacred in Tragic Life," challenges Agamben's account of biopolitics, which presents the twentieth-century death camp with its biopolitical production of bare life as a catastrophic break with any previous epoch and, at the same time, begins its genealogy of biopolitics with Aristotle. Nikolopoulou argues that classical Greek tragedy provides us with a rich imagery for articulating the imprint of nature upon our individual and social existence, but one that eludes the key conceptual distinctions of the contemporary discourse on biopolitics.

Chapter 5, "Beyond Biopolitics and Juridico-Institutional Politics: Aristotle on the Nature of Politics" by Adriel M. Trott, examines the extent to which the conception of nature that underlies Aristotle's account of politics can be seen as "biopolitical." Trott argues that Aristotle's approach exceeds both a merely biological conception of nature and a juridico-institutional understanding of politics. In Trott's view, Aristotle's third alternative is grounded on an approach to politics as a natural activity and relies on an inclusive sense of nature that is not reducible to biological processes; this approach counteracts the modern tendency to contrast politics with nature and the soul with the body.

Chapter 6, Jussi Backman's "*Bene vivere politice*: On the (Meta)biopolitics of 'Happiness,'" studies, in turn, the alleged "biopolitical" dimensions of the ideal of "happiness" in ancient political theory. Backman suggests an under-standing of biopolitics focused on the conceptualization of the final aim of the political community, rather than techniques of government. Backman argues that the Aristotelian *eudaimonia* and the Thomistic *beatitudo* are in fact "metabiopolitical" ideals centered on contemplation as an activity that lies beyond the communal and biological concerns of everyday life. With the help of Arendt, the chapter also investigates the momentous "biopolitical" transformation of the concept of happiness into "quality of life" in modern political thought, especially in Thomas Hobbes.

Part III ("Biopolitical Interpretations of Ancient Thought") includes criti-cal discussions of contemporary interpretations of ancient thought in a bio-political framework. In chapter 7, "Hannah Arendt's Genealogy of Biopolitics: From Greek Materialism to Modern Human Superfluity," Ville Suuronen outlines a historical account of biopolitics based on Arendt's inter-pretation of ancient political ideals and their transformation through Christianity. In Suuronen's view, Arendt enables us to discover the funda-mental element of biopolitics in the "materialism" of classical Greek political philosophy that regarded politics in terms of ruling and managing the necessities of biological life, ultimately aiming at making possible the contemplative life. Describing the various transformations that the Western conception of the significance of the biological life-process underwent from classical antiquity through Christianity and modernity, Suuronen explains how Arendt connects modern biopower with the rise of the *animal laborans* and the corresponding ideal of biological life as the "highest good." In Suuronen's interpretation, for Arendt, this development also forms a basic precondition for the emergence of totalitarian domination.

Chapter 8 by Sergei Prozorov, "From Biopolitics to Biopoetics and Back Again: On a Counterintuitive Continuity in Foucault's Thought," suggests a new interpretation of Foucault's later works by shedding light on the relationship between his account of biopolitics and his interpretation, in his final lectures of the 1980s, of the ancient "biopoetic" techniques of constituting the self. Prozorov illuminates the unity and coherence of the various lines of research sketched out by the later Foucault: for Foucault, Prozorov argues, the biopoetics of the Hellenistic period is a solution to essentially biopolitical problems. In this context, Prozorov analyzes the biopolitical meaning of Foucault's interpretations of both Stoic philosophy and the Cynics, and their relevance for current debates on affirmative biopolitics.

The last contribution of the volume, chapter 9, "Agamben's Aristotelian Biopolitics: Conceptual and Methodological Problems" by Antonio Cimino, discusses a number of issues arising from Agamben's interpretation of Aristotelian texts. Cimino concentrates both on Agamben's reading of the relationship between *bios* and *zōē*, and on some tenets of the Agambenian "genealogy" of biopower. Cimino argues that Agamben's reading does not do justice to Aristotle's conception of life, because it is based on a peculiar use of Schmitt's notion of exception. Moreover, Cimino contends that Agamben does not substantiate his narrative of the history of biopower in a persuasive manner. Despite these negative conclusions, Cimino is to a certain extent sympathetic to Agamben's thesis about the ancient origins of biopower.

References

Agamben, Giorgio. 1995. *Homo sacer: Il potere sovrano e la nuda vita*. Turin: Einaudi.
Agamben, Giorgio. 1998. *Homo Sacer: Sovereign Power and Bare Life*. Translated by Daniel Heller-Roazen. Stanford, CA: Stanford University Press.
Almeida, Miguel Régio de. 2014. "Rudimentos de biopolítica no direito Romano." *Humanitas* 66: 207–29. https://doi.org/10.14195/2183-1718_66_11.

Arendt, Hannah. 1998. *The Human Condition*. 2nd ed. Chicago: University of Chicago Press. First published 1958.

Arnhart, Larry. 1988. "Aristotle's Biopolitics: A Defense of Biological Teleology against Biological Nihilism." *Politics and the Life Sciences* 6 (2): 173–91. https://doi.org/10.1017/S0730938400003233.

Binding, Karl. 1920. *Zum Werden und Leben der Staaten: Zehn staatsrechtliche Abhandlungen*. Munich: Duncker & Humblot.

Campbell, Timothy, and Adam Sitze, eds. 2013. *Biopolitics: A Reader*. Durham, NC: Duke University Press.

Clough, Patricia Ticineto, and Craig Willse, eds. 2011. *Beyond Biopolitics: Essays on the Governance of Life and Death*. Durham, NC: Duke University Press.

Dennert, Eberhard. 1920. *Der Staat als lebendiger Organismus: Biologische Betrachtungen zum Aufbau der neuen Zeit*. Halle an der Saale: Müller.

Di Leo, Jeffrey R., and Peter Hitchcock, eds. 2020a. *Biotheory: Life and Death under Capitalism*. New York: Routledge.

Di Leo, Jeffrey R., and Peter Hitchcock. 2020b. "Biotheory: An Introduction." In *Biotheory: Life and Death under Capitalism*, edited by Jeffrey R. Di Leo and Peter Hitchcock, 1–19. New York: Routledge. https://doi.org/10.4324/9781003021506-1.

Esposito, Roberto. 1998. *Communitas: Origine e destino della comunità*. Turin: Einaudi.

Esposito, Roberto. 2002. *Immunitas: Protezione e negazione della vita*. Turin: Einaudi.

Esposito, Roberto. 2004. *Bíos: Biopolitica e filosofia*. Turin: Einaudi.

Esposito, Roberto. 2008. *Bíos: Biopolitics and Philosophy*. Translated by Timothy Campbell. Minneapolis: University of Minnesota Press.

Esposito, Roberto. 2010. *Communitas: The Origin and Destiny of Community*. Translated by Timothy Campbell. Stanford, CA: Stanford University Press.

Esposito, Roberto. 2011. *Immunitas: The Protection and Negation of Life*. Translated by Zakiya Hanafi. Cambridge: Polity.

Fehér, Ferenc, and Ágnes Heller. 1994. *Biopolitics*. Aldershot: Avebury.

Finlayson, James Gordon. 2010. "'Bare Life' and Politics in Agamben's Reading of Aristotle." *The Review of Politics* 72 (1): 97–126. https://doi.org/10.1017/S0034670509990982.

Forti, Simona. 2006. "The Biopolitics of Souls: Racism, Nazism, and Plato." *Political Theory* 34 (1): 9–32. https://doi.org/10.1177/0090591705280526.

Foucault, Michel. 1976. *Histoire de la sexualité*. Vol. 1, *La volonté de savoir*. Paris: Gallimard.

Foucault, Michel. 1978. *The History of Sexuality*. Vol. 1, *An Introduction*. Translated by Robert Hurley. New York: Pantheon.

Foucault, Michel. 1984. *The Foucault Reader*. Edited by Paul Rabinow. New York: Pantheon.

Foucault, Michel. 1997. *"Il faut défendre la société": Cours au Collège de France (1975–1976)*. Edited by Mauro Bertani and Alessandro Fontana. Paris: Gallimard; Seuil.

Foucault, Michel. 2000. *Essential Works of Foucault, 1954–1984*. Vol. 3, *Power*. Edited by James D. Faubion. New York: New Press.

Foucault, Michel. 2001. *Dits et écrits*. Vol. 2, *1976–1988*. Edited by Daniel Defert and François Ewald with Jacques Lagrange. Paris: Gallimard.

Foucault, Michel. 2003. *"Society Must Be Defended": Lectures at the Collège de France, 1975–76*. Translated by David Macey. New York: Picador.

Foucault, Michel. 2004a. *Naissance de la biopolitique: Cours au Collège de France (1978–1979)*. Edited by Michel Senellart. Paris: Gallimard; Seuil.

Foucault, Michel. 2004b. *Sécurité, territoire, population: Cours au Collège de France (1977–1978)*. Edited by Michel Senellart. Paris: Gallimard; Seuil.

Foucault, Michel. 2008. *The Birth of Biopolitics: Lectures at the Collège de France, 1978–79*. Translated by Graham Burchell. Basingstoke: Palgrave Macmillan.

Foucault, Michel. 2009. *Security, Territory, Population: Lectures at the Collège de France 1977–78*. Translated by Graham Burchell. Basingstoke: Palgrave Macmillan.

Frías Urrea, Rodrigo. 2013. "Foucault y los orígenes griegos de la biopolítica." *Revista de filosofía* 69: 119–32. https://doi.org/10.4067/S0718-43602013000100010.

Gómez Camarena, Carlos. 2014. "Biopolitics." In *Encyclopedia of Critical Psychology*, edited by Thomas Teo, 164–7. New York: Springer. https://doi.org/10.1007/978-1-4614-5583-7_27.

Hardt, Michael, and Antonio Negri. 2000. *Empire*. Cambridge, MA: Harvard University Press.

Hardt, Michael, and Antonio Negri. 2004. *Multitude: War and Democracy in the Age of Empire*. New York: Penguin.

Hardt, Michael, and Antonio Negri. 2009. *Commonwealth*. Cambridge, MA: Harvard University Press.

Harris, G. W. 1911. "Bio-politics." *The New Age: A Weekly Review of Politics, Literature, and Art*, December 28, 1911.

Hawkins, Tom. 2018. "Agamben, 'Bare Life,' and Archaic Greek Poetry." *Mouseion: Journal of the Classical Association of Canada* 15 (1): 49–70. https://doi.org/10.3138/mous.15.1.5.

Heidegger, Martin. 1975. *Gesamtausgabe*. Vol. 24, *Die Grundprobleme der Phänomenologie*. Edited by Friedrich-Wilhelm von Herrmann. Frankfurt am Main: Klostermann. Original lecture course 1927.

Heidegger, Martin. 1988. *The Basic Problems of Phenomenology*. Translated by Albert Hofstadter. Bloomington: Indiana University Press.

Heller, Ágnes, and Sonja Puntscher Riekmann, eds. 1996. *Biopolitics: The Politics of the Body, Race and Nature*. Aldershot: Avebury.

Herder, Johann Gottfried. 1796. *Briefe zur Beförderung der Humanität*. Vol. 7. Riga: Hartknoch.

Jobe, Kevin Scott. 2015. "Foucault and Ancient *Polizei*: A Genealogy of the Military Pastorate." *Journal of Political Power* 8 (1): 21–37. https://doi.org/10.1080/2158379X.2015.1011378.

John of Salisbury. 1855. *Patrologia Latina*. Vol. 199, *Joannis Saresberiensis opera omnia*. Edited by Jacques Paul Migne. Paris: Migne.

Kjellén, Rudolf. 1905. *Stormakterna: Konturer kring samtidens storpolitik*. Vol. 1, *Rent europeiska stormakter*. Stockholm: Geber.

Kjellén, Rudolf. 1916. *Politiska handböcker*. Vol. 3, *Staten som lifsform*. Stockholm: Geber.

Kjellén, Rudolf. 1920. *Grundriss zu einem System der Politik*. Leipzig: Hirzel.

Lemke, Thomas. 2007. *Gouvernementalität und Biopolitik*. Wiesbaden: VS Verlag für Sozialwissenschaften.

Lemke, Thomas. 2010. "From State Biology to the Government of Life: Historical Dimensions and Contemporary Perspectives of 'Biopolitics.'" *Journal of Classical Sociology* 10 (4): 421–38. https://doi.org/10.1177/1468795X10385183.

Lemke, Thomas. 2011. *Biopolitics: An Advanced Introduction*. Translated by Eric Frederick Trump. New York: New York University Press.

Lemm, Vanessa, and Miguel E. Vatter, eds. 2014. *The Government of Life: Foucault, Biopolitics, and Neoliberalism*. New York: Fordham University Press.

Milbank, John. 2008. "Paul against Biopolitics." *Theory, Culture & Society* 25 (7–8): 125–72. https://doi.org/10.1177/0263276408097801.

Mills, Catherine. 2018. *Biopolitics*. London: Routledge.

Minca, Claudio. 2015. "The Biopolitical Imperative." In *The Wiley Blackwell Companion to Political Geography*, edited by John Agnew, Virginie Mamadouh, Anna J. Secor, and Joanne Sharp, 165–86. Malden, MA: John Wiley & Sons. https://doi.org/10.1002/9781118725771.ch14.

Moheau, Jean-Baptiste. 1778. *Recherches et considérations sur la population de la France*. Paris: Moutard.

Ojakangas, Mika. 2013. "*Erēmos aporos* as the Paradigmatic Figure of the Western (Thanato)political Subject." *Alternatives: Global, Local, Political* 38 (3): 194–207. https://doi.org/10.1177/0304375413497843.

Ojakangas, Mika. 2016. *On the Greek Origins of Biopolitics: A Reinterpretation of the History of Biopower*. London: Routledge.

Ojakangas, Mika. 2017. "Biopolitics in the Political Thought of Classical Greece." In *The Routledge Handbook of Biopolitics*, edited by Sergei Prozorov and Simona Rentea, 23–35. London: Routledge. https://doi.org/10.4324/9781315612751-2.

Prozorov, Sergei, and Simona Rentea, eds. 2017. *The Routledge Handbook of Biopolitics*. London: Routledge.

Rose, Nikolas. 2007. *The Politics of Life Itself: Biomedicine, Power, and Subjectivity in the Twenty-First Century*. Princeton, NJ: Princeton University Press.

Skornicki, Arnault. 2015. "Les origines théologico-politiques du biopouvoir: Pastorale et généalogie de l'État." *Sociología Histórica* no. 5: 43–66.

Uexküll, Jakob von. 1920. *Staatsbiologie: Anatomie, Physiologie, Pathologie des Staates*. Berlin: Paetel.

Van den Daele, Wolfgang, ed. 2005. *Biopolitik*. Wiesbaden: VS Verlag für Sozialwissenschaften.

PART I
BIOPOLITICS IN ANCIENT THOUGHT

1

Biopolitics and the "Boundless People"

An Iliadic Model

Sara Brill

1. Population, Animality, and the People

In her recent exploration of the "posthuman turn" in philosophy, Adriana Cavarero offers a concise formulation of Hannah Arendt's diagnosis of Plato's "most serious fault": "[H]e has sacrificed the plural world to the totalizing effect of the One" (Cavarero 2019, 40). For Cavarero, and a number of other thinkers, this reduction implicates Platonic philosophy in totalitarian politics, and requires us to view this politics less as an aberrant pathology than, as Simona Forti puts it, as "a fragment of a general deconstructive operation of our history"—"ours," I infer, because it attempts to bring to political expression a defining feature of that history of philosophy that would come to be called "Western," namely, the metaphysics of form (Forti 2006, 26). Regardless of whether one views this metaphysics as Plato's own or as a product of the early commentaries that would become "Platonism," Forti reminds us that such a reductive tendency is marked in this history and requires rigorous and persistent interrogation.

On the one hand, Aristotle seems to share a similar concern, both with the metaphysics of forms as such and, more importantly for this chapter, with the politics it informs. It is precisely the emphasis on unity, as it is attained by the collapse of the private family, the collective ownership of property, and the education of men and women in common, for which Aristotle criticizes the Socrates of Plato's *Republic*. He does so on the grounds of what he insists is the irreducibly heterogeneous character of rule and of the *polis* itself. Too much unity destroys the city by transforming it into something else (*Pol.* 2.2.1261a15–23). It is a mark of the tyrant to reduce his citizens to a single mass forced into serving his private will (5.11.1313a41–1314a29), a perverse mirror image of the king's deployment of the eyes and hands of others whom he treats as co-rulers (*synarchous*; 3.16.1287b30).

Sara Brill, *Biopolitics and the "Boundless People": An Iliadic Model* In: *Biopolitics and Ancient Thought*. Edited by: Jussi Backman and Antonio Cimino, Oxford University Press. © Oxford University Press 2022. DOI: 10.1093/oso/9780192847102.003.0002

And yet, Aristotle's insistence on the heterogeneity of rule, and on the need to maintain essential differences against the forces of homogenization and idiosyncrasy, does not stop him from instrumentalizing citizen life. While in the first book of the *Politics*, Aristotle asserts that the political expert does not create his "material" but receives it and puts it to use, just as the weaver does not create wool but receives it and makes something with it (*Pol.* 1.10.1258a20–7), by the seventh book he insists that the political expert must strive to create the citizen, both collectively in a form of public education and individually in a system of legislation designed to produce citizens whose very bodies are amendable to the will of the legislator (7.16.1335a5). When Aristotle compares citizens to the material (*hylē*) of the weaver (7.4.1325b40–1326a4), when he treats them as property of the city (8.1.1337a27–9), when he claims that the lives of citizens should be far more regimented than the lives of their slaves (*Metaph.* 12.10.1075a19–23), when he characterizes those slaves as living tools (*Pol.* 1.4.1253b30–4), he perhaps most clearly approaches the kind of formulation of "the human" that, for very good reason, concerns Cavarero and Forti, that is, Arendt's "One Man of gigantic dimension," stripped of novelty, contingency, and history (Arendt 1973, 466).

Aristotle's emphasis on engineering the bodily as well as psychical character of citizens recommends comparison with contemporary theories of biopolitics, a comparison Mika Ojakangas (2016) has drawn with particular clarity. To be sure, Aristotle's eugenics legislation is designed to hold the generation of life under the harness of the political partnership, such that one's *genesis* belongs to the *polis* itself, an entity that exercises its ownership of citizens in a variety of laws, but especially in laws pertaining to the production of human beings. By means of these laws, it arrogates to itself the creation of *zōē* as an act of choice on the part of the city, and a civic duty on the part of its residents, who are required to farm out their sperm and wombs as liturgy to the *polis* (*Pol.* 7.16.1335b27–1336a1).

But it is far from clear that *bios* is the sole, or even main, target here and we should guard against assuming too quickly the synonymy of the Greek *bios* and the prefix "bio-."[1] Put differently, we cannot take for granted that there is anything in ancient Greek thought that corresponds to a "population" in the sense so indispensable to Foucault's thinking, from his development of biopower and biopolitics in his lectures on social medicine in the early 1970s, to his later transition to governmentality, where population emerges as designating a "pertinent" collection of human beings whose health and living

---

[1] A point made particularly clearly in Holmes 2019.

are understood as consisting in a set of homogeneous biological processes that will form the horizon of governmental care, a collection distinct from and placed over against "the people."[2] Thus conceived, "population" emerges as a product of a calculation designed to render a multiplicity of individuals into an anonymous mass whose biological needs delimit what will and will not count as significant and worthy of protection and security.

When, in the central books of the *Politics*, Aristotle considers the various forms that collectives of humans may take—multitude (*plēthos*), people (*dēmos*), the many (*hoi polloi*), for example—he does so precisely in order to observe the differences both between and within kinds, and the work these differences do in forming communities with very particular characters. Aristotle's emphasis on *different kinds* of human collectives connects his political theorizing with his zoological research, and with broader cultural tropes that treat vitality in close proximity to vividness.[3] That is to say, while the specific legislation Aristotle designs invites comparison with biopolitical concerns, the end at which this legislation aims is determined within a conception of *zōē* whose political valence has not yet been fully charted.[4]

Thus, even granting some ambiguity to Foucault's use of "population," the sense operative throughout his development of the features of governmentality, that is, the homogenization of humans into a numerical "population," is, to borrow from Bruce Curtis, "a statistical artefact" produced in a very specific set of historical conditions and interests that "made it possible for number to take the place of status" (Curtis 2002, 508–9, 530).[5] Such an understanding complicates the applicability of the concept to Aristotle's political theory, not simply because Aristotle could not perform the calculations necessary but because he wouldn't have. The abrogation of status to number would have been inimical to Aristotle, both because it would violate

---

[2] See Foucault's comments about the formation of "population" early on in the 1977–8 lecture course published in English translation as *Security, Territory, Population* (Foucault 2007, 41–4). As Cisney and Morar (2016) observe, the connection between biopolitics and governmentality is such that the former simply recedes in favor of the latter in Foucault's later lectures. On the role of "population" in the relation between the two, see Cisney and Morar 2016, 7–14; see also Curtis 2002.

[3] On the connection between vitality and vividness, see the sources gathered in Brill 2020, 1–7.

[4] The flaws in the contemporary theoretical framework that has dominated discussion of *zōē* in Aristotle, that of Giorgio Agamben, has been the subject of several recent studies, including Ojakangas's own (see also Finlayson 2010; Dubreuil 2006; Holmes 2019; Miller 2020; Brill 2020).

[5] Curtis (2002) tracks this ambiguity as largely equivocating between a concern with "populousness," which attempts to hold a set of relations between different groups steady and employs an organic model, and the aggregation of human beings into a numerical set called a "population," which employs an atomic model. By these terms, Ojakangas's justification of his alignment of *plēthos* with population on the grounds of Aristotle's emphasis on the determinate number of human beings within a political partnership (Ojakangas 2016, 39) correctly identifies Aristotle's concern with populousness, but not with population. On the effects of Aristotle's concern with the size and quality of *polis* inhabitants on medieval demography, see Biller 2000. On the role of statistics in producing the concept of population, see Cole 2000; the contributions collected in Caplan and Torpey 2001; Curtis 2001.

differences he saw as essential to the *polis* and because, as he remarks in the *Nicomachean Ethics*, one shouldn't seek mathematical precision in the study of the kinds of phenomena politics addresses, that is, the beautiful and the just (*Eth. Nic.* 1.3.1094b12–30). It would have to be up to individual statesmen to determine the correct number of births or marriages, for instance, in order to attain the aim Aristotle does stipulate: "the greatest excess of number with a view to self-sufficiency of life that is readily surveyable [*hē megistē tou plēthous hyperbolē pros autarkeian zōēs eusynoptos*]" (*Pol.* 7.4.1326b23–5).[6]

There are certainly resonances here with Foucault's interest in surveillance and panopticism. It is not as though we simply could not say of Aristotle that he treats the human multitude in terms similar to those Foucault uses to trace the treatment of population emergent from the science of policing, that is, "as a mass of living and co-existing beings" (Foucault 1989, 106). The living (*zēn*) of citizens is central to Aristotle's political theory and his emphasis on the sharing of life (*syzēn*) is an emphasis on their coexistence. But the difference that must be insisted upon resides within the conception of living itself. The living at stake in biopolitics consists of a set of biological processes bound up with reproduction, maturation, and death.[7] For Aristotle, the living (*zēn*) from which living being (*zōion*) derives its sense is most vividly expressed in those activities that most clearly demarcate kinds of living beings. For humans, these are the activities of perceiving and understanding (*Eth. Nic.* 9.9.1170a16–19: *aisthēseōs ē noēseōs*; *Eth. Eud.* 7.12.1244b24–6: *to aisthanesthai kai to gnōrizein*). To treat human life as coextensive with the processes of reproduction and nutrition, for instance, is to deny its distinctive character as human life, the very life that citizenship in a *polis* is designed to most fully realize. This is a reductive homogenizing that Aristotle aligns with deviant regimes and explicitly criticizes. He does indeed study and theorize different stages of life (following a long history of Greek thinking) or what we might call a "life cycle," keyed to major reproductive and maturational events, most clearly in the collection of texts known to us as the *Parva naturalia*.[8] As we shall see, the human "life cycle" plays a decisive role in his envisioning of the best human city. Nevertheless, it does so in service to the performance of those deeds that, for Aristotle, most distinguish the living of human beings and bring them as close to the divine as possible.[9]

---

[6] Unless otherwise noted, all translations from Aristotle's *Politics* are my own, in consultation with those of Saunders and Lord. The Greek text is that of Ross.

[7] For further specification of the understanding of life at work in Foucault's development of biopolitics, see Rose 2006; Mader 2016; Mills 2016.

[8] On the concept of life cycle in the *Parva naturalia*, see King 2001, and more broadly in Aristotle, see Garland 1990.

[9] On the role of the biological in Aristotle's political theory, see also chapters 5 and 6 by Adriel M. Trott and Jussi Backman in this volume.

Yet, precisely in his description of the character and lives of the citizens of the best city, Aristotle does not escape a homogenizing of a different kind, one that illuminates an instrumentalization and commodification embedded in his understanding of the political valence of *zōē*. The city's "ownership" of its citizens is an extension of Aristotle's broader orientation toward human political life. Humans are meant for a city (for example, *Pol.* 1.2.1253a2), the shared perception of justice as it is realized in the pursuit of virtue is the foundation of human political life (1.2.1253a15–17; 7.8.1328a33–b3), and this perception is made possible by the possession of *logos* (1.2.1253a13–15). Indeed, it is through this shared perception that humans enact the common task that distinguishes *politikos* animals from those that are not (*Hist. an.* 1.1.488a), and it is the capacity for *logos*, the capacity that allows them to perceive justice and injustice, which makes humans especially political (*Pol.* 1.2.1253a7). In fact, we find an emphasis on the expansions and contractions of perception throughout Aristotle's writing on human political life, where the calibration and "normalization" of perception prove essential to the political bond.[10] Moreover, none of these observations is made in isolation from a study of the bodies that have living as a capacity, from the morphology, physiology, and anatomy of living beings and the forces of their embodiment. Nor from a study of "organicity" as such, as these "zoological" inquiries, in turn, cannot be separated from an assertion about *zōē* itself: "[F]or living requires many instruments [*pollōn gar organōn deitai to zēn*]" (7.8.1328b6–7). For Aristotle, to be alive is to instantiate a force that infuses the *kosmos*, moving the heavenly bodies and animating all living beings (see *Cael.* 1.9.279a17–b3). The living being, as Aristotle considers it, is an especially clear expression of this power.

Aristotle's conjoining of living and ruling is invited by the etymological connection between *agelē* (herd), *agelaion* (the character of being gregarious), and *agō* (to lead), which asserts a connection between the sociality of living beings (or the lack thereof) and the nature of political life. Aristotle will claim, in fact, that it is in a living being "first" that we observe forms of rule. If living being serves as a paradigm of substance in the *Metaphysics*, this

---

[10] In addition to the juxtaposition we observed above of the king's amplification of perception through making his supporters co-rulers with the tyrant's concentration of perception to serve his own private ends, Aristotle also compares the authority of the people (or the many) that is attained by the aggregation of their perceptions to the sovereign perception of the god-like human (*Pol.* 3.11.1281a42–b7). At the level of individual perception, he contrasts the accuracy of self-perception of the great-souled person with the flaws in self-perception of the small-souled and the vain (*Eth. Nic.* 4.3.1123a35–b12). He will emphasize the unity of perception of the virtuous with the shattering of perception of the vicious, that is, the same things always appear as good and pleasant to the virtuous person, and are so, while the vicious person is at war with himself and regrets on one day what he perceived as good the previous day (*Eth. Eud.* 7.5.1240b14–21). And in general, he will observe that humans are bad judges of their own worth because their perception of themselves is skewed (7.4.1239a15–17).

is so, at least in part, because living being is also an expression of rule, as Aristotle asserts very clearly in the *Politics*: it is in a living being that "one can first observe both the rule characteristic of a master and political rule" (*Pol.* 1.5.1254b3–4). The very frame by which Aristotle investigates the kinds of human multitudes and peoples in the *Politics* is explicitly structured by his conception of animality: "[I]f we chose to acquire a grasp of kinds of animals, we would first enumerate separately what it is that every animal must necessarily have" (4.4.1290b25–7), in order to discern its necessary parts and all of their possible combinations; "[one may proceed] in the same manner in the case of the regimes spoken of; for cities are composed not of one but of many parts, as we have often said" (1290b37–8).

To be sure, a comprehensive study of Aristotle's thinking about the political valence of animality would well exceed a single chapter. Here I aim to highlight the importance of such a study for contemporary assessment of Aristotle's political theory by providing a genealogical lens for viewing Aristotle's thinking about the nature of the human multitude, that is, by tracing some of the most influential among such formulations prior to Aristotle, namely, those that are used in the *Iliad* to designate the collective Achaean and Trojan forces. After all, the examples of nonhuman political animals Aristotle offers in the *History of Animals*—bees, wasps, ants, and cranes (*Hist. an.* 1.1.487b33)—are anticipated by the poem's imagery for collective human action, which draws precisely on these and other animal collectives. When we examine the iconography of shared life that appears in the *Iliad*— the imagery it employs to depict the actions of the Achaean and Trojan forces—we encounter elements of, to borrow from Michèle Le Dœuff (1990), a "philosophical imaginary" that profoundly shaped how Aristotle thinks about the work of the *polis*.[11]

My primary claim is that Aristotle's sense of the sharing of the perception of justice as the common deed that comprises human political life is informed by an Iliadic model, the harnessing of *aisthēsis* and *logos* alike for the pursuit of a common task. As with Aristotle, the root of this model is found in the very conception of living as it is accomplished by a variety of animal kinds. In both cases, *zōē* emerges as a collectively pursued enterprise requiring fluid combinations of coalescences and diffusions of force and capacity, a variety of organizations in a very particular, that is, transindividual, sense. In the

---

[11] "For there exists a certain task of a city too, so that the city most capable of bringing this to completion is the one that must be supposed the greatest" (*Pol.* 7.4.1326a12). I should add that a focus on the armies is not by any means the only way to get at depictions of shared life in the *Iliad*; indeed, such a focus leaves out consideration of the few brief but powerful depictions of the life shared within the family, which would include the life shared between men and women. Such a broader consideration is necessary for a comprehensive treatment of the topic, but would exceed the scope of a single chapter.

Iliad, prior to the "reduction" of people to things, armies have become packs and swarms, heroes have become walls and rivers, peoples have become sand and stars.[12] I aim, then, to trace the conception of political power—as the power to generate what Homer calls the "boundless people [*dēmos apeirōn*]" (*Il.* 24.776)—that emerges from the animal imagery for human collective action employed throughout the *Iliad*, in order to illuminate the context from which Aristotle develops the conception of *zōē* that undergirds his understanding of the formation of people and that complicates our assessment of the "biopolitical" character of Aristotle's thought.[13]

In order to make good on these claims, I will first turn to the *Iliad* itself in order to chart its favored images for conveying the efficacy of human collective actions and the forms of force to which these images give rise (section 2). Aristotle famously also privileges the human as particularly political on the grounds of its possession of *logos*. And on this, too, Homeric epic is not silent. For when we turn to assess what vision of shared life emerges from the poetic constellation of these images, the possession of *logos* comes to the fore as an essential, if also ambivalently treated, feature. Thus, in section 3, I will trace the poem's depiction of the arc of utterance available to Achaean and Trojan armies as collectives in order to locate Homer's approach to *logos* within the broader context of communicative sound and further specify the model of power that emerges from the poem. I will then return to Aristotle to focus on his understanding of the formation of peoples, the variety of kinds the human multitude may take, and the regimes of force they exhibit (section 4).

2. Swarms, Flocks, Herds

The collection of metaphors Homer uses in order to describe the actions of the Achaean and Trojan armies is wide-ranging but consistently returns to favored tropes drawn from: (a) plant, animal, insect, and human life, whereby Achaean and Trojans are likened to leaves and grass; to swarms of bees, flies, wasps, and locusts; to flocks of birds, goats, and sheep; to schools of fish; to packs of wolves, hounds, and jackals; to reapers, farmers, weavers, loggers, and tanners; (b) elemental forces, likened to waves, wind, storms, fire, rivers, and stars; and (c) inanimate and inert environmental features: walls of stone,

---

[12] On the caution with which we should characterize the poem's materialist impulses as reductive, see Purves 2015.

[13] Unless otherwise noted, all translations of the *Iliad* are those of Lattimore.

cliffs of granite, beaches of sand.[14] Each of these groups of metaphors emphasizes different but interlocking aspects of collectives of men. The imagery of animals and plants presents animal and vegetal *heterogeneous* unity, respectively: swarms and flocks stress not only the communal nature of the action—the unity of purpose that holds together large numbers of individuals around a common deed—but also the varieties of organization, the malleability of structure, and the shifting morphology of which such groups are capable; leaves and grasses juxtapose the fragility of human life with the endurance of human deeds, emphasizing the tension between the strength in their number, on the one hand, and the ephemeral and vulnerable nature of their individual constituents, on the other. Wave and fire comprise a *homogeneous* unity that conveys the efficacy held by the Achaean and Trojan hosts. Stone, especially granite, contains this efficacy and holds it together. We see nothing here of "inert," "passive," or "mere" matter; even the stones are animated by purpose.[15] Rather, taken together, these images provide a metaphorics for describing different regimes of force. If it is true, following Simone Weil's (1945) formulation, that force is the poem's ultimate protagonist, it is equally the case that force is not only treated as monolithic in the *Iliad*; rather, the poem highlights a number of organizations and dispersions of force, and it is particularly inclined to use animal collectives in order to do so, presenting a variety of what we could call *zōē*-regimes.[16] Through such imagery Homer confronts his audience with a spectrum of capacity, such that the power of herd and field, for instance, coalesces into the force of wave or storm, and then crystallizes into stone and occasionally shatters into sand or refracts into stars.

The actions this imagery seeks to illuminate, the deeds that are allotted to the Achaeans and the Trojans *en masse*, can be relatively clearly identified. They *gather* for assembly or for battle, and here imagery of flocks of birds and beasts abounds, but also of gathering waves and thunderheads, as well as

---

[14] (a) leaves: *Il.* 2.467–8 (and flowers), 2.800–1, 6.146–9, 535; bees: 2.86–8, 12.167–72; birds: 2.459–66, 3.1–6; wasps: 16.259–62; flies: 2.469–71, 16.641–4; goats: 2.474–7; sheep: 4.433–8; wolves: 11.72–3, 16.156–63, 16.352–5; hounds: 17.725–9; jackals: 11.474–80; schools of fish: 21.22–4; locusts: 21.12–16; reapers: 11.67–9; woodcutters: 11.86–9; farmers: 12.421–3; weavers: 12.433–5; loggers: 16.633–4; tanners: 17.389–93. (b) waves: 2.144–6, 2.209–10, 2.394–7, 4.422–6, 7.63–6, 9.4–8, 13.795–800, 14.392–401, 15.381–4, 17.262–5; wind and storm: 4.275–9, 5.522–7, 12.278–87, 13.334–8, 14.394–401, 16.384–93, 16.765–9, 19.357–61; fire: 2.455–8, 2.780, 13.39–44, 13.673, 14.392–401, 17.366, 18.1; rivers: 4.452–6; stars: 8.555–61, the dog star: 298. (c) stone walls and granite cliffs: 15.617–20, 16.212–14; sand: 2.800. For studies of individual elements, see, for example, Whitman 1958, 128–53; Fenno 2005.

[15] See Purves 2015 as well as relevant new materialism sources, for example, Bennett 2010a, 2010b, and the work collected in Coole and Frost 2010.

[16] As Holmes (2015) observes, since Weil's influential study, force is read as central to the poem, a position affirmed more recently in Dimock 2008, 73–106. See also Bonnafé 1984 on the dominance of animal life similes in the *Iliad*.

one of the few references to swarms of bees.[17] They *affirm*; here the imagery of roaring waves is again frequently evoked and serves to portray the collective Achaean army less as a deliberative body than an evaluative body, or even, insofar as their participation in assembly is characterized most frequently as giving assent to a particular path of action, as an affirming body. They *disperse*, either to reconvene on the battlefield, or to their respective camps and campfires (likened to stars), or in a few instances in terror to ships or behind city walls (swarming). They *fight*, and are likened to fire, river, and a variety of animals. Their fighting can be further divided into defensive (wall of stones and cliff of granite) and offensive, which in turn can be broken into two modes, distance fighting (archery) and hand-to-hand combat (images of *technē* are particularly predominant here). Of the scenes of hand-to-hand combat, some of the bloodiest are those skirmishes around the corpse of a fallen hero. Here the imagery of packs picking off a weakened member of a flock and of insects swarming predominates.

Many of these scenes strain the boundaries of deliberative communal action; at times, they depict groups organized by shared fighting habits and backgrounds, at others, assemblages of fighters drawn together by the exigencies of the battlefield. Indeed, the lines between these actions are not always clear, and Homer's imagery just as often troubles these distinctions as it asserts them. In some passages, multiple metaphors are used to get at the action being described, as, for instance, in the first description of the armies gathering on the plain, in which they are likened to fire, flocks of birds, leaves, flowers, and swarms of flies:

> As obliterating fire lights up a vast forest
> along the crests of a mountain, and the flare shows far off,
> so as they marched, from the magnificent bronze the
>   gleam went
> dazzling all about through the upper air to the heaven.
> These, as the multitudinous nations of birds winged
>   [*hōs t' ornithōn peteēnōn ethnea polla*, 459],
> of geese, and of cranes, and of swans long-throated
> in the Asian meadow beside the Kaystrian waters

---

[17] "Like the swarms of clustering bees [*ēute ethnea eisi melissaōn hadinaōn*] / that issue forever in fresh bursts from the hollow in the stone, / and hang like bunched grapes as they hover beneath the flowers in springtime / fluttering in swarms together that way and that way, / so the many nations of men [*hōs tōn ethnea polla*] from the ships and the shelters / along the front of the deep sea beach marched in order / by companies to the assembly, and Rumor walked blazing among them, / Zeus' messenger, to hasten them along" (*Il.* 2.87–94). The only other reference to bees in the *Iliad* is at 12.167–72. All other references here are cited in footnote 14 above.

this way and that make their flights in the pride of their
    wings, then
settle in clashing swarms and the whole meadow echoes
    with them,
so of these the multitudinous tribes from the ships and
shelters poured to the plain of Skamandros, and the earth
    beneath their
feet and under the feet of their horses thundered horribly.
They took their position in the blossoming meadow of
    Skamandros,
thousands of them, as leaves and flowers appear in
    their season.
Like the multitudinous nations of swarming insects [ēute
    myiaōn hadinaōn ethnea polla, 469]
who drive hither and thither about the stalls of the sheepfold
in the season of spring when the milk splashes in the
    milk pails:
in such numbers the flowing-haired Achaians stood up
through the plain against the Trojans, hearts burning to
    break them.

                                      (*Il.* 2.455–73)

In book 14, wave, fire, and wind are used to describe the war cries of both Achaean and Trojans and none is adequate—the metaphorics exhausts itself:

The two sides closed together with a great war cry.
Not such is the roaring against dry land of the sea's surf
as it rolls in from the open under the hard blast of the
    north wind;
not such is the bellowing of fire in its blazing
in the deep places of the hills when it rises inflaming
    the forest,
nor such again the crying of the wind in the deep-haired
oaks, when it roars highest in its fury against them,
not so loud as now the noise of Achaians and Trojans
in voice of terror rose as they drove against one another.

                                      (*Il.* 14.393–401)

In other passages the same imagery is used to describe a variety of actions, producing a series of elisions. This is especially the case for assembly and battlefield, whose delineation is often blurred by the persistent imagery of waves to describe the gathering for assembly (*Il.* 2.209–10), the roaring of assent (2.394–7), the amassing for battle (4.422–9, 7.61–6), and the fighting itself (13.795–801, 14.394–401, 15.381–6, 17.263–5). Gathering for battle and fighting are also elided at times; for instance, both the amassing of the armies and the fighting around a corpse evoke imagery of swarms of insects (for example, flies: 2.469–73, 16.641–3; wasps: 16.259–65). And the connection between assembly and fighting implicit in this chain of images is furthered by the connection between the roaring in assembly, the sound of cries and screams on the battlefield, and the increasing indistinctness of these battlefield utterances from the sounds of weapons clashing and blows thudding.[18] This is also an elision of the roaring of mouths and the thundering of feet, of utterance and deployment. With the addition of clashing of shields and spears, we find an elision of hand with mouth and foot, a disarticulation of the body.[19]

The portrait of the Achaean and Trojan armies that emerges from this poetic constellation is that of a body subject to a variety of coalescences and diffusions of force. In this they are not distinct from the bodies of heroes themselves, save in the particular forms their coalescences and diffusions take (the particular actions of which they are capable), and even these can be performed by heroes under extreme circumstances. Indeed, one of the indexes of Achilles' uncanny greatness is that he becomes like an army, swarming around and into the Trojan ranks.[20] In these instances, the line between the Achaean host and its heroes is not as distinct as it might appear to be elsewhere, and as it has often been taken to be. The heroic *bios*, the life of shining words and deeds, does not merely occur against the backdrop of the "masses"; these masses, the "boundless people" (*dēmos apeirōn*; *Il* 24.776), are themselves treated as protagonists, as political actors.[21] Heroes become microcosmic armies, armies become macrocosmic heroes.

---

[18] The elision is prefigured by the use of the same wave imagery to describe both the roaring of the men in assembly and the sound of their marching as they amass on the battlefield. On the significance on associating the heroic war-cry (*iachō*) with the people, see Hammer 2002, 154–5.

[19] And, to follow Purves (2015), a re-articulation, of hand and shield, for instance.

[20] We can see the imagery applied to the Achaeans also applied to Achilles, the images not just of organic motion, but of elemental force (he is accused of being fed on salt water and birthed by the sea) and inert material (like a stone). See Holmes 2015; Purves 2015.

[21] We might then consider individuals and collective as differing not in their ability to undergo coalescence and diffusion, but in the ease with which they can embody or accept a variety of forms of coalescence and diffusion. If we do so, we can identify (a) the coalesced army, gathered for assembly or battle, fighting in units in some instances determined by where they have come from and in others by the particularities of the battlefield, and (b) the diffuse army, the army routed by panic and fear, or the army leaving assembly and returning to fires around which each man cooks his own meal. And we can identify (a) the coalesced hero, distinguishing himself by his strength, intelligence, and/or fighting, often aided by the gods, and even a single hero amassing sufficient force as to spill over an entire army and body of water like

3. One or Several Tongues?

In presenting their collective action in assembly and on the battlefield, Homer emphasizes the role of speech in accomplishing both coalescences and diffusions of force. He thus presents the capacity for *logos* as a source of vulnerability as well as strength. Deliberation is not consistently privileged; assent can be given to bad advice as well as good, as when, for example, the Trojans give assent to Hector rather than Polydamas, their wits having been clouded by Athena (*Il.* 18.310–13). Homer describes an arc of human utterance from *mythoi* (speeches) to *epainoi* (shouts of approval) to *iachai* (cries), and it is worth lingering over the *Iliad*'s illustration of those contexts in which linguistic idiosyncrasy recedes into the background and shared utterance comes to the fore.[22] The effect of such passages is to both illustrate human aggression and reveal its limits. For instance, Achilles' assertion of a radical alienation between Hector and himself is called into question by the very medium in which he utters it.[23] When the cries of battle mesh with the clash of weapons and the thudding sound of blows and falling bodies, the *Iliad* blurs the boundary between speech and cry, draws attention to the murmur underneath the speeches at the assembly, the hum of the army that could at any moment burst into cry, and confronts its audience with the underlying connection between word and deed.[24] When this connection mingles with the other elements of the spectacle of war, the glittering, dazzling, rippling play of weapons and men as well as the grinding, foggy, dusty obscuring work of war, the poem suggests an ambivalence and even suspicion about speech and its connection with other forms of human utterance.

Homer complicates this play between attachment and isolation in his characterization of the organization of the Trojan forces. Disguised as Priam's son Polites, Iris addresses the Trojan assembly gathered in front of Priam's door:

---

a swarm or flock himself, prompting mass fighting even amongst the gods, and in turn we have (b) the diffusion of the hero in his death and the spilling of his blood or in the derangements sent from the gods or the scattering and separation accomplished by fear. On the political significance of such a formulation of the "boundless people," see Elmer 2013, 177–203.

[22] For an analysis of systematic differences between Achaean and Trojan speech patterns, see Mackie 1996; Ross 2005.

[23] "As there are no trustworthy oaths between men and lions, / nor wolves and lambs have spirit that can be brought to agreement / but forever hold feelings of hate for each other, / so there can be no love between you and me, nor shall there be / oaths between us, but one or the other must fall before then / to glut with his blood Ares the god who fights under the shield's guard" (*Il.* 22.262–7).

[24] These scenes of vocal collective assent-giving provide the performance of unity through univocity. In Aeschylus's *Suppliants* (965–8), the description of a vote, the first extant of its kind, provides a similar performance.

> Old sire, dear to you forever are words beyond number
> as once, when there was peace; but stintless war has arisen.
> In my time I have gone into many battles among men,
> yet never have I seen a host like this, not one so numerous.
> These look terribly like leaves, or the sands of the sea-shore,
> as they advance across the plain to fight by the city.
> Hector, on you beyond all I urge this, to do as I tell you:
> all about the great city of Priam are many companions,
> but multitudinous is the speech of the scattered nations [*allē*
>   *d' allōn glōssa polyspereōn anthrōpōn*]:
> let each man who is their leader give orders to these men,
> and let each set his citizens in order, and lead them.
>
> (*Il.* 2.796–806)

Iris's advice echoes that of Nestor to Agamemnon earlier, insofar as she suggests an organization of troops that breaks them into smaller fighting units. Once Agamemnon's near-disastrous testing of the armies has been righted and the chaos it created quelled, Agamemnon receives some advice from Nestor about how to organize the Achaean troops:

> Set your men in order by tribes, by clans [*kata phyla kata*
>   *phrētras*], Agamemnon, and let clan go in support of clan,
>   let tribe support tribe.
> If you do it this way, and the Achaians obey you,
> you will see which of your leaders is bad, and which of
>   your people,
> and which also is brave, since they will fight in divisions,
> and might learn also whether by magic you fail to take this
> city, or by men's cowardice and ignorance of warfare.
>
> (*Il.* 2.362–8)

The relationship between organization and disclosure that Nestor's advice asserts merits attention. The fighting capacities of both captains and men will become apparent if the army is organized into smaller groups determined by shared living and fighting habits. Nestor claims that such an arrangement will reveal the courage or cowardice of the captain and the fighting prowess or lack thereof of the men—such formations disclose what is praiseworthy or blameworthy, they bring something to light and allow it to be assessed with respect to its excellence or lack thereof. What allows this kind of formation to be disclosive is that it forms smaller groups of praise and blame, smaller contexts of surveillance, loyalty, and fear of dishonor, a smaller collectivity whose members feel answerable to one another. Such a grouping harnesses senses of loyalty, competition, and shame in such a way as to further collective action rather than compete for it or shatter it; it acts as a way of separating out that in fact unifies toward a single purpose.

However, because the Trojan army consists not only of Trojans but of troops not bound by a single language, this organization includes an isolation of one fighting mass from another. Because individual heroes can speak to one another across Achaean and Trojan lines, it is in the collective of Trojan and *epikouroi* forces that the effects of linguistic heterogeneity are felt (see Ross 2005).[25] That this lack of linguistic cohesion can produce a lack of fighting cohesion is suggested by the description of the troops' deployment subsequent to their organization:

> Now when the men of both sides were set in order by their
>   leaders,
> the Trojans came on with clamour and shouting, like wildfowl
>   [*klangēi t' enopēi t' isan ornithes hōs*],
> as when the clamour [*klangē*] of cranes goes high to the
>   heavens,
> when the cranes escape the winter time and the rains
>   unceasing
> and clamorously [*klangēi*] wing their way to the
>   steaming Ocean,
> bringing to the Pygmian men bloodshed and destruction:
> at daybreak they bring on the baleful battle against them.
> But the Achaian men went silently [*sigēi*], breathing valour,
> stubbornly minded each in his heart to stand by the others.
>
> (*Il.* 3.1–9)

Here, Homer explicitly juxtaposes the utterances of the Trojan forces with the silence of the Achaean troops. Perhaps ironically, what the possession of a single "tongue" affords the Achaeans is silent deployment. This point is further illustrated in a lengthy passage, whose mingling of speech with spectacle merits close attention (*Il.* 4.422–50); I will attend to the most germane aspects here. The Danaans "went silently [*sigēi*], you would not think all these people with voices kept in their chests were marching; silently, in fear

---

[25] Further, Achaeans and Trojans can achieve sufficient consensus to form the (albeit short-lived) truce of books 3 and 4. See Elmer 2012.

of their commanders; and upon all glittered as they marched the shining armor they carried" (4.427–32). By contrast, the Trojans marched

> as sheep in a man of possessions' steading
> stand in their myriads waiting to be drained by their
>   white milk
> and bleat interminably as they hear the voice of their
>   lambs, so
> the crying of the Trojans went up through the wide army.
> Since there was no speech nor language common to
>   all of them
> but their talk was mixed, who were called there from many far
>   places [*ou gar pantōn ēen homos throos oud' ia gērys, alla*
>   *glōss' ememikto: polyklētoi d' esan andres*].
>
> (*Il.* 4.433–8)

Note the initial disjunction of Achaean silence and Trojan shouting; the passage that follows emphasizes the sound of fighting which includes not only the clash of weapons but the shouts and cries of men (*Il.* 4.450–6). Here, the silence of the Achaeans as well as the "clamor" of the Trojans and the speeches that preceded this action all devolve into the cries and screams of battle. And these utterances, these cries and screams, are taken up with the gleaming and glittering of weapons and shields and their clanging and clashing to produce the spectacle of battle. Thus, that the Trojan forces lack common voice does not always prove an impediment for the action is attested to in many passages in which speech has devolved into battle cries. The difference between the two armies vis-à-vis linguistic homogeneity becomes less and less important as battle intensifies.[26]

In its portrayal of Achaean or Trojan armies giving assent or voicing (enacting) dissent, the *Iliad* offers us a glimpse of the preconditions for frank political speech (*parrhēsia*). Neither "mere" noise nor argument, and yet deeply efficacious (a speaking that is a doing), these expressions of affirmation and

---

[26] As, for instance, a passage from book 13: "So he spoke and led them way, and the rest of them followed him / with unearthly clamour [*ēchēi thespesiēi*], and all the people shouted [*iache*] behind him. / But the Argives on the other side cried out [*epiachon*], and would not forget / their warcraft, but stood the attack of the brave Trojans, / and the clamour [*ēchē*] from both was driven high to Zeus' shining aether" (*Il.* 13.833–7). And from book 14: "Not such is the roaring against dry land of the sea's surf / as it rolls in from the open under the hard blast of the north wind; / not such is the bellowing of fire in its blazing / in the deep places of the hills when it rises inflaming the forest, / nor such again the crying voice of the wind in the deep-haired oaks, / when it roars highest in its fury against them, / not so loud as now the noise of Achaeans and Trojans / in voice of terror [*phōnē deinon*] rose as they drove against one another" (14.394–401).

dissent provide both the linguistic and deliberative substratum from which political speech emerges and the end toward which this speech aims. They are, in this sense, both the first and the final causes of political speech. When we attend to the full range of utterance of which the armies are capable, noting also the significance of the capacity for silence granted by a shared speech, we see that these assertions of assent provide the basis for the efficacy of shared life, they make it possible to move or resist with the force of water, fire, and granite.[27]

But also, in its elision of expressing affirmation, gathering for assembly, amassing for battle, and fighting, that is, in its elision of linguistic, deliberative, and martial deeds, the *Iliad* conveys the vulnerability of *logos* in two senses.[28] First, there is the vulnerability that belongs to *logos*, the tenuous line between speech and noise. Second, there is the vulnerability that *logos* opens up, the vulnerability to err to which humans are exposed by being the animal that "has" *logos*, and thus as subject to linguistic division as well as unity, and to the possibility of being persuaded to act against one's interest.

This ambivalence toward *logos* points to the real issue at stake here, the organization of force toward a common end. *Logos* emerges as an aspect of human animality that can be more or less successfully harnessed to a single purpose. Throughout the poem, the group cohesion and communication of animal collectives illuminate the political bond between human forces as well as its rupture. The clamor of cranes and the swarming of bees, for instance, figure the coalescence and diffusion of force to which the human collectives are subject. What emerges from this imagery is a sense of the power of a common end to generate people, and the power of the people to bring about an end. What most directly forms the "boundless people" is the shared grief over the loss of Hector, grief that is given voice by Hecuba, Andromache, and Helen, in a lamentation that cannot be separated from the cries and wails it elicits in response. This vision of the generation of a *dēmos* does not result in a democracy in the contemporary sense; it is less a rule of the people than a production of people via the rule of shared life. In this, the human collective gives expression to a rule that is taken to be indicative of animality itself, that takes the living body as a regime, and embodiment as already a politics.

---

[27] They also provide a tacit critique of excessive individualism and hyperbolic masculinity. For example, the Achaeans suffer fewer losses in the fight for Patroclus's body because they remembered "always to stand massed and beat sudden death from each other" (*Il.* 17.364–5).

[28] I am using *logos* here primarily in the sense of speech or, more broadly, linguistic capacity. The ambivalence I chart is consistent with the actual appearances of *logos* in both Hesiod and Homer; for analysis, see Lincoln 1997.

Even if we see here nothing of mere inert matter, and thus nothing of a population in the sense of an anonymous material over which power works, we nevertheless see the seeds of such a formulation in the very working of power that is the herd, the pack, and the swarm, that crystallizes into a wall of stone or a cliff of granite, and shatters into grains of sand, a force whose very efficacy can be turned against it, an instrumentalization of life that simply expresses in vivid terms what Aristotle will go on to formulate as a principle of *zōē* itself, namely that life instantiates a form of rule (*Pol.* 1.5.1254a35).

4. Multitudes, Peoples, Masses

Midway through Aristotle's account of the various multitudes that make up the parts of a *polis*, he pauses to reflect on the power of the sea to form peoples, to shape communities on the basis of the desires it meets, for conquest, for instance, or commerce, travel, or sustenance (*Pol.* 4.4.1291b20–2). The very preponderance of fishermen in Tarentum, for example, or warship crews in Athens, gives texture to the city and provides evidence of the observation that, when given authority, the differing kinds of *dēmoi* form different kinds of democracy. Of these, Aristotle numbers five, from the kind in which both poor and rich participate in the regime in similar fashion, "so far as possible" (1291b35–7), such that the rule of the people is secured only by their greater number, to the democracy in which "the multitude, rather than the law, have authority [*kyrion d' einai to plēthos kai mē ton nomon*]" (1292a5). This fifth democracy, the most debased in Aristotle's opinion, is most vulnerable to demagoguery, for "where laws are without authority, there popular leaders arise" (1292a10–11). In such a condition, "the people become a monarch, from many combining into one—for the many have authority not as individuals but all together [*monarchos gar ho dēmos ginetai, synthetos heis ek pollōn: hoi gar polloi kyrioi eisin ouch hōs hekastos alla pantes*]" (1292a11–13). Aristotle pauses here to wonder whether the Homeric reference in the *Iliad* to "many-headed rule [*polykoiraniēn*]" (2.204) conveys concern over this very structure of power, before concluding that such a rule of the people resembles tyranny (*Pol.* 4.4.1292a18), and risks its very status as a regime, "for where the laws do not rule there is no regime" (1292a32).

The anxiety about a form of "democracy" that tends toward tyranny was not unique to Aristotle. But Aristotle's concentrated use of a variety of forms of reference to human collectives—multitude (*plēthos*), people (*dēmos*), the many (*hoi polloi*)—conveys the sense that any attempt to negotiate rule and authority carries with it the possibility of forming or deforming a human multitude, of producing either a *dēmos* or a *tyrannos*, or even a *dēmos* that becomes a *tyrannos*. It is for this very reason that expertise in politics requires training to discern the many kinds of multitudes and peoples. And it is at least in part as an effort to shore up vulnerability to the threat of tyrannical rule "by the people" that Aristotle spends that latter part of the *Politics* designing not only the outline of a system of education for citizens of the aspirational *polis* (the city of prayers, as he describes it) but also a system for the production of citizen children in the eugenics legislation that forms one of the clearest points of intersection with contemporary biopolitics.

The aim of this management of human birth and early education is the production of what Aristotle describes as a political multitude (*Pol.* 7.7.1327b18), whose labor must be organized according to the needs of the best city. A self-sufficient *polis* must accomplish the provision of sustenance, of the arts, of weapons, of funds, superintendence with respect to the divine, and finally, "the most necessary thing of all [*pantōn anankaiotaton*]," judgment concerning what is advantageous and what is just (8.8.1328b5–15). Accordingly, the political multitude must include farmers, artisans, a fighting element, a well-off element, priests, and judges of things necessary and advantageous.

Aristotle next sorts out how to divide up the human multitude as regards these tasks and roles. Because the aim of the city is virtue, neither the vulgar element nor the farmer can be granted fully enfranchised citizenship, the former because their way of life is "ignoble and opposed to virtue" (*Pol.* 7.9.1328b39–41), the latter because they lack the necessary leisure: "for there is need for leisure both as regards the creation of virtue and as regards political actions" (1328b41–1329a2). The farming class, then, should be made up of "slaves or barbarian subjects [*doulous ē barbarous perioikous*]" (1329a26).[29] The military and deliberative elements are determined not by different groups of people, but by different aspects of the life cycle of the same group of people, "insofar as each task belongs to a different prime of life [*hēi men gar heteras akmēs hekateron tōn ergōn*]" (1329a8). This would allow the city to take advantage of the presumed greater capacity of the young and greater prudence of the middle-aged (1329a14–17). Priestly duties are allocated to these same men in their old age (1329a27–34).

Aristotle is clear that it is this collection of men, whose early adulthood will be spent in military pursuits, middle age in deliberation and command, and old age in attending to the gods, who are the citizens of the city (*Pol.* 7.9.1329a19). In restricting citizenship in this way, Aristotle ties the life

---

[29] Here I follow Lord in bracketing the *ē* of the MSS, which would read "barbarians or subjects."

of the citizen to the life cycle of an exclusive category of men whose living is regulated at all stages, from a system of education that comprises a supervision of their complete sensorium—from what they eat, see, and hear, to how they touch and are touched—to the training in war and peace that occurs over the course of their adult life. When they are beyond child-producing age, they are released from procreative duty but will continue in their role as ruling and being ruled in turn, transitioning to the priesthood in later life. They are supported by a host of slaves and other laborers, and by legislation providing for their private ownership of other humans and things and limiting the size of the human collective to which they belong. This is all to say that the entire structure of their lives is built upon the systemic, ingrained exploitation of a massive labor class made possible by a model of private ownership, understanding of possessions, and system of education that are formed by Aristotle's conception of the instruments required by *zōē*.

In the city of prayers, then, Aristotle envisions a complete regulation and synchronization of citizens' entire life cycle. The aim of this comprehensive regulative structure is the production of a citizen body and soul best capable of producing noble deeds, and a city whose *bios* (its *politeia*; *Pol.* 4.11.1295a40–b1) is best able to realize the excellence that Aristotle takes to be most definitive of humans. The partnership of such citizens comprises, for Aristotle, a city able to sustain itself in perpetuity, defend itself from its neighbors, rule those who need ruling, and carry on in the closest proximation to the eternal orbits of the divine that is humanly possible. The city emerges from this account as synonymous with the partnership of these men, and they themselves, like the forms of human multitude and the plurality of *politeiai*, are, in the end, conceived of as expressions of the force of *zōē*.

5. Conclusion

The differing forms of human multitude that Aristotle traces in the central books of the *Politics*, like the differing forms of force available to living collectives that Homer limns, attest to a plurality and multiplicity of *zōē*-regimes. While some of these regimes are formed on the basis of deliberation, some arise simply by the exigencies of performing the shared deed that constitutes their foundational motivation. In this sense, there is less a "population" than many "multitudes," not all of which are created by the forces of *human* rule. And the *physis* that has something to do with the preponderance of fishermen on Tarentum or naval crews in Athens cannot be assumed to align perfectly with the "nature" and "natural law" that Foucault sees as regulative ideals in the emergence of contemporary biopolitics (Foucault 2007, 55–86). Moreover, while Aristotle will broach a human multiplicity stripped of identifying features, an anonymous mass, he will do so as an expression of a deviant political structure, a tyrannical *dēmos* that tends toward the popular leader who would institute full tyranny if given the chance. This is the very multitude that inspires Aristotle to consider the Homeric concern about multiheaded rule (*polykoiraniēn*; see *Pol.* 4.4.1292a13).

And yet, while the best city is designed, in part, to avoid this particular anonymous mass, its approach to its citizens—the wool the seasoned statesman must weave—bears more than a passing resemblance to the tyrant's. What is aberrant about the tyrant is less the degree of his control of his citizens than the end toward which this control aims, that is, his own private good as opposed to the common good. The best city will strive to regulate every aspect of the life cycle of its citizens, from conception, birth, and early childhood education to shared public education, and on into public service that includes military service, public administration, religious observance, and submission of one's bodily fluids and capacities to the production of future citizens. The distinction between the tyranny and the city of prayers, we are led to believe, lies in a transhuman ideal of godlike capacity invoked in the very prayer in which this city finds its expression, and embedded in the conception of *zōē* that forms the aim and end of Aristotle's political theory. Indeed, it is *zōē* that is at stake in and must be assured by human political life. The result of Aristotle's efforts to do so include forms of legislation designed to regulate life processes for optimal living as he perceives it, an orientation toward the *polis* as the site in which such regulation is best realized, and a vision of the aspirational *polis* whose excellence resides in its sensitivity to the dominant life-cycle events of its citizens, all of which are informed by a detailed body of knowledge about the lives and natures of animals.

There are clear intersections with the concerns of biopolitics, governmentality, and security as Foucault discusses them in his later lecture courses. But the vision of *zōē* that resides at the heart of Aristotle's political theory—as a cosmic force, as expression and index of power, as assured by the eternality of the heavens—cannot be assumed to map so easily on to the aims of contemporary biopolitical forces. Where those lines converge and diverge cannot be seen without a detailed account of Aristotle's orientation toward animality as such, and its place within his larger conceptions of *physis* and *kosmos*.

References

Aeschylus. 1991. *The Suppliants*. Translated by Peter Burian. Princeton, NJ: Princeton University Press.

Arendt, Hannah. 1973. *The Origins of Totalitarianism*. New York: Harcourt Brace Jovanovich.

Aristotle. 1884. *Ethica Eudemia*. Edited by Franz Susemihl. Leipzig: Teubner.

Aristotle. 1894. *Ethica Nicomachea*. Edited by Ingram Bywater. Oxford: Clarendon Press.

Aristotle. 1924. *Metaphysics*. 2 vols. Edited by William David Ross. Oxford: Clarendon Press.

Aristotle. 1957. *Politica*. Edited by William David Ross. Oxford: Clarendon Press.

Aristotle. 1964–9. *Histoire des animaux* [*Historia animalium*]. Vols. 1–3. Edited by Pierre Louis. Paris: Les Belles Lettres.

Aristotle. 1965. *Du ciel* [*De caelo*]. Edited by Paul Moraux. Paris: Les Belles Lettres.

Aristotle. 1981. *The Politics*. Translated by Thomas Alan Sinclair, translation revised by Trevor J. Saunders. Harmondsworth: Penguin Books.

Aristotle. 1984. *The Politics*. Translated by Carnes Lord. Chicago: University of Chicago Press.

Bennett, Joan. 2010a. *Vibrant Matter: A Political Ecology of Things*. Durham, NC: Duke University Press.

Bennett, Joan. 2010b. "A Vitalist Stopover on the Way to a New Materialism." In *New Materialisms: Ontology, Agency, and Politics*, edited by Diana Coole and Samantha Frost, 47–69. Durham, NC: Duke University Press. https://doi.org/10.1215/9780822392996-002.

Biller, Peter. 2000. *The Measure of Multitude: Population in Medieval Thought*. Oxford: Oxford University Press.

Bonnafé, Annie. 1984. *Poésie, nature et sacré*. Vol.1, *Homère, Hésiode et le sentiment grec de la nature*. Lyon: Maison de l'Orient.

Brill, Sara. 2020. *Aristotle on the Concept of Shared Life*. Oxford: Oxford University Press.

Caplan, Jane, and John Torpey, eds. 2001. *Documenting Individual Identity: The Development of State Practices in the Modern World*. Princeton, NJ: Princeton University Press.

Cavarero, Adriana. 2019. "The Human Reconceived: Back to Socrates with Arendt." In *Antiquities beyond Humanism*, edited by Emanuela Bianchi, Sara Brill, and Brooke Holmes, 31–46. Oxford: Oxford University Press. https://doi.org/10.1093/oso/9780198805670.003.0002.

Cisney, Vernon, and Nicolae Morar. 2016. "Introduction: Why Biopower? Why Now?" In *Biopower: Foucault and Beyond*, edited by Vernon Cisney and Nicolae

Morar, 1–25. Chicago: University of Chicago Press. https://doi.org/10.7208/CHICAGO/9780226226767.003.0000.

Cole, Joshua. 2000. *The Power of Large Numbers: Population, Politics, and Gender in Nineteenth-Century France.* Ithaca, NY: Cornell University Press.

Coole, Diana, and Samantha Frost, eds. 2010. *New Materialisms: Ontology, Agency, and Politics.* Durham, NC: Duke University Press.

Curtis, Bruce. 2001. *The Politics of Population: Statistics, State Formation, and the Census of Canada, 1840–1975.* Toronto: Toronto University Press.

Curtis, Bruce. 2002. "Foucault on Governmentality and Population: The Impossible Discovery." *The Canadian Journal of Sociology/Cahiers canadiens de sociologie* 27 (4): 505–33. https://doi.org/10.2307/3341588.

Di Leo, Jeffrey R. and Peter Hitchcock, eds. 2020. *Biotheory: Life and Death under Capitalism.* New York: Routledge.

Dimock, Wai Chee. 2008. *Through Other Continents: American Literature across Deep Time.* Princeton, NJ: Princeton University Press.

Dubreuil, Laurent. 2006. "Leaving Politics: *Bios, Zōē,* Life." Translated by Clarissa C. Eagle and Laurent Dubreuil. *Diacritics* 36 (2): 83–98. https://doi.org/10.1353/dia.2008.0013.

Elmer, David. 2012. "Building Community Across the Battle-Lines: The Truce in *Iliad* 3 and 4." In *Maintaining Peace and Interstate Stability in Archaic and Classical Greece,* edited by Julia Wilker, 25–48. Berlin: Verlag Antike. https://doi.org/10.13109/9783946317845.25.

Elmer, David. 2013. *The Poetics of Consent: Collective Decision Making and the "Iliad."* Baltimore, MD: Johns Hopkins University Press.

Fenno, Jonathan Brian. 2005. "'A Great Wave against the Stream': Water Imagery in Iliadic Battle Scenes." *The American Journal of Philology* 126 (4): 475–504. https://doi.org/10.1353/ajp.2006.0005.

Finlayson, James Gordon. 2010. "'Bare Life' and Politics in Agamben's Reading of Aristotle." *The Review of Politics* 72 (1): 97–126. https://doi.org/10.1017/S0034670509990982.

Forti, Simona. 2006. "The Biopolitics of Souls: Racism, Nazism, and Plato." *Political Theory* 34 (1): 9–32. https://doi.org/10.1177/0090591705280526.

Foucault, Michel. 1989. *Résumé des cours, 1970–1982.* Paris: Julliard.

Foucault, Michel. 2007. *Security, Territory, Population: Lectures at the Collège de France, 1977–78.* Translated by Graham Burchell. New York: Palgrave Macmillan.

Garland, Robert. 1990. *The Greek Way of Life: From Conception to Old Age.* London: Bristol Classical Press.

Hammer, Dean. 2002. *The Iliad as Politics: The Performance of Political Thought.* Oklahoma City: University of Oklahoma Press.

Holmes, Brooke. 2015. "Situating Scamander: 'Natureculture' in the *Iliad.*" *Ramus* 44 (1–2): 29–51. https://doi.org/10.1017/rmu.2015.2.

Holmes, Brooke. 2019. "Bios." *Political Concepts: A Critical Lexicon*, no. 5. Accessed January 27, 2020. https://www.politicalconcepts.org/bios-brooke-holmes.

Homer. 1951. *The Iliad*. Translated by Richmond Lattimore. Chicago: University of Chicago Press.

Homer. 1998–2000. *Ilias*. 2 vols. Edited by Martin Litchfield West. Stuttgart: Teubner.

King, R. A. H. 2001. *Aristotle on Life and Death*. London: Duckworth.

Le Dœuff, Michèle. 1990. *The Philosophical Imaginary*. Translated by Colin Gordon. Stanford, CA: Stanford University Press.

Lincoln, Bruce. 1997. "Competing Discourses: Rethinking the Prehistory of *Mythos* and *Logos*." *Arethusa* 30 (3): 341–67.

Mackie, Hilary. 1996. *Talking Trojan: Speech and Community in the Iliad*. Lanham, MD: Rowman & Littlefield.

Mader, Mary Beth. 2016. "Foucault, Cuvier, and the Sciences of Life." In *Biopower: Foucault and Beyond*, edited by Vernon Cisney and Nicolae Morar, 121–37. Chicago: University of Chicago Press. https://doi.org/10.7208/chicago/9780226226767.003.0006.

Miller, Paul Allen. 2020. "Against Agamben: or Living your Life, *Zōē* versus *Bios* in the late Foucault." In *Biotheory: Life and Death under Capitalism*, edited by Jeffrey Di Leo and Peter Hitchcock, 23–41. New York: Routledge. https://doi.org/10.4324/9781003021506-3.

Mills, Catherine. 2016. "Biopolitics and the Concept of Life." In *Biopower: Foucault and Beyond*, edited by Vernon Cisney and Nicolae Morar, 82–101. Chicago: University of Chicago Press. https://doi.org/10.7208/chicago/9780226226767.003.0004.

Ojakangas, Mika. 2016. *On the Greek Origins of Biopolitics: A Reinterpretation of the History of Biopower*. London: Routledge.

Purves, Alex. 2015. "Ajax and Other Objects: Homer's Vibrant Materialism." *Ramus* 44 (1–2): 75–94. https://doi.org/10.1017/rmu.2015.4.

Rose, Nikolas. 2006. *The Politics of Life Itself: Biomedicine, Power, and Subjectivity in the Twenty-First Century*. Princeton, NJ: Princeton University Press.

Ross, Shawn A. 2005. "*Barbarophonos*: Language and Panhellenism in the *Iliad*." *Classical Philology* 100 (4): 299–316. https://doi.org/10.1086/500434.

Weil, Simone. 1945. "The Iliad, or the Poem of Force." Translated by Mary McCarthy. *Politics*, November 1945, 321–31.

Whitman, Cedric H. 1958. *Homer and the Heroic Tradition*. Cambridge, MA: Harvard University Press.

2
Plato and the Biopolitical Purge of the City-State

Mika Ojakangas

1. Introduction

In *Homo Sacer*, one aim of which is to correct Michel Foucault's thesis on the history of biopolitics, Giorgio Agamben introduces Plato's "law of nature" as an antidote to the sophistic confusion of violence and law. Citing a passage from the *Laws* (3.690b–c) in which Plato supplements Pindar's axiom of sovereignty, according to which it is natural that the strong rule the weak, with his own axiom of the natural superiority of the prudent ones, Agamben writes:

> In the passage from the *Laws* cited above, the power of law is defined as being in accordance with nature (*kata physin*) and essentially nonviolent because Plato is most of all concerned to neutralize the opposition that, for both the Sophists and Pindar (in a different way), justified the "sovereign" confusion of *Bia* and *Dikē*.
>
> (Agamben 1998, 34)

In this chapter focusing on Plato's mature works, I argue that Plato's law "according to nature" is neither nonviolent nor an antidote to violence, inasmuch as for Plato, the use of violence in the mode of political and legal therapy is not only a necessity in a well-ordered city-state but also entirely in accordance with nature.[1] Although it is true that Plato criticizes the sophistic idea that violence creates justice, it is also evident that the Platonic natural justice is not antithetical to violence as such. In Plato's view, it is naturally just to be violent (for instance, to kill those whose body or soul is so "deformed" that it is incurable), particularly if and when this violence contributes to the well-being of the city-state—like amputation contributes

---

[1] With the expression "mature works" I refer to the *Republic* and the (presumably authentic) books written (again, presumably) after it, including primarily the *Sophist*, the *Statesman*, the *Timaeus*, and the *Laws*. A few references are also made to *Gorgias*, where Plato first introduces his medical model of politics.

Mika Ojakangas, *Plato and the Biopolitical Purge of the City-State* In: *Biopolitics and Ancient Thought*. Edited by: Jussi Backman and Antonio Cimino, Oxford University Press. © Oxford University Press 2022.
DOI: 10.1093/oso/9780192847102.003.0003

to the health of one's body if an organ is deformed by a disease. Plato does not believe that violence *creates* justice, but he believes that the implementation of justice *presupposes* violence.

Furthermore, I argue that Platonic violence is essentially biopolitical, representing what Foucault identifies as biopolitical state racism, in particular. Just like biopolitical rationality in general, biopolitical state racism aims to improve the welfare of the population in terms of its physical and mental health, morality, and intelligence. Yet biopolitical state racism adds a significant twist to biopolitical rationality: the welfare of the population presupposes the elimination of the bad elements of the very same population (Foucault 1990, 135–9; 2003b, 239–64). Hence, a state racist mentality looks at the population as a gardener looks at her garden: without weeding, the garden does not flourish. This is the mentality that permeates Plato's political philosophy. In Plato's view, this mentality is lacking in the Greek democratic city-state in which the weeds (the inferior many) repress the flowers (the superior few), but it is not altogether absent from Greek society as he discovers it in a variety of other practices from selective animal breeding to the art of medicine. A good statesman, as Plato argues in the *Laws* (5.735b–736a), imitates stockbreeders who separate the healthy from the unhealthy and the purebreds from the degenerate stock, keeping only the purebreds and healthy animals to look after. Otherwise, animals endowed with healthy and pure bodies and characters are contaminated by the faults of the sick and impure through interbreeding.

2. Health as the Paradigm of Justice

In *Homo Sacer*, Agamben maintains that Plato's "law of nature" aims at undermining the sovereign confusion of violence and law. Yet it is well-known that the notion "law of nature" (*nomos physeōs*) appears only once in Plato's works, more precisely, in the *Gorgias* in a passage in which Callicles defends his thesis that it is the right of "the superior rule the inferior" (*ton kreittō tou hēttonos archein*; *Grg.* 483d). Asking by what right Xerxes marched against Greece, or his father against Scythia, Callicles famously proclaims:

> I believe that these men do these things in accordance with the nature of what is just [*kata physin tēn tou dikaiou*]—indeed, by Zeus, in accordance with the law of nature [*kata nomon ge ton tēs physeōs*], and presumably not with the one we insti-
> tute. We mold the best [*beltistous*] and the most powerful [or: the

healthiest—*errōmenestatous*] among us, taking them while they are still young, like lion cubs, and with charms and incantations we subdue them into slavery, telling them that one is supposed to get no more than his fair share, and that is what is admirable and just. But I believe that if a man whose nature is equal to it were to arise, one who had shaken off, torn apart, and escaped all this, who had trampled underfoot our documents, our tricks and charms, and all our laws that violate nature [*nomous tous para physin*], he, the slave, would rise up and be revealed as our master, and here the justice of nature [*tēs physeōs dikaion*] would shine forth.   (*Grg.* 483e–484b)

Hence, it is not unproblematic to refer to Plato's doctrine of "natural law," unless one erroneously thinks that Callicles' position in *Gorgias* is actually that of Plato. In fact, even the expression "justice of nature" (*tēs physeōs dikaion*) is absent from the texts supposedly representing Socrates' or Plato's views. On the other hand, it is true that in Plato's late works, nature (*physis*) *is* the criterion of justice. Real justice is based not on customs or opinions but on nature. According to Plato, in fact, everything that is "according to nature" (*kata physin*) is just, while anything that is "contrary to nature" (*para physin*) is unjust. Hence, Agamben is at least partially correct when he speaks about Plato's "law of nature." But to what extent is this "law of nature" an *antithesis* of that of the sophists? Callicles argues that it is according to nature that the best (*beltistous*) and the strongest (*errōmenestatous*) rule; but if we read Plato's *Republic* or the *Laws*, it becomes immediately obvious that also Plato advocates the rule of the best. In the *Republic*, the guardians are "the best [*beltistai*] of all the citizens"—and to the extent that health, psychic health in particular, is one of the essential features of the best, they are in this sense also the strongest. In Plato's view, it is also "according to nature" (*kata physin*) that the superior rule the inferior (*Resp.* 5.474b–c).

What, then, is the difference between Callicles and Plato? The difference resides in their conceptions of the *intention* of nature. While Callicles believes that nature expresses itself in the degrees of power preferring the strong to the weak, Plato's concept of nature resembles that of ancient physicians. Justice is the natural balance between the different parts of the soul in the same sense as health (*hygieia*) in medicine is the natural balance between the different parts of the body. As the body is healthy when each of its parts performs its proper function in the hierarchical constitution of the body, the soul is just and virtuous when each of its parts performs its proper function (*ergon*) in the hierarchical constitution of the soul in which the rational part dominates the appetitive and the spirited parts. As Plato writes in the *Republic*:

To produce health [*hygieian*] is to establish the relation of ruling and being ruled between the elements of the body according to nature [*kata physin*], while to produce disease [*noson*] is to establish the relation of ruling and being ruled contrary to nature [*para physin*].

That's right.

Then, to produce justice is to establish the relation of ruling and being ruled between the parts of the soul according to nature [*kata physin*], while to produce injustice is to establish the relation of ruling and being ruled contrary to nature [*para physin*].

Precisely.

Virtue [*aretē*] seems, then, to be a kind of health [*hygieia*] and beauty [*kallos*] and good disposition of the soul [*euexia psychēs*], and badness [*kakia*] would be disease [*nosos*], ugliness [*aischros*], and weakness [*astheneia*].

(*Resp.* 4.444d–e; translation modified)

In the *Republic*, the same pattern holds true with entire city-states. As there are three different parts of the soul, there are three different natural classes (*genē physeōn*) in the city-state. Consequently, to produce justice in the city-state is to establish the relation of ruling and being ruled between the classes according to nature (*kata physin*), while to produce injustice is to establish the relation of ruling and being ruled contrary to nature (*para physin*; *Resp.* 4.434a–c). Further, to the extent that the soul is just if it is dominated by the reasonable part, the city-state is considered to be just if it is dominated by the class in which the reasonable part of the soul is the leading part. Or, more precisely, the city-state is just if each individual performs the function (*ergon*) proper to the nature (*physis*) of that individual and the class or race (*genos*) he naturally belongs to (435b),[2] meaning the class of manual laborers, auxiliaries, or leaders, respectively.

3. Democratic Anomaly

This conception of justice is not an antithesis of Callicles' natural justice. From Plato's point of view, in fact, Callicles is on the right track by assuming that justice has its basis not in customs or in opinions, but in nature. Callicles' mistake is just that he misinterprets nature's intention: he believes that nature expresses itself in the degrees of power. According to Plato, however, it is not power but health, understood as the natural balance between the parts of the

---

[2] *Genos* can be translated as either "race" or "class," depending on the context. On the notion of *genos* in Plato, see, for example, Kamtekar 2002.

whole in the hierarchical structure of the soul and the city-state, that is the true end of nature. Although they both agree that it is natural that the best and the strongest rule, Callicles' mistake is, according to Plato, that he identifies excellence, strength, and health with physical power. In Plato's view, it is not only physical but also—and above all—mental excellence, strength, and health that should determine, if we are to follow the intention of nature, the hierarchy of the positions of power in the city-state. Instead of Callicles, or Thrasymachus for that matter,[3] Plato's real adversary is Greek *democracy*. In the democratic city-state, there are neither rulers nor hierarchy (*Resp.* 8.558c), as it distributes equality to "both equals and unequals alike" (558c). Such a leaderless equality is contrary to nature, as "it is by nature fitting [*prosēkei physei*] for some... to lead the city, whereas for others [it is fitting] to obey the leader" (5.474b–c; translation modified). It is also contrary to nature because natural equality does not entail equal share but "dispenses more to the greater and less to the smaller" (*Leg.* 6.757c; translation modified). In democracy, secondly, because there are no leaders in the state and everybody (including foreigners, women, and even slaves) is equal with one another, everyone is also absolutely free. Even domestic animals enjoy this democratic equality and freedom:

> Even horses and donkeys are accustomed to roam freely and proudly along the streets, bumping into anyone who does not get out of their way; and all the rest are equally full of freedom.   (*Resp.* 8.563c)

In Plato's view, justice prevails when each individual performs the function (*ergon*) proper to the nature (*physis*) of that individual and the class (*genos*) he belongs to, but in the democratic city-state there is no proper place or function either for the individuals or for the classes (as there are none)—not even for animals. Justice finds its place in the well-ordered city-state ruled by the superior race, but in the democratic city-state, there is no order or rule whatsoever. This disorder and unruliness is the main characteristic of the democratic city-state—and the same unruliness describes the soul of the democratic individual:

> And so he lives on, yielding day by day to the desire at hand. Sometimes he drinks heavily while listening to the flute; at other times, he drinks only water and is on a diet; sometimes he goes in for physical training; at other times, he's idle and neglects everything; and sometimes he even occupies himself with what he takes

---

[3] Because Thrasymachus in the *Republic* does not employ the *nomos/physis* framework in his defence of the concept of justice as the advantage of the stronger, I leave it aside in this analysis.

to be philosophy. He often engages in politics, leaping up from his seat and saying and doing whatever comes into his mind. If he happens to admire soldiers he's carried in that direction, if money-makers, in that one. There's neither order [*taxis*] nor necessity [*ananke*] in his life, but he calls it pleasant [*hedyn*], free [*eleutherion*], and blessedly happy [*makarion*], and he follows it for as long as he lives.

(Resp. 8.561c–d)

Rather than Callicles' natural law, it is this unruliness (form of life without a proper form, without a proper function, without necessity), which, for Plato, is a logical consequence of absolute equality and freedom, that annoys him the most.[4] The democratic soul and the city-state are thoroughly contrary to nature (*para physin*)—and to the extent that they are contrary to nature, they are manifestations of injustice *par excellence*. Democratic man calls his life pleasant and blessedly happy, but in Plato's estimation, happiness (*eudaimonia*) is possible only for a well-ordered soul in a well-ordered city-state organized according to natural justice: "The whole point of our legislation is to allow the citizens to live supremely happy lives" (*Leg.* 5.743c).[5] Instead of happiness, the democratic soul and the city-state characterized by unbounded and unnatural freedom are in a state of miserable disease. Against this disease of freedom, Plato establishes a system of natural hierarchy by means of the total control of individuals and populations:

The vital point is that no one, man or woman, must ever be left without someone in charge of him [*anarchon*]; nobody, whether at work or in play, must get into the habit of acting alone and independently. In peace and war alike, we must give our constant attention and obedience to our leader, submitting to his guidance even in tiny details.   (*Leg.* 12.942a–b; translation modified)

---

[4] Recently, there has also appeared a tendency to depict Plato as a *defender* of democracy. In her *Poetic Justice*, for example, Jill Frank argues that the negative representation of democracy in the *Republic* does not apply to democracy as such but only to its imperial form assumed by Athenian democracy, seeking for "power, glory, and honor" (Frank 2018, 143). She justifies her argument by stating that the *Republic* stages the need to develop human capacities, offering an education in ethical and political self-governance. Due to this noble aim, the *Republic* endorses democracy, Frank claims. However, such an interpretation is not very plausible. Nowhere in the *Republic* do we find criticism of *democratic* desire for power, glory, and honor—simply because they were not considered as democratic values either by Plato or by the Greeks. For Plato, they were timocratic values. Further, although the role of education (*paideia*) is central in the *Republic*, there is, in the Greek context, nothing particularly democratic about it. For the Greeks, *paideia* was an aristocratic ideal. The main values of the Greek democracy were freedom and equality ("freedom based on equality"; *Pol.* 6.2.1317b16–17), and, based on these principles, the right to live as one likes (1317b10–15; see also Hdt. 3.83; Thuc. 2.37, 7.69; pseudo-Xenophon, *Ath. pol.* 1.10–12). For Plato, they were precisely these fundamental democratic values—particularly the one that gives everyone the right (*exousia*) to "arrange his own life in whatever way pleases him" (*Resp.* 8.557b)—that were the main faults of democracy. Hence, rather than criticizing Athenian imperial democracy seeking for power and glory, he is criticizing democracy as such—democracy based on individual freedom and equality.

[5] "We take ourselves," Plato writes also in the *Republic* (4.420c), "to be fashioning the happy city, not picking out a few happy people and putting them in it, but making the whole city happy [*eudaimon*]."

4. Disease of Injustice

Now, although Plato believes that both the soul and the city-state can be just or unjust, it is the condition of the soul—the disposition (*hexis*) and character (*ēthos*) of men—that determines the condition of the city-state, including the form of its government.[6] Hence, a city-state cannot be just if there are bad men among its inhabitants: "Statecraft truly according to nature [*kata physin*] will never voluntarily compose a state of good [*chrēstōn*] and bad [*kakōn*] men" (*Plt.* 308d; translation modified). This is why Plato pays so much attention to the physical and mental qualities of the individuals in his books on politics, rather than the institutional structures of the city-state. Further, because Plato thought that heredity, in particular, but also the environment, especially in childhood, determine the physical and mental quality of individuals,[7] he not only deals extensively with such biopolitical issues as sexual intercourse, marriage, pregnancy, childbirth, childcare, healthcare, physical training, and education, but regards them as the most *essential* issues of politics and legislation (see, for example, *Leg.* 8.842d–e). Only if the city-state guarantees all of its inhabitants a healthy inborn nature, a healthy physical environment, healthy childcare, a healthy diet, a healthy physical training, and good education, will they be of high quality, which in turn is the precondition for the just city-state governed according to nature.

Yet Plato admits that even in the best-governed city-state, bad individuals may be born. Healthy parents sound of body and mind may sometimes produce a deformed child (*Resp.* 5.460c). Bodily diseases, even transient ones, may also give rise "to all manners of rashness and cowardice, and of forgetfulness also, as well as of stupidity" (*Ti.* 87a). In Plato's view, moreover, it is almost a natural necessity that even the leaders of the best-governed city-state at some point join brides and grooms at the wrong time with the

---

[6] As Plato puts it in the *Republic* (8.544d): "And do you realize that of necessity there are as many forms of human characters as there are constitutions? Or do you think that constitutions are born 'from oak or rock' and not from the characters of the people?"

[7] Plato believes that for the most part physical and mental traits are inborn—though in his view, even acquired habits may be inherited (see *Leg.* 6.775d–e). This explains why he pays so much attention not only to the regulation of sexuality and reproduction but also to the parents' physical and mental condition before and during the sexual act in the *Republic* and the *Laws*. For a more detailed analysis of the regulation of sexuality and reproduction in Plato, see Ojakangas 2016, 59–100. However, Plato is not a determinist in matters of heredity. In his view, healthy parents may give birth to a deformed child (*Resp.* 5.460c). Moreover, a bad environment may ruin even the best individuals (8.550b). The physical environment has also an effect on the bodies and characters of individuals (*Leg.* 5.747d–e). Nonetheless, Plato *is* a determinist: for him, the combination of heredity and environment (from the physical environment to the political organization of the city-state) determines the character and the conduct of man. It is not good or bad will but the combination of inborn nature (*physis*), nurture (*trophē*), and education (*paideia*) that renders a man good or corrupts him. On biopolitical and reproductive social justice in Plato, see also chapter 3 by Kathy L. Gaca in this volume.

consequence that the children will be neither well-formed (*euphyeis*) nor fortunate (*eutycheis*; *Resp.* 8.546c–d). Now, if there are no well-governed city-states consisting of both good and bad men, an urgent question arises: What to do with the bad ones?

Before looking at what Plato suggests with regard to the unjust ones, let us consider his definition of injustice. We recall what Plato said in the *Republic*: injustice is a disease (*nosos*), ugliness (*aischros*), and weakness (*astheneia*) of the soul. This passage already indicates that for Plato, justice and injustice are attributes not of *action* but those of *disposition* (*hexis*) or *character* (*ēthos*). A bit earlier in the same book, he states this explicitly. Justice "does not concern man's external action but what is inside him" (*Resp.* 4.443c–d; translation modified). The same holds with injustice. While justice is a balance of the soul, injustice is its imbalance: a disturbed state of the soul, be it permanent or transient. Hence, an individual can be unjust *irrespective* of what the individual possessing such a disturbed soul has done or left undone: "My general description of injustice is this: the mastery of the soul by anger, fear, pleasure, pain, envy and desires, whether they lead to any actual damage or not" (*Leg.* 9.863e). An individual endowed with a disturbed soul is not bad because he is guilty of an unjust offense, but because his soul is in a bad condition. He is unjust because there are bad acquired and natural habits (*Resp.* 10.618d) in his soul. Inversely, an injury when caused by a just man is *not* an injustice, simply because his disposition is just: if justice prevails in the soul of man, his actions are always just, even if he happens to err (*Leg.* 9.864a). Further, the acquired and inborn habits *determine* the bad man to be unjust against his will: "All bad men are, in all respects, unwillingly bad" (860d; translation modified).[8] Thus, instead of being an autonomous person endowed with a free will, responsible for his actions, and, therefore, a site of legal imputation, a bad man is determined to be bad either by his (sick) body or by his (corrupted) environment, "both entirely beyond [his] control" (*Ti.* 87b). Indeed, he himself—that is, his soul—is suffering from a disease.

We should not take the metaphor of disease too lightly. On the one hand, disease of the soul (*psychēs nosos*) is one of the most often employed metaphors of moral badness in Plato's corpus (*Grg.* 480a–b, 524e; *Resp.* 4.444d–e, 10.610a–611a; *Soph.* 228d–e; *Ti.* 86b–87b; *Leg.* 9.853d, 854b–c, 862c).[9] Given Plato's assumption that nobody is voluntarily bad, the metaphor of disease is

---

[8] In the *Timaeus* (86d–e; translation modified), Plato likewise writes: "No one is voluntarily bad but the bad man becomes bad by reason of some bad condition of body [*ponēra hexis tou sōmatos*] and unskilled nurture [*apaideutos trophē*]." Plato does not explicitly say that a good man is also determined to be good, but given Plato's anthropological determinism, this should be the case.

[9] On medical metaphors in Plato, see Lidz 1995. On medical metaphors in Greek political language in general, see Brock 2013, 69–76, 147–56.

also an apt metaphor for injustice: surely, nobody *wants* to be sick. Yet the real reason why we should not take this metaphor lightly is that in Plato's late writings, some exceptions aside, it is not a metaphor in the first place: injustice *is* a disease. For Plato, all psychosomatic imbalances are diseases: "Disease [*nosos*] and discord [*stasis*] are the same thing" (*Soph.* 228a). While a disease of the body is a discord (*stasis*) between the parts of the body, a disease of the soul is a discord between the parts of the soul.[10] In Plato's estimation, injustice is also such a disease of the soul. Ordinary people call it wickedness (*ponēria*), but "it is very clearly a disease (*nosos*)," as Plato asserts in the *Sophist* (228d). Hence, rather than a metaphor, injustice is literally a disease of the soul. Evidently, not all the diseases of soul are moral diseases.[11] Yet, as already said, injustice entails discord in the soul, and is therefore always a disease. Further, because injustice is a disease of the soul, it should be *treated* like a disease. Instead of being punished, individuals suffering from the vices in their soul must be provided with "the therapy [*therapeias*] of body and mind" (*Ti.* 87c; translation modified).

5. Political Therapy

Now we are perhaps ready to answer the question what to do with the unjust ones. They should be cured by therapy. This holds true with all unjust people and as we will see, even with those bad men who happen to commit crimes and cause injuries. Yet instead of the art of medicine, this therapy is the task of politics. The task of the art of politics, Plato writes in the *Laws* (1.650b; translation modified), is to "give therapy [*therapeuein*] to men's souls."[12] In the *Gorgias* (464b), Plato famously divides this political therapy into two branches: preventive and rehabilitative. Legislation is preventive activity, as its aim is to prevent diseases and promote health of the soul, while the administration of justice, needed only if somebody's soul is unhealthy, aims at healing his disease:

I'm saying that of this pair of subjects [body and soul] there are two different arts. The one for the soul [*psychē*] I call politics [*politikēn*]; the one for the body [*sōmati*], though it is one, I can't give you a name for offhand, but while the

[10] In the *Timaeus*, diseases, including the diseases of soul, are not so much a result of an imbalance between the elements of the body or the parts of the soul but of the imbalance *between* body and soul: "In determining health and disease or virtue and vice no proportion [*symmetria*] or lack of it [*ametria*] is more important than that between soul and body" (*Ti.* 87d).

[11] On a detailed analysis of mental illness in Plato's works, see Ahonen 2014, 35–67.

[12] Even the entire city-states can be given therapy (see Plato, *Plt.* 278e, *Resp.* 4.443e).

therapy [*therapeias*] of the body is a single art, I'm saying it has two parts: gymnastics [*gymnastikēn*] and medicine [*iatrikēn*]. In politics, the counterpart of gymnastics is legislation, and the part that corresponds to medicine is the administration of justice [*dikaiosynēn*].   (*Grg.* 464b; translation modified)[13]

In other words, legislation is preventive health care of the soul ("mental hygiene") and jurisdiction is treatment of mental diseases ("psychiatry") in the same sense as gymnastic is preventive healthcare of the body and medicine is treatment of bodily diseases.

In Plato's view, preventive health care of the soul must start early in childhood—in fact, already in the womb (*Leg.* 7.792e)—for "any living creature that flourishes in its first stages of growth gets a tremendous impetus towards its natural perfection and the final development appropriate to it" (6.765e).[14] However, if a statesman neglects this issue and a child's upbringing therefore becomes misguided, the child will become "the wildest animal on the face of the earth" (766a). He will become a bad citizen suffering from a disease of the soul, be it ambition, anger, avarice, cowardice, desire, fear, folly, ignorance, impulse, insanity, jealousy, lust, pain, pleasure, senility, sloth, or whatever.[15] As already said, the task of politics in general—and also of the famous Socratic method (elenchus)[16]—is to prevent these kinds of diseases of the soul in the city-state. Yet if an individual suffering from such a disease happens to cause *injuries*, justice (courts and judges) must intervene.[17]

In a well-ordered city-state in which there are only people of good quality, thanks to good inborn nature and well-organized nurture and education, there is no need for doctors or judges (*Resp.* 405a–b), but to the extent that such a city-state is exceptional, even nonexistent, both doctors and judges are needed. Judges are the doctors of the soul. However, in what way are they supposed to heal diseases of the soul that cause injuries? In Plato's works, perhaps surprisingly, the most frequently mentioned therapy for the morally sick soul that has caused injuries is *penalty*. Given his definition of injustice

---

[13] See also *Soph.* 228a–229a. Here, gymnastics corresponds to instruction and medicine to what Plato calls the art of discipline (*kolastikē technē*).

[14] For a detailed analysis of childcare in Plato's *Laws*, see Ojakangas 2016, 88–90.

[15] Trevor J. Saunders (1991, 187–8) enumerates as many as twenty-four states of mind that Plato considers psychic injustices in the *Laws* alone.

[16] The aim of the elenchus is to cure citizen's intellectually or morally ill souls by admonishing, reproving, and disgracing them so that citizens will become better. From this perspective, it is not surprising that Socrates in the *Gorgias* (521d) calls himself the best of politicians.

[17] In his detailed analysis of Plato's penal code in the *Laws*, Saunders (1991, 142–5) demonstrates that although injustice for Plato is always involuntary, injuries (*blabai*) are not. An unjust man may cause injuries voluntarily, but injuries themselves are not the criterion of injustice. For instance, when a just man causes an injury, it does nor render him unjust, because a just man—due to his disposition—does not have an unjust intent to injure and therefore, his injury should be considered as a mere accident (see *Leg.* 9.861e–862b).

as disease, this sounds paradoxical. Indeed, Plato himself writes: "The unjust man deserves just as much pity as any other sufferer" (*Leg.* 5.731c–d). Why, then, punish him? How is penalty supposed to heal a sick soul? The answer may be found in Plato's understanding of penalty.

6. Curative Penalty

In an Athenian court, punishment had the status of recompense and retribution: a criminal was punished according to his crime in order to inflict suffering on an offender in return for suffering inflicted. In Plato, the status of punishment is entirely different. Firstly, a criminal is not to be punished according to his crime but according to his state of mind: "Penalty [*dikēn*] is to be inflicted not because of the crime (what is done cannot be undone), but for the sake of the future," that is, in order to change the character of the offender (*Leg.* 11.934a–b). Accordingly, punishment must be tailored to each individual separately, focusing not on the crime he has committed but on the disturbed state of mind from which he is suffering. In the *Laws* in particular, with regard to punishment, even the seriousness of one's crime is often irrelevant (see *Leg.* 12.941c–942a)—even though Plato also seems to believe that the more serious the crime, the more severe the mental illness of the criminal. For Plato, secondly, punishment does not entail suffering but *relief*. To be sure, some punishments cause pain, but so do some medical operations such as surgery. In other words, although a punishment may cause pain, its *aim* is not to cause pain but, on the contrary, to relieve the criminal from suffering from the disease of his soul. Penalty is a remedy and hence, in a sense, not a penalty at all but a *reward*. One who pays no penalty for the wrong he has done, Plato writes in *Gorgias* (479e), is the most miserable man on earth. Therefore:

> If he or anyone else he cares about acts unjustly [*adikēsēi*], he should voluntarily go to the place where he'll pay his due as soon as possible; he should go to the judge as though he were going to a doctor, anxious that the disease [*nosēma*] of injustice shouldn't be protracted and cause his soul to fester incurably.
>
> (*Grg.* 480a–b)

Finally, the number of remedies available to the judges of the Platonic city-state, in the *Laws* in particular, is virtually infinite. Hence, a penalty inflicting pain is only one among many other penalties—or, rather, remedies. In the

Laws, the judge, in order to cure the patient, may use any imaginable method. He may use actions, words, pleasure, pain, honor, dishonor, fines, and even gifts—or, as Plato continues, "absolutely any means" (*Leg.* 9.862d). This is quite remarkable, particularly if we take into account the historical context. Indeed, even to a modern reader—to whom the idea of a criminal suffering from personality disorder or the idea of justice as restorative rather than retributive is certainly familiar—the idea that criminals should be given *gifts* may sound paradoxical. From the point of view of the Platonic penology, however, it is not a paradox. The aim of a penalty is to heal, not to punish, and if a judge, after the diagnosis of the mental illness the offender is suffering from, concludes that the best way to cure his illness is a gift, it is then the best possible penalty for him. To be sure, Plato does not single out a case in which a gift would be an appropriate penalty, but he suggests, for example, that a fit punishment for a coward is to let him live "according to his nature" (*kata physin*), that is, *without danger* (12.945a).

In Foucault's estimation, that a lawbreaker is suffering from mental illness or that the task of the state is to heal such a disorder are eminently modern ideas (see Foucault 1995, 2003a), but if our analysis is correct, these ideas are as old as Western political philosophy itself.[18] This also holds true with the institution Plato introduces in the *Laws*—for although at odds with the ancient Greek system of penalty, it was nonetheless introduced in the context of ancient Greek society, and thus well before modernity.[19] Plato calls this institution *sōphronistērion* and its purpose is to reeducate foolish (*anoia*) individuals suffering from atheism, agnostic ideas, heretical views, or idolatry. The inmates of this institution are isolated from everybody else but the members of the Nocturnal Council, the highest authority in the city-state (*Leg.* 12.961a–969a).[20] The members of this council meet regularly the inmates of the *sōphronistērion* in order to restore their mental health:

> Those who [among the impious] have simply fallen victim to foolishness [*anoias*] and who do not have a bad impulse and character [*aneu kakēs orgēs te kai ēthous*] should be sent to the reform center [*sōphronistērion*] by the judge in accordance

---

[18] Foucault admits that the premodern tradition recognized the idea of crime as a disease of the social body but not the idea of the criminal as someone suffering from a disease (Foucault 2003a, 91). In Plato's texts, both conceptions are clearly present.

[19] As Kenneth R. Moore (2012, 79) puts it, nothing comparable to a *sōphronistērion* was "properly established until the nineteenth or twentieth centuries."

[20] On the role of the Nocturnal Council in the *Laws*, see Klosko 1988.

with the law for a term not less than five years, and during this period no citizen must come into contact with them except the members of the Nocturnal Council, who should pay visits to admonish [*nouthetēseî*] them and ensure their spiritual salvation [*tēs psychēs sōtēriaî*]. When his imprisonment is over, a prisoner who appears to be enjoying mental health [*sōphronein*] should go and live with sensible people, but if appearances turn out to have been deceptive, and he is reconvicted on a similar charge, he should be punished by death.   (*Leg.* 10.908e–909a)

7. The Incurable

As the quotation above indicates, not all diseases are curable—and it is here that Plato's biopolitical program is gradually transformed into thanatopolitical state racism. If an inmate of the *sōphronistērion* has not come to his senses (*sōphroneō*) in five years, he will be punished by death. It should also be noted that it is not only foolish individuals who have turned out to be incurable after five years of imprisonment that must be put to death but also all those who, unlike the curable inmates of the *sōphronistērion*, do have a bad natural impulse (*orgē*) and character (*ēthos*; *Leg.* 10.908e). Only the curable individuals should be cured, while the incurable must be destroyed:

Suppose the lawgiver finds a man who is beyond cure [*aniatōs*]—what legal penalty will he provide for this case? He will recognize that the best thing for all such people is to cease to live—best even for themselves.   (*Leg.* 9.862e)

Indeed, to the same extent that a good physician, according to Plato, understands that there are lives beyond cure and therefore not worth medical treatment, a good statesman must kill those people whose souls are ill-formed and incurable:

Together they'll [medicine and jurisprudence] look after those who are naturally well endowed [*euphyeis*] in body and soul. But as for the ones who are not, such as are defective in body, they will suffer to die, and those whose souls are ill-formed and incurable [*kata tēn psychēn kakophyeis kai aniatous*], they will themselves put to death.   (*Resp.* 3.410a; translation modified)

Further, it is not only that a good judge is like a good physician when he treats diseases of the soul, but a good physician is also a good statesman (*politikos*) when he treats diseases of the body. A good physician, according to Plato, leaves a man incapable of living the "established order of life" to suffer and die (*Resp.* 3.407e). Hence, Karl Popper is right when he asserts that "Plato interprets medicine as a form of politics" (Popper 2005, 147), but the same can be said of Werner Jaeger, who in his *Paideia* maintains that Plato understand politics as a form of medicine (Jaeger 1947, 135). Together they—medicine and politics—constitute the Platonic medico-political sanitary machine:

> Now, these two groups [democratic leaders and their supporters] cause problems in any state, just as phlegm and bile in the body. And it is against them that the good doctor and lawgiver of a city must take advance precautions, first, to prevent their presence and, second, to cut them out of the hive as quickly as possible, cells and all, if they should happen to be present.
>
> (*Resp.* 8.564b–c; translation modified)

8. State Purge

As the quotation above indicates, a disease in the psychophysical constitution of an individual is also a disease of the city-state (*poleōs nosēma*). This is why the Platonic therapy of the soul—even the Platonic therapy of the body—is inevitably always also political therapy of the city-state. The Platonic city-state is not an abstract entity hoovering above the inhabitants of the city but the sum of these inhabitants. The inhabitants of the city are like the members of the body—and if one member of the body suffers from a disease, so does the whole body (*Resp.* 5.462c–d). What, then, are the consequences of the mental illness of immorality in the city-state? On the one hand, it is a burden to the city-state because a mentally ill individual is "of no use to the state" (3.410a). On the other hand, it is more than a mere burden: it is deadly dangerous because it is *contagious*. Moral illness is contagious through example but particularly through *interbreeding*. Through interbreeding, moral illness necessarily leads to the destruction of the entire city-state.

In the *Republic* (8.547a), the intermixture of different classes and races, and the intermixture of the superior and the inferior individuals in the guardian race, in particular, entails an "anomaly out of harmony" (*anōmalia anarmostos*) in the city-state and is thus the primary cause of its ruin. Therefore, in Plato's view, certain drastic measures are needed to preserve the purity of the race of guardians (5.460c). Firstly, bodily and mentally inferior guardians must be prevented from reproducing (459d). Secondly, if it nonetheless happens that they have sex and a woman becomes pregnant, the fetus must be aborted (461c). Thirdly, if such a child is born, he or she must be left without nurture (461c).[21] The same holds true even with the children born to the superior guardians endowed with a sound body and mind, in case their children, for some reason, are born with defective traits:

> They'll [officials appointed for the purpose] take the children of good parents to the nurses in charge of the rearing pen situated in a separate part of the city, but the children of inferior parents, or any child of the others that is born defective [anapēron], they'll hide in a secret and unknown place, as is appropriate.
>
> (Resp. 5.460c)

In the *Republic* (5.459a–b), this eugenic program is illustrated employing selective animal breeding as an analogy.[22] A good statesman must not only train his "tame animals" as a dog-trainer trains his dogs. He must also pay attention to the unions (*gamos*) and procreations (*paidopoiia*) of the human herd (*agelē*) as a breeder of dogs pays attention to these in order to improve the quality and to prevent the degeneration (*kheiron*) of the race (*genos*) of his dogs (459a–b).[23]

In the *Statesman*, Plato deals with the same theme employing the analogy of weaving. As a weaver, or anyone practicing "constructive science" (*synthetikos epistēmē*), rejects the bad and takes only the good and fitting materials when he starts to work, the statecraft "according to nature" (*kata physin*), when it is about to construct a city-state, purges it from the bad elements (*Plt.* 308c–d). After testing all the inhabitants, to those who appear to be incurably vicious, it inflicts "the punishments of death and exile and deprivation of the most important civic rights," while those who "wallow in ignorance and craven humility" it places under the yoke of slavery (308e–309a). For the interweaving and binding together of the bad (*kakos*) with the bad or of the good (*agathos*) with the bad will never create an enduring fabric, and thus no art—be it weaving or statecraft—ever seriously engages in such a business. With regard to the city-state, a good fabric can be woven only if the materials used in it are of "noble nature from their birth [*tois eugenesi*]

---

[21] "If our herd [*poimnion*] is to be of the highest possible quality, the former's [superior individuals] offspring must be reared but not the latter's [inferior individuals]" (*Resp.* 5.459d–e).

[22] On Plato's eugenic policies in the *Republic*, the *Statesman*, and the *Laws*, see Rankin 1965; Fortenbaugh 1975; Klosko 1991; Halliwell 1993; Ajavon 2001; Popper 2005; Ojakangas 2016.

[23] When Plato speaks of different races (*genē*) of dogs, he means qualitatively different dogs *within* a breed of dogs. Some dogs are of high quality, superior by nature (*euphyeis*), while others are of low quality, inferior by nature (*kakophyeis*). It is these two groups of dogs, distinguished from each other by their inherited qualities, that constitute two different races of dogs—and the same holds true for human beings.

genomenois] and have been nurtured in accordance with nature [*kata physin*]" (309e–310a; translation modified).

In the *Laws*, after the so-called introductory part (*Leg.* 5.734e), Plato returns to the weaving analogy he introduced in the *Statesman* but abandons it right away, shifting instead to selective animal breeding theme again—even though now, the breeder of dogs is replaced by a stockbreeder. A good statesman, Plato starts his argumentation, should perform a similar purge (*katharmos*) in the state as a good cattleman performs in the stock of his animals. He must separate (*dialegō*) the healthy from the unhealthy and the purebreds from the degenerate stock (*ta te hygiē kai ta mē kai ta gennaia kai agennē*), keeping only the purebreds and healthy animals to look after. Otherwise, animals endowed with healthy (*hygiēs*) and pure (*akēratos*) body (*sōma*) and character (*ēthos*) will be contaminated by the faults of the sick and impure through interbreeding. As Plato writes:

> He knows that otherwise he would have to waste endless effort on sickly and refractory beasts, degenerate by nature and ruined by incompetent breeding, and that unless he purges the existing stock these faults will spread in any herd of animals that are still physically and temperamentally healthy and unspoiled.
>
> (*Leg.* 5.735b–c)

In other words, degenerate and defiled animals are a burden to the whole stock, not only because they are weak—and therefore a burden to the sound—but also and above all because the healthy and undefiled are contaminated by the faults of the weak.

Of course, Plato is not interested in animal breeding and only mentions it "by way of illustration" (*Leg.* 5.735c). He is interested in humans: "With human beings it is vitally important for the legislator to search out and declare the appropriate measure in each case regarding the purge and other modes of treatment" (735c–d). Thus, it is more important and definitely more necessary to use these horse breeder's methods to improve the human stock than with the horses themselves: "Every legislator must do it, by one way or another" (736a; translation modified). Among humans, Plato continues, the leaders of the city-state may use either mild or drastic measures, depending on the form of government. A tyrant may use harsh methods and carry out a "state purge" (*katharmos poleōs*) drastically, "which is the best way"—for "like drastic medicines, the best purge is a painful business" (735d). It takes the punishment to the point of exile or death. In the non-tyrannical city-states, based on people's consent, the purge must be milder because people do not necessarily accept tyrannical methods. For Plato, however, if the leaders of a non-tyrannical state are clever enough, they can achieve the same good results as tyrants. Although people do not normally accept harsh methods, they may accept them at a moment of crisis, especially if the leaders of the state are able to convince them that the unhealthy and degenerate people are the cause of the crisis. The same method can be applied to the poor:

> When there is a shortage of food, and the poor show themselves ready to . . . attack on the property of the rich, they are to be regarded as a disease that has developed in the body politic [*hōs nosēmati poleōs empephykotí*]—and in the friendliest possible way they should be, as it will tactfully be put [*di' euphēmias apallagēn*], "transferred to a colony."   (*Leg.* 5.735e–6a; translation modified)

We may speculate on what this euphemism ("transferred to a colony") actually means. What no longer requires any speculation, however, is whether Platonic politics is biopolitical state racism. It is biopolitical state racism at its purest. The physical and mental health and happiness of the population legitimates and necessitates the elimination of the "sick" and the "poor"—and it does so because their inherent weakness, irrespective of whether they have done something illegal or immoral, is contagious: without a thorough purge, the rest of the population will degenerate too. Such racism must be distinguished from traditional ethnic racism (antibarbarism), prevalent in Plato's lifetime in Greek society (see, for example, Isaac 2004; Lape 2010). Plato's racism is not antibarbarism (even though his writings occasionally show antibarbaric sentiments) but an entirely new kind of racism based on medico-political principles of psychosomatic health: one must not kill barbarians but the members of one's *own* community suffering from a "defective body" or an "ill-formed soul" (*Resp.* 3.410a; translation modified).

9. By Way of Conclusion: Tyranny

This said, it is obvious that the "law of nature" of the sophists is not an antithesis of Plato's "natural justice," as both the sophists and Plato intimately link justice and violence. Yet this link is not identical in them either. In Callicles' view, violence *creates* justice, while in Plato, justice *presupposes* violence. The incurable must be either killed or expelled from the city, since otherwise there can be neither justice nor happiness in the city-state. Rather than the natural law of the sophists, the true antithesis of Plato's justice according to nature is democratic freedom and equality—the democratic form of life without a proper form, function, or necessity. In democracy, everyone—including the incurably deformed souls (*Resp.* 8.558a)—has the license "to arrange his own life in whatever manner pleases him" (557b), but for Plato, for whom justice is based on the hierarchical order of nature, such a license is contrary to nature in every respect: it is a license to destroy the entire city-state.

However, would it be more correct to say that *tyranny*, rather than democracy, is the antithesis of Plato's political order based on justice according to nature? We know well that in the *Republic*, tyranny is the end point of the piecemeal process of degeneration of the souls and city-states, the point reached only after the collapse of democracy. Not democracy but tyranny is the "ultimate disease of the state" (*eschaton poleōs nosēma*; *Resp.* 8.544c; translation modified). Further, if the sophistic natural law of the strongest is interpreted as legitimation of a tyrannical mode of government (Callicles praises tyranny in the *Gorgias*), we may conclude that it is, after all, the sophistic natural law and not democratic equality that is the ultimate target of Plato's criticism.

Before concluding, however, we must take a closer look at what Plato says about tyranny. Although the *Republic* dedicates a number of pages to the analysis of tyranny, Plato says relatively little about tyranny as a form of government, focusing mainly on the tyrant's character. In the *Statesman*, however, we find a lengthy passage on the institutional arrangements of different forms of government in which Plato discusses the nature of tyranny in detail. Here, Plato distinguishes as many as seven forms of government: democracy governed by laws, democracy governed without laws, aristocracy, oligarchy, kingship governed by laws, kingship governed without laws, and tyranny (always governed without laws). Then he states that the worst and the best forms of government are both monarchies—forms of government in which there is a single ruler (*monarchia*). The worst possible form of government is tyranny (always governed without laws) and the best possible one is kingship (*basileia*) but again, *without* laws.[24] Hence, when it comes to the fundamental institutional principles, the worst and the best forms of government are *identical* (excluding the name). They are forms of government in which there is but one ruler and he rules without laws (and, if possible, preferably also without people's consent; see *Plt.* 293b–c).[25] The only difference pertains to the *character* of the monarch. In the best form of government, the monarch is

---

[24] In a well-governed city-state, there are no laws because laws are dogmatic and inflexible, incapable of taking into consideration "the differences of man and of actions" (*Plt.* 294b). Therefore, as the captain of a ship relies on his art (*technē*) rather than on written rules when steering his ship, a good statesman makes his "art [*technēs*] more powerful than the laws [*nomōn*]" when governing the city-state (296e–297a; translation modified).

[25] Here, Plato employs the medical analogy again: "Whether [physicians] cure us against our will or with our will, by cutting us or burning us or causing us pain in any other way, and whether they do it by written rules or without them, and whether they are rich or poor, we call them physicians just the same, so long as they exercise authority by art or science, purging [*kathairontes*] us or reducing us in some other way, or even adding to our weight, provided only that they who treat their patients treat them for the benefit of their health" (*Plt.* 293b–c). On *katharmos* as a philosophical method, see *Soph.* 226d–227d.

wise, inspired by knowledge, while in the worst he is ignorant, inspired by desire (301b–c).

From this perspective, it is not surprising that in the *Laws*, tyranny is *not* depicted as the worst form of government. On the contrary, if the tyrant happens to be kinglike (to have a good memory, quick intelligence, courage, and nobility of manner by nature), tyranny is the *best* form of government: "The best state will be the product of tyranny, thanks to the efforts of a first-rate legislator and a virtuous tyrant" (*Leg.* 4.710d; translation modified). But why call him a tyrant and not a king? The answer may pertain to the problematic nature of kingship. In the *Statesman*, after asserting that kingship without laws and people's consent is the best form of government (*Plt.* 293a–d), Plato nevertheless returns, at the end of the dialogue (301d–302e), to the traditional understanding of kingship as a form of government based on the rule of law and the consent of the people—not only because of the rarity of truly royal characters but also in order to distinguish it from tyranny. In the *Laws*, however, it seems that Plato has learned the lesson: Why call tyranny kingship, if the only difference between the best form of kingship and tyranny is the character of the monarch? Indeed, if a tyrant is as virtuous as a king, tyranny is a better form of government than kingship because the king needs the consent of the people but the tyrant does not: a tyrant may invoke whatever methods when governing the city-state. In particular, he may carry out the inevitable state purge drastically, which is the best way to do it ("the best purge is a painful business"; *Leg.* 5.735d). The only problem with tyranny is that the tyrant is not usually virtuous and therefore, he is not able to figure out the biopolitical aim of the government (the happiness of the entire city-state). This is also the reason why his state purge goes astray. Like a good king, a tyrant performs a state purge in his city-state, but unlike a king who like a good doctor "draws off the worst and leaves the best," a tyrant "does just the opposite" (*Resp.* 8.567c). Yet if a tyrant be wise enough to draw off the worst and leave the best, tyranny would be the best form of government absolutely. For it does not matter whether the city-state is governed by laws or without laws, with people's consent or without it (*Plt.* 293a)—the most essential is to purge the city-state and render it thus better and happier:

And whether they [statesmen] purge [*kathairōsin*] the state for its good by killing or banishing some of the citizens, or make it smaller by sending out colonies somewhere, as bees swarm from the hive, or bring in citizens from elsewhere to make it larger, so long as they act in accordance with knowledge [*epistēmēi*] and justice [*dikaiōi*] and preserve and benefit it by making it better than it was, so far as is possible, that must at that time and by such characteristics be declared to be the only right form of government [*politeian*].   (*Plt.* 293d–e; translation modified)

In Agamben's estimation, the Platonic law in accordance with nature (*kata physin*) is essentially nonviolent, but if my analysis is correct, in Plato everything according to nature, be it law, knowledge, or justice, presupposes the violent elimination of everything that is incurably contrary to nature (*para physin*). A happy city-state inhabited by healthy characters and dispositions is possible only by means of the expulsion or extermination of the incurable. And to the extent that there are always such incurables around, it is not a mere option. It is a necessity: "Every legislator must do it, by one way or another" (*Leg.* 5.736a).

References

Agamben, Giorgio. 1998. *Homo Sacer: Sovereign Power and Bare Life.* Translated by Daniel Heller-Roazen, Stanford, CA: Stanford University Press.

Ahonen, Marke. 2014. *Mental Disorders in Ancient Philosophy.* Cham: Springer.

Ajavon, François-Xavier. 2001. *L'eugénisme de Platon.* Paris: L'Harmattan.

Aristotle. 1944. *Politics.* Translated by Harris Rackham. In *Aristotle in Twenty-Three Volumes,* vol. 21. Cambridge, MA: Harvard University Press.

Brock, Roger. 2013. *Greek Political Imagery from Homer to Aristotle.* London: Bloomsbury.

Fortenbaugh, W. W. 1975. "Plato: Temperament and Eugenic Policy." *Arethusa* 8 (2): 283–305.

Foucault, Michel. 1990. *The History of Sexuality.* Vol. 1, *An Introduction.* Translated by Robert Hurley. New York: Vintage Books.

Foucault, Michel. 1995. *Discipline and Punish.* Translated by Alan Sheridan. New York: Vintage Books.

Foucault, Michel. 2003a. *Abnormal: Lectures at the Collège de France 1974–1975.* Translated by Graham Burchell. New York: Picador.

Foucault, Michel. 2003b. *"Society Must Be Defended": Lectures at the Collège de France 1975–1976.* Translated by David Macey. New York: Picador.

Frank, Jill. 2018. *Poetic Justice: Rereading Plato's Republic.* Chicago: University of Chicago Press.

Halliwell, Stephen. 1993. Introduction to Plato, *Republic 5,* edited by Stephen Halliwell, 1–38. Warminster: Aris & Phillips.

Herodotus. 1920. *The Histories.* Translated by Alfred Denis Godley. Cambridge, MA: Harvard University Press.

Isaac, Benjamin. 2004. *The Invention of Racism in Classical Antiquity.* Princeton, NJ: Princeton University Press.

Jaeger, Werner. 1947. *Paideia: The Ideals of Greek Culture.* Vol. 2. Translated by Gilbert Highet. Oxford: Blackwell.

Kamtekar, Rachana. 2002. "Distinction without a Difference: Race and *Genos* in Plato." In *Philosophers on Race*, edited by Julie K. Ward and Tommy L. Lott, 1–16. Oxford: Blackwell. https://doi.org/10.1002/9780470753514.ch1.

Klosko, George. 1988. "The Nocturnal Council in Plato's *Laws*." *Political Studies* 36 (1): 74–88. https://doi.org/10.1111/j.1467-9248.1988.tb00217.x.

Klosko, George. 1991. "'Racism' in Plato's *Republic*." *History of Political Thought* 12 (1): 1–13.

Lape, Susan. 2010. *Race and Citizen Identity in the Classical Athenian Democracy.* Cambridge: Cambridge University Press.

Lidz, Joel Warren. 1995. "Medicine as Metaphor in Plato." *The Journal of Medicine and Philosophy* 20 (5): 527–41. https://doi.org/10.1093/jmp/20.5.527.

Moore, Kenneth Royce. 2012. *Plato, Politics and a Practical Utopia: Social Constructivism and Civic Planning in the Laws.* New York: Continuum.

Ojakangas, Mika. 2016. *On the Greek Origins of Biopolitics: A Reinterpretation of the History of Biopower.* London: Routledge.

Plato. 1921. *Sophist.* Translated by Harold N. Fowler. In *Plato in Twelve Volumes*, vol. 7. Cambridge, MA: Harvard University Press.

Plato. 1925. *The Statesman.* Translated by Harold N. Fowler. In *Plato in Twelve Volumes*, vol. 8. Cambridge, MA: Harvard University Press.

Plato. 1929. *Timaeus.* Translated by Robert Gregg Bury. In *Plato in Twelve Volumes*, vol. 9. Cambridge, MA: Harvard University Press.

Plato. 1997a. *Gorgias.* Translated by Donald J. Zeyl. In *Plato: Complete Works*, edited by John M. Cooper. Indianapolis, IN: Hackett.

Plato. 1997b. *The Laws.* Translated by Trevor J. Saunders. In *Plato: Complete Works*, edited by John M. Cooper. Indianapolis, IN: Hackett.

Plato. 1997c. *Republic.* Translated by George Grube, translation revised by C. D. C. Reeve. In *Plato: Complete Works*, edited by John M. Cooper. Indianapolis, IN: Hackett.

Popper, Karl. 2005. *The Open Society and Its Enemies.* Vol. 1, *The Spell of Plato.* London: Routledge.

Pseudo-Xenophon. 1984. *Constitution of the Athenians.* Translated by Edgar Cardew Marchant. In *Xenophon in Seven Volumes*, vol. 7. Cambridge, MA: Harvard University Press.

Rankin, H. D. 1965. "Plato's Eugenic *euphēmia* and *apothesis* in *Republic*, Book V." *Hermes* 93 (4): 407–20.

Saunders, Trevor J. 1991. *Plato's Penal Code: Tradition, Controversy, and Reform in Greek Penology.* Oxford: Clarendon Press.

Thucydides. 1881. *History of the Peloponnesian War.* Translated by Benjamin Jowett. Oxford: Clarendon Press.

3

Sovereign Power and Social Justice

Plato and Aristotle on Justice and Its Biopolitical Basis in Heterosexual Copulation, Procreation, and Upbringing

Kathy L. Gaca

1. Introduction

Biopolitics is vital for understanding classical antiquity, the age of the *polis* and of philosophical dialogue and research into *polis* governance (*politeia*), notably the work of Plato in the *Republic* and *Laws*, and of Aristotle and the Peripatetics in Aristotle's *Politics* and the *Constitution of Athens*.[1] Michel Foucault, who shaped "biopolitics" as one of his signature ideas, explicates its time frame as though biopolitics were a recent development in state-sponsored "power mechanisms ... established since the eighteenth century" and designed to sort, process, and control human populations (Foucault 2003, 259).[2] Yet when he explains the working of biopolitics, he on noteworthy occasion has recourse to a historical exercise of this power that has ample precedents going back to the ancient Mediterranean—rulers exerting the sovereign power over the life and death of their subjects (Foucault 1980, 135–59; 2003, 239–64),[3] and of additional peoples sought, conquered, and taken as their subjects. While "biopower" in Foucault's sense is not reducible to the rulers' sovereign power over the life and death of subjects, it is one of his succinct ways of referring to the ruler or ruling council exercising this biopolitical power.[4] Even though Foucault only describes relatively recent and modern adaptations of biopolitics as sovereign power under the rule of

[1] My deep thanks to Jonathan E. Bremer, Jussi Backman, and Antonio Cimino for their many helpful insights and suggestions on this chapter. All translations of Greek sources are my own unless otherwise indicated.
[2] In the first volume of *The History of Sexuality*, Foucault sees this "power over life" as starting in the seventeenth century and taking on mutable forms in European society from then on (Foucault 1980, 139).
[3] For a worthwhile discussion of Foucault's lectures on biopolitics along with essays exploring their significance for recent and modern times, see Morton and Bygrave 2008.
[4] Foucault (1980, 139–40) presents his neologism "biopower" in connection with governmental "regulatory controls" that make for "a biopolitics of the population."

Kathy L. Gaca, *Sovereign Power and Social Justice: Plato and Aristotle on Justice and Its Biopolitical Basis in Heterosexual Copulation, Procreation, and Upbringing* In: *Biopolitics and Ancient Thought*. Edited by: Jussi Backman and Antonio Cimino, Oxford University Press. © Oxford University Press 2022. DOI: 10.1093/oso/9780192847102.003.0004

force, including Nazi Germany's forced labor and extermination camps along with other less nefarious examples, biopower along this spectrum discloses sovereign power at work in antiquity too. This includes, for instance, the democratic assembly (*ekklēsia*) and empire of Athens during the Peloponnesian War (431–04 BCE) having their forces ravage and liquidate the Melian Greeks through massacre and enslavement in 415 BCE and King Philip II of Macedon having the same done to the Olynthian Greeks in 348 BCE. Once applied to incidents such as these, Foucault's biopolitical focus on sovereign power provides a valuable historical and moral framework for better understanding and motivating Plato's and especially Aristotle's biopolitical arguments against sovereign power.

In classical antiquity and thereafter, rulers exerted biopolitical sovereign power through strategies of intimidating demagogic persuasion and shows of force in colonialist conquest, warfare, and enslavement to turn previously self-determining peoples into conquered and subservient collectives and to keep them as such. But if the peoples resisted collective submission or became subdued as though submissive but then rebelled, conquering rulers did not hesitate to have their loyal forces unleash a ravaging liquidation on them. They ravaged the resistant or rebellious peoples to break down their standing as an associated kin group, to dissolve their shared heritage, and to forcibly and sexually remix with the rulers' loyalist forces the captive girls and women, mainly young women, wanted alive as slaves from the insubordinate peoples. In so doing, sovereign rulers worked to reconstitute the enslaved women and their ensuing generations of daughters as a downtrodden but obedient subservient non-combatant multitude raised by sexually violent fathers. As added deterrent to resistance and rebellion, the loyalist forces turned into fathers through ravaging rape inculcated obedience to the conquerors, especially in the boys produced. The men and the boys having come of adolescent age as men formed the combatant branch of the conquerors' subservient multitude and had to follow their rulers' orders with proficient alacrity, with the boys learning this doctrine from birth.

Ravaging, recognized as warfare in antiquity, and finally starting to be recognized as genocidal since then too,[5] both literally and culturally, was a harsh alternative way to impose conquest by terminating the men's lineage of the resistant people and turning the slain men's sisters, daughters, and wives into slave plunder property reallocated to the conquerors' brigades for these men to invasively rape and impregnate them and have the offspring brought up

---

[5] For ravaging as warfare (e.g., *leisteia* in Thucydides and the hendiadys *in bello latrociniisque* in Caesar), see Thuc. 4.41.3; Hdt. 4.103.2; Caesar, *BGall.* 6.35.7; Xenophon, *An.* 4.4.1, 6.1.28; for ravaging as genocide, see Van Wees 2016; Gaca 2022.

aligned as loyalist devotees for the conquerors, thus overthrowing the bereaved women and throwing down the memory of their ravaged people from the sexual and procreative ground up. This form of enslaving or lethal rape through ravaging warfare is heterosexually specific and is here termed ravaging rape.[6] The organized violence of ravaging accordingly proceeded as follows. The rulers had their forces kill off the men or the men and the boys of all ages and then seize, maul, enslave, and redistribute the girls and young women wanted alive as slave plunder property among themselves for the men to use as their coerced sustenance providers, procreative vessels, and forced prostitutes, while killing the women not wanted alive or leaving them injured and likely to die.

Thucydides carefully unfolds one ravaging incident in his Melian Dialogue. Here, Athenian forces were the aggressors demanding surrender and collective submission from the Spartan island colony and *polis* of Melos in 415 BCE, and threatening to ravage them if they refused. Upon hearing the Melians' spirited refusal and determination to fight to retain their autonomy, the Athenians laid siege to and ravaged the Melians for refusing to submit to the Athenian empire (Thuc. 5.85.1–116.4). Ravaging is also what Philip II of Macedon had his forces do to the Greek *polis* of Olynthus in 348 BCE, likewise because the Olynthians resisted collective submission and tried to thwart Philip's drive to extend his sovereign power by taking over Olynthus (Polyb. 9.28.2–3). In both cases, the Athenian and Macedonian forces killed off the fighting-age men and mauled the women and children, keeping the girls and young women wanted alive as slaves and procreative vessels to produce, through ravaging rape, offspring who would be raised to obey and follow their Athenian and Macedonian commanders and conquerors with alacrity. The Athenian and Macedonian forces slaughtered the women's menfolk and took over the men's place with the women for this purpose, imposing an oblivion about Melian and Olynthian Greek ancestry and martially "Athenianizing" and "Macedonianizing" the offspring—especially the boys, who enrolled as forces for their conquerors in early manhood. The biopolitical tenor of sovereign power over the life and death of conquered subjects is thus glaring and graphic in ravaging warfare—massacre, mass enslavement of the women and children wanted alive, mass ravaging rape of the girls and young women, and an agenda of compulsory procreation to increase the subservient multitude in service to the conquerors and identifying with their

---

[6] This and upcoming brief discussions in this chapter about the organized violence and aims of ravaging warfare and rape highlight salient points argued in Gaca 2008, 2011a, 2011b, 2011c, 2014, 2015, 2016a, 2016b, 2018a, 2018b. On forced impregnation and compulsory procreation in ravaging warfare and its aftermath, see Gaca 2018a.

ethnoreligious identity. All of this was at the conquerors' triumphal expense of the conquered peoples whose bereaved women's lineages had to submit to their archenemies if they wanted to survive.

In antiquity, rulers and ruling councils were already asserting the moral high ground to make ravaging seem an unimpeachable expression of sovereign power. For instance, Xenophon (ca. 428–347 BCE) buys into this viewpoint from his mercenary experience, for he maintains that conquest imparted to the conqueror unilateral power over the life and death of the overthrown peoples. He even presents this view as though it were a kind of eternal and universal law. "It is a law in perpetuity among all people that when a city is taken in war, the persons and property of the inhabitants belong to the captors" (Xenophon, *Cyr.* 7.5.73)[7] for them to do with as they will, including enslaving or killing them with impunity. This martial law the Romans and Romanized Celts likewise called "the power to inflict [debased] life or painful death" (*vitae necisque potestas*) on the conquered, with slavery epitomizing debased life (Caesar, *BGall.* 1.16.5–6, 5.56.2; see also 6.23.1–5, 7.4.9–10). However, this claim of sovereign power over the conquered was not yet seemingly august and cloaked in ermine as it later came to be under the Christian doctrine of the divine right of kings in Europe and among the Spanish conquistadors in the New World. Conquest through collective submission or ravaging was still known to be a violent and extractive imposition on the regional inhabitants, an imposition that meant "nothing good for them" (Appian, *Mith.* 188), hence the resistance from the likes of Melos and Olynthus. Thus, as borne out by ancient sources, Foucault had a sound historical intuition that biopolitics should foreground and track the working of sovereign power, even though his foray did not reach earlier than the eighteenth century.

2. Plato and Aristotle

Plato and Aristotle are biopolitical thinkers in their own right, in ways not tethered to sovereign power and articulately critical of its doings. While Foucault's examination of biopolitics as sovereign power helps disclose its massive sexually mediated and lethal violence and oppression, their arguments

---

[7] For this action to be defensible in his view, Xenophon requires that the ravaged city either be an abhorred enemy and in the wrong (*adikon te kai echthran polin*), or that it simply be inhabited by war enemies (*tous polemious*), *Mem.* 4.2.15, 2.2.2. The *Dissoi logoi* presents the ravaging only of war enemies as legitimate (frag. 90.3.5 DK; see also Polyb. 2.58.10, 5.11.3–4). See further De Sensi Sestito 1999, 111–14, especially nn. 1–11.

and insights are invigorating. Moreover, Foucault's account of biopolitics only lightly discusses sexual copulation, procreation, and childrearing (Macey 2008),[8] but the ravaging conquest customs of rape, enslavement, and compulsory procreation show that the sexual treatment of women and girls in body and mind is a pivotal concern for social justice. Plato and Aristotle had the perspicacity to understand this and to demonstrate why this is the case. In so doing, they illuminate ways of making biopolitics a liberating move that releases society from sovereign power and subservience, women and children first but men too.

Biopolitics is in evidence in Plato's works, mainly the *Republic* and the *Laws*, where Plato presents sexual, procreative, and childrearing customs as a first customary law or set of first laws for social justice.[9] For Plato, if human beings get these customs right, then the human capacity to craft justice is sound and the society and its norms of justice are upright; if the customs are wrong, then this human capacity is unsound and society and its norms of justice turn crooked. To develop and instate sound customs of procreation and upbringing conducive to justice is consequently a major project in both dialogues. Through these reforms in the *Republic* and as further modified in the *Laws*, Plato was trying to bring the reproductive and childrearing basis of social justice more readily within the reach of peoples living in a *polis* modeled on his proposed reforms.

In book 5 of the *Republic*, Plato urges the need to override private families of freeborn men perpetuating the custom of treating women and children as possessions on the principle of "to each his own" (*ktēseis gynaikōn kai paidōn*; Plato, *Resp.* 5.462c3–6, *Plt.* 271e8), be the children and women freeborn or slave. In order to attain an ideally just society, communalism must be established in procreation and in the upbringing of the guardian class. Aristotle rightly took the communalizing proposal seriously but was unreceptive to it. However, he was still persuaded by Plato's core biopolitical conviction that sexual relations, reproduction, and upbringing were pivotal to instating and maintaining social justice or injustice.[10] This provided added impetus for Aristotle and the Peripatetics to incorporate sexual and procreative customs in the investigation of the *politeiai* of numerous Greek cities in the Mediterranean—that is, of their local governance and other social norms,

---

[8] For thoughtful studies of Foucault's spare comments on the biopolitical significance of women's sexuality and procreativity, see Deutscher 2012 and Mills 2017.

[9] My position on this general point is consonant with that of Ojakangas (2016). See also chapter 2 by Ojakangas in this volume.

[10] Aristotle, *Pol.* 2.1.1261a2–2.5.1264b25, and Gaca 2003, 47n77, 90. The serious aim of the sexual communalism in Plato's *Republic* 5 is decisively borne out by Plato's *Laws* (5.739b8–e3), and see further Gaca 2003, 41–8, along with the bibliography cited there.

both codified and uncodified. This research made the Peripatetics attentive to gender and age and interested in the heterosexual customs of sexual copulation, reproduction, and upbringing among men, women, and children living in these cities. What is more, the Peripatetics' findings highlighted to them the violent inequities of Greek and Macedonian forces overrunning and ravaging Greek and non-Greek cities. In addition to the ravaging of Melos and Olynthus, other such incidents include the ravaging of Greek Orchomenus and Pellene by, respectively, Ionian Greeks and Sicyonian Greeks in the early Archaic period, and the ravaging of Apulian Italian Carbina by Tarentine Greeks in the early fifth century BCE. One aim in this aggression was to enslave war-captive girls and women seized therein, and to subject them to rape as coerced vehicles of forced impregnation and compulsory procreation, while also using the enslaved female captives as forced sustenance and service providers for the ravaging forces (Gaca 2018a, 2018b). These incidents were not anomalies, for ravaging warfare and the compulsory procreative functions of enslaving rape were a basic part of martial state-building projects to reinforce colonialist conquest and to turn productive civil inhabitants into a subservient multitude under sovereign rule.

As briefly sketched above in connection with Foucault on sovereign power, ravaging is a historically prevalent and strikingly gendered form of punitive and acquisitive total warfare starting in antiquity and still persisting today, but it has not been studied in breadth and depth prior to my own work on its organized violence and biopolitical motives from antiquity to modernity. In this type of aggression, martial elite commanders send their subordinate forces on campaigns to punitively attack targeted peoples, either because they resist being turned into subservient forced laborers and tribute bearers or because they submit to this status under pressure, only to underperform in following orders or to rebel against doing so. This punishment is also acquisitive in nature and is regularly oriented to enslave women and girls, and often also preadolescent boys through the aforementioned organized violence of ravaging, exterminating either the entire male lineage of all ages, including boys and male infants, or the fighting-age adult males, and then seizing and enslaving the captured girls and women wanted alive and subjecting them to ravaging rape (Gaca 2010, 2011b; 2015, 282). Ravaging aggression also involved killing, and to a degree raping and killing, numerous other female captives or leaving them injured and likely to die (Gaca 2011c, 96n37). The latter were mainly women and girls who resisted being raped, for as ravaged captives they were coercively required to yield and submit to this lethal sexual maltreatment as the price for staying alive. Alternatively, they were perceived as not worth keeping alive on other grounds, such as being considered too old or ugly or lame and hence unable "to walk suitably" (*decenter ambulare*; William of Adam, *Saracens*, 80) as part of the forces' female baggage of sustenance providers and reproductive vehicles in the camps and on campaigns.

My main interest here is in the enslaved girls and women, for they were subjected to forced impregnation and compulsory procreation for the rearing of male and female offspring under the aegis of ravaging warfare among the martial companies (Gaca 2018b, 2022). Through the use of coercive techniques in war-god devotion (Gaca 2016a), the male offspring produced through ravaging rape and their sons in turn were raised to identify as assimilated yet subordinated ethnoreligious men's lineages of fathers, brothers, and sons populating and identifying as the lower-echelon contingents of their conquering and colonizing warrior elite superiors. The female offspring were raised as ancillary slave women coerced to provide offspring and sustenance for the contingents, while only being partially assimilated to them as women's lineages of mothers, daughters, and sisters.

Nonetheless, to sense the stark objectification of the female captives kept alive and enslaved as coerced submissives, it is worthwhile to appreciate how the women who were judged not worth keeping alive were treated, for many of these killings served as a warning to the enslaved women. In the thirteenth century, Byzantine forces under the commander John Cantacuzenus in their ravaging of Rhodes in 1249 broke into houses and then "slept with," that is, raped and enslaved, "the women of the Rhodian men, unless this or that one was over-age or not good-looking—these they pushed out the door" (*synekoitazonto de kai tais toutōn gynaixin, ei mē tina exōron ousan ē to eidos ouk agathēn apēlasan exō*; George Acropolites, *Annales* 48). While the higher-ranking aggressors among the warrior elite gained the confiscated houses and the women in them who were judged worth keeping alive as slaves, women pushed out the door were in effect marked as sexually usable without restrictions by the elite's subordinate forces camped outside. As such, they were gang-rape targets at high risk of being killed, just like the women elders (*grandaevae feminae*) in Roman-ravaged Cremona in 69 CE. The forces of Trajan's faction under Antonius Primus sadistically sported with and killed elder women and men in Cremona (Tacitus, *Hist.* 3.33).

The other reason for raping and killing women was because they resisted rather than yielded to being raped. This set a dire example so that the rest of the girls and women witnessing their slaughter would yield in order to avoid being killed. As part of the uncodified but still normative law or standard custom of the ravaging conqueror among martial companies (Xenophon, *Cyr.* 7.5.73), aggressor forces sought to turn it into a capital affront for ravaged captive girls and women in their hands to resist punitive enslaving rape. In a reversal of ancient civil laws against heterosexual rape that required proof of resisting, such as the attacked woman trying to be heard shouting for help, as in the apocryphal biblical tale *Daniel and Susanna* 24, martial forces required the female captives to submit to being raped or to be punished with death as defiant resisters. This has been the case since antiquity. For instance, in the ravaging of Thebes in 335 BCE by Macedonian forces under Alexander, Plutarch notes that a relatively high-ranking Macedonian soldier also named Alexander gained Timocleia, a young woman who was the sister of the Theban hero Theagenes. He spent the night with her alternating between threatening to kill her or to continue sexually having her from then on as his slave wife. He required that she submit to being raped to stay alive.[11]

The mock legalism of the martial law of the conqueror still continues as an ongoing practice; it is articulated in a sobering recent incident from the ravaging 1992–6 Bosnian War waged by Serb forces largely against Bosnian Muslims but also Croat Catholics. In this war, a Bosnian Muslim woman Kadira was imprisoned in the Doboj high school gymnasium turned into a women's detention camp, where the women and girls imprisoned there were packed in wall-to-wall, about two thousand total. As Kadira attests, "I saw about seven or eight little girls who died after they were raped. I saw how they [the Serb forces] took them away to be raped and then brought them back unconscious," in the sense of lifeless. "They threw them down in front of us, and... then they'd announce: 'Look, that's what'll happen to you too if you resist and disobey Serbian law'" (Stiglmayer 1994, 116–21). Given this so-called law of the conqueror first recorded by Xenophon, the forces in Doboj were proclaiming it a capital crime in ravaging warfare for the captive Bosnian Muslim and Croat Catholic girls and women to resist and struggle against being raped by the Serb captors in control of them, as the seven or eight little girls evidently did.

To exercise such lethal extremism over resistant girls and women in order to exert enslaving rape control over the rest of them has been a routine practice in ravaging warfare since antiquity, with sustained accounts of such organized violence appearing in the *Iliad* and the Hebrew Bible. Aristotle and the Peripatetics are key witnesses to such practices. Thanks in part to

---

[11] As this account would have it, the soldier Alexander's tyranny of life-and-death power over Timocleia did not last long, however, for the next day she and her slave maids played off his cupidity and ingeniously killed him (Plutarch, *De mul. vir.* 259f3–4 [in *Mor.*]).

Plato's idea of the sexual and procreative customary law needed to attain social justice, they produced candid research on the habitual norms of ravaging warfare and rape, which were manifestly contrary to norms of social justice.

Though Plato and Aristotle differed in the directions they went to develop equitable norms of sexual intercourse, procreation, and childrearing as a groundwork set of social laws or customs (Plato, *Leg.* 4.720e10–721a8), they were of like mind in formulating a sexually grounded biopolitics toward this end. They both argued that in order to attain social justice, practices of copulating, childrearing, and education should undergo judicious reform to make them mutually beneficial for the sexual agents and their communities. Responsible political governance should therefore accord a leading place to these functions of human sexuality on its agenda. As discussed below, for Aristotle and the Peripatetics, one among several goals in this regard was to overrule ravaging aggression and the martial ethos driving it. In their stead they sought to instate secure customs of mutually respectful, nonviolent sexual relations and nurture.

The matter of equitable sexual, reproductive, and childrearing relations became of deep and direct concern for Aristotle when he was still at Plato's Academy and at a relatively early point in his philosophical career, when he was about thirty-five. In 349 BCE, Philip II of Macedon had his forces ravage Aristotle's home *polis* of Stagira. This led Aristotle to appeal to Philip to allow Stagira to be refounded and the remnant refugee survivors, family and friends among them, to return, rebuild, and resettle without being threatened with further destruction (Plutarch, *Alex.* 7.3 [in *Vit.*]; Hornblower 2012).[12] In a later part of the received Peripatetic tradition that there is no good reason to doubt, the remnant Stagirites, in gratitude for Aristotle's intervention, honored him with an annual festival, the *Aristoteleia* (*Vita Marciana* 17; in Düring 1957, 96–106). As one indicator of the surprisingly low status of the present scholarly knowledge about ravaging warfare and its devastating gendered harms to ancient civil society in the Mediterranean, this incident in Aristotle's life has drawn the attention and acknowledgment of hardly any scholars apart from the astute historian Hornblower, yet the evidence is solid. I now turn to Plato's formative biopolitical ideas and to Aristotle's and the Peripatetics' constructive response to develop them further.

---

[12] Aristotle's intervention to rescue his remaining people and reestablish his home city gave him the paradoxical distinction of being, in one person, both a native son and founder of his city (Dio Chrys. *Or.* 47.9).

3. Plato on the First Laws of Social Justice and Aristotle's Response

As Plato states in an evocative sketch toward an argument in the *Laws*, the socially normative mating customs of human copulation and procreation are a "first law or custom [*prōtos nomos*]" or a set of "first lawful customs [*nomoi prōtoi*]" of social order. "So long as these are well set forth, in all probability their establishment will lead to what is right in every city," that is, to social equity or fair dealings for the inhabitants (*gamikoi dē nomoi prōtoi kindyneuousin tithemenoi kalōs an tithesthai pros orthotēta pasēi polei*; *Leg.* 4.720e10–721a8). Here social equity is pictured as the *orthotēs* of a builder—straightness or uprightness, plumb-line true as opposed to crooked and badly made. Unless people have well-formulated procreative and related sexual customs by which to live as political animals, a badly built social disorder and crooked ways of injustice and inequality become ingrained. Plato presents this view here in the *Laws* as a brief aside, without unfurling its implications in the immediate context. Elsewhere in the *Republic* and *Laws*, however, he discloses his sustained efforts to shape customs of heterosexual copulation, reproduction, childrearing, and education rightly in the interest of social justice, such as the communal sexual reforms for the guardians of Kallipolis in *Republic* 5 (Gaca 2003, 23–93). Thus, it was no incidental sidebar in Plato's ethics and political philosophy to make sound normative customs of human copulation, procreation, and upbringing a first customary law of social order. It was a position he was committed to, and one that he worked out at length in his two major dialogues of political philosophy. To make justice accessible for all meant that philosophers should put this concern first on their agenda to identify and work to correct inequitable customs of heterosexual copulation, procreation, childrearing, and education. To have politics without a reflective and judicious biopolitics would lead the social constituents astray.

Aristotle and his fellow Peripatetics took to heart that Plato's first law was of pivotal import. As Aristotle puts it, the customs of the women in a city, especially their reproductive sexual activity, childrearing, and education, are of primary import as to whether a society proceeds "rightly or not rightly" (*peri tou orthōs kai mē orthōs*; *Pol.* 2.9.1270a11). This is Aristotle's allusion to Plato's stance that human copulation and procreation are a "first law [*prōtos nomos*]" of social order where well-crafted reproductive customs work "for that which is right in every city" (*pros orthotēta pasēi polei*; *Leg.* 4.721a7), that is, for equity and justice. In the *Politics*, Aristotle accordingly coins new words for two important steps and skills in the art of living that he names "mating" (*gamikē*) and "child-making" (*teknopoiētikē, Pol.* 1.3.1253b8–11), and he offers a range of specific reforms (7.15.1334b6–17.1337a7), some in response to problems in specific cities, such as the city of Troezen having girls married and procreating at too young an age (7.16.1335a19–22). The procreative and upbringing education skills offered by Aristotle would, he states, instill in the offspring a shared ethos of beliefs and behaviors that promote the best-quality development of their moral reasoning and mind as a whole. As with the reproductive custom in Troezen, Peripatetic *politeia* research was directed toward elucidating the ethos of social customs and norms in the city inhabitants' everyday lives as well as their governance policy, procedures, and laws, not only their constitutions. Thus their research contained substantive local social history and ethnography of considerable biopolitical import.

4. The Peripatetics on Ravaging Rape

While Plato along with the early Stoics offered extensive communal sexual and procreative reforms to attain social justice (Gaca 2003, 23–93), Aristotle and the Peripatetics took a different route toward this end. In their inquiries, they investigated a major but until then tersely discussed practice of sexually grounded injustice: the rape of war-captive girls and women through ravaging warfare. This behavior was promoted among martial companies (Xenophon, *Cyr.* 7.5.73), despite the serious harms of ravaging rape as coercive mating practices with far-reaching repercussions of injustice across generations, including slavery, forced concubinage, coerced wifehood, and the compulsory procreation of subordinate offspring raised to do little more than mind their assigned gender stations at the lower end of the martial hierarchy: the male offspring as expendable subordinate forces, the female offspring as their ancillary providers.

As Aristotle observed, numerous aggressor martial forces in antiquity were in the grip of being fixated (*katokōchimoi*) primarily on heterosexual copulation, as mythologized in tales about Ares and Aphrodite (*Pol.* 2.9.1269b23–31), but also on male homoerotic copulation, fixations stimulated with intense violence as rape in ravaging warfare, and as pederasty in a vein that was also violent and coercive. This observation from Aristotle is informed in part by his stay in the court of Pella as tutor of the young Alexander, for some of his specific evidence in support of this claim comes from violent sexual intrigues among the Macedonian warrior elite, notably the double outrage that the Macedonian Pausanias felt at being sexually assaulted by Attalus and Philip making light of it (*Pol.* 5.10.1311b1–3). In reaction, Pausanias assassinated Philip in 330 BCE. Aristotle thus confirms the gist of Theopompus that the Macedonian warrior elite were randy and violent. Theopompus calls the elite Macedonian forces of Philip II "man-slayers" (*androphonoi*) and "man-whores" (*andropornoi*) committed to the "plundering and massacre techniques" (*harpazein kai phoneuein*) of ravaging warfare (Theopomp. frag. 225b [*FGrH* #115]). In so doing, they were a good example of what Aristotle is driving at when he states that one of the biggest problems with martial power is "injustice having weapons" (*adikia echousa hopla*; *Pol.* 1.2.1253a33–4). This evocative phrase provides a succinct historical insight into the core problems of martial power: it is violent, rapacious, and unfair. The injustice cut both ways, as the subordinate forces assigned to carry out ravaging aggression were deterred from developing their capacity for moral reasoning and responsible agency. They too were under threat of torment and death if they refused to follow the ravaging and other orders issued by their warrior elite commanders (Gaca 2016b).

The Peripatetics' explicit coverage of ravaging rape stands in contrast to the terse discourse about the practice by earlier Greek historians whose writing of history preceded the Peripatetic development of moral biography and history. Herodotus, Thucydides, and Xenophon in their historiography indicate that captive girls and women were martially mauled and turned into slaves of the forces in ravaging warfare, but often leave its sexual tenor to be understood. For example, Herodotus makes it clear that the Persian king Darius received his delivery in the pretty young girls from Miletus ravaged for its role in the Ionian Rebellion, but he does not say what was sexually done to them (Hdt. 6.32). Further, numerous Athenian men enslaved, moved in, and household-settled with ravaged and enslaved girls and women of the Dolopes and of the Melian Greeks upon killing off their menfolk before and during the Peloponnesian War, but Thucydides does not explicitly specify the habitual rape involved in household-settlement takeover in the wake of ravaging warfare (Thuc. 1.98.3, 5.116.4).

Finally, many of Xenophon's fellow mercenaries each had their favorite "recently captured woman or child war-captive," a number of the children girls, seized from their ravaging forays on route back from Persia to Greece, but Xenophon does not state what the forces sexually did with them (*An.* 4.1.12). Only once does Herodotus expressly indicate the rape in the mauling and enslavement meted out to ravaged war-captive girls and women, falsely leaving the impression that this was an anomalous practice. During the Persian Wars, subordinate forces of Thessalians and Persians under Xerxes' control gang-raped and killed a number of Phocian women fleeing for cover during his ravaging campaign against Athens, Eretria, and the rest of the men's lineages in Greece who refused to become Persian subjects: "They chased down some of the Phocians near the mountains, and they killed some of the women, copulating with them in a gang manner" (*kai tinas diōkontes heilon tōn Phōkeōn pros toisi oresi kai gynaikas tinas, dephtheisan misgomenoi hypo plētheos*; Hdt. 8.33).[13] Unlike the Thessalians, the Phocians refused to become Persian subjects during Xerxes' invasion of Greece, and so ravaging was their punishment from the Thessalians as their long-term rivals, with unrestricted lethal gang rape meted out to the women not wanted alive as slaves.

We enter an altogether different world of sexual discourse in Peripatetic and Peripatetic-derived discussions of rape in ravaging warfare. A Peripatetic-derived source is explicit about the rape of the women and their daughters involved in the andrapodizing—that is, ravaging—of the Peloponnesian Greek city of Pellene near Sicyon around 600 BCE. Dating to the second century CE, yet drawing on Peripatetic research on governance customs, this papyrus fragment (*POxy.* 10.1241 = 2069 MP³) discloses that rape is carried out in the ravaging of targeted peoples and uses an idiomatic martial compound verb starting with *kata* that stresses the intense sexual violence used.[14] Pellene near Sicyon "was andrapodized by force" ([*exandra*]*podisthēnai*), and the women and daughters were sexually assaulted "as spear-taken war captives." This meant that "the women and daughters were treated completely as whores [*kataporneuthēnai*]" once they were seized "as war captives" (*POxy.* 10.1241, col. 3.2–12). This ravaging was carried out by forces under the command of Cleisthenes of Sicyon, the grandfather of Cleisthenes of the Athenian democratic reforms (Gaca 2011c, 95–6). Cleisthenes of Sicyon had his men subject the women and girls of ravaged Pellene to a thorough (*kata-*) whoring (*porneuein*) or to what should be called "the total-whore treatment" by the same or similar methods of *polemiōn hybris* that Carthaginian forces used all night long against daughters and women in their ravaging of Selinous in 409 BCE (Diod. Sic. 13.57.6). The verb *kataporneuein* regularly signifies limited serial rape that is primarily used to enslave the captive girls and women or to unrestricted gang rape against them that has a strong propensity to be lethal (see, for example, Aelian, *VH* 9.8).

---

[13] In contexts of martial aggression, as here in Hdt. 8.33, *diaphtheirein, phthora*, and cognates mean "do away with, kill, bring to a mortal end," not simply "corrupt." See, for instance, Thuc. 3.68.2; Diod. Sic. 17.12.5.

[14] On this papyrus and its published editions, see Gaca 2011c, 94n30.

In total-whore aggression small or large-scale, the men further punish their slain male enemies indirectly and the affiliate enemy women's lineage directly by sexually mauling the girls and women (Strabo 4.1.13, 6.1.8; Plutarch, *Tim.* 13.7–10 [in *Vit.*]). The women and girls of Pellene, by being so assaulted, were stripped of their social standing and dignity—wives, mothers, sisters, and daughters before the attack, slaves and whores afterwards, if they survived, an important contingency to remember given the capacity of ravaging rape to be lethal. The capacity of these sexual attacks to kill girls and women should not be overlooked simply because the practice is often named, as in *POxy.* 10.241, for the main propensity of ravaging warfare to take and enslave "women and daughters" (*tas gynaikas … kai tas thygateras*) as "war-captives" (*aichmalōtistheisas*),[15] turning them into maids and whores (*pornai*) for the ravaging forces, here those of Cleisthenes of Sicyon, and having them produce debased male offspring as coerced subordinate forces and female offspring to take their place in their ancillary providers and support staff. Though fragmentary, the Peripatetic-derived information about Cleisthenes' forces slave-whoring out the war-captive women and daughters of Pellene leaves us in the rare position of having more information about what was done to the women and their daughters in this ravaging incident than about what was done to the men, but the Greek historian Anaxandridas independently confirms that Pellene was subjected to andrapodizing. He indicates that only a remnant of men from Pellene survived this aggression, likely as refugees who took flight or went into hiding to elude being slaughtered. These men stayed together and were determined to rebuild Pellene once they consulted and received approval from Apollo at Delphi to do so (Anaxandridas frag. 2 [*FGrH* #404]).

Further, as recounted in a brief but revealing fragment from the first century BCE, the Peripatetic historian Nicolaus of Damascus (b. ca. 64 BCE) is likewise explicit. He states that in the early Archaic period, when some Ionian Greeks were at war with the Greek inhabitants of the city of Orchomenus, they ravaged the villages around the city. In this incident, they took and hauled off many of the women there as their spear-taken captives (*aischmalōtous pollas ēgagonto*). They "turned these women totally into concubines" (*katapallakeuontes autas*) and produced children (*paidas*) from them (Nic. Dam. frag. 53 [*FGrH* #90]). The male offspring were raised to identify as Ionian-devoted subordinate forces upon reaching fighting-age adolescence, for the upbringing custom was to raise the boys produced through ravaging rape to identify with the ethnoreligious identity of their

---

[15]   On the reliability of these epigraphical readings in Greek, see further Gaca 2011c, 94–6.

aggressor rapist fathers, not with the people of their ravaged, raped, and enslaved mothers, as Euripides makes clear. In his *Trojan Women*, he states that ravaged Trojan women were enslaved to produce male offspring for Greece as a source of grief for the remnant Trojans, and especially for the surviving enslaved Trojan women forced to produce male offspring, only to see them raised to identify with their enemy as Greek (Euripides, *Tro*. 565–7).[16]

The Peripatetics' greater frankness about ravaging rape is well signaled in their use of the compound verbs *kataporneuein* and *katapallakeuein*. Martial Greek vernacular is partial to using *kata-* compounds to describe the enormity of the violence in the steps of ravaging warfare: *katadramein, katastrephein, katasphaxai, kataporneuein, katapallakeuein*, "totally overrun," "totally overthrow," "totally slaughter" (the targeted men or the men and boys), "totally whore" (treat as total or as abject whores), and "totally concubine" as in effect a verb (treat as total or as abject concubines). In this Peripatetic evidence, there is no reluctance about being sexually explicit about the enormity of the rape aggression against the girls and women of peoples targeted with ravaging.

Similarly, the Peripatetic Clearchus (ca. 340–ca. 250 BCE), who was a student of Aristotle, provides additional information about the sexual ravaging against war-captive girls and women, as presented in a fragment from the fourth book of his *Lives* (*Bioi*), a work with a recurrent theme of exploring dissolute human lives and social norms. Clearchus is explicit about this practice, and he uses the tripartite *paides, parthenoi*, and *gynaikes* to underscore that only the women were fully adult and that preadolescent girls and marriageable-aged virgin girls were sexually mauled along with the grown women.[17] As quoted by Athenaeus, in the 470s BCE, after Tarentine Greek forces overthrew the Iapygian (that is, Apulian) and Messapian city of Carbina in the Sallentine heel of southern Italy, the fighters rounded up and stripped naked the girls, virgins, and young women of Carbina. They then subjected them to ravaging rape in the most outrageous public setting imaginable—the very temple precincts of the gods in the city. In short, they desecrated the city's sacred ground by turning it into a rape camp. The fighters "rounded up girls, virgins, and the women at their sexual peak into the sacred precincts of the inhabitants of Carbina" (*paidas kai parthenous kai tas en akmēi gynaikas athroisantes eis ta tōn Karbinatōn hiera*). "Then they staged the bodies of these female captives naked for everyone to view during the

---

[16]   On this coercive procreative purpose as forced recruitment of boys from birth into the martial ethnoreligious identity of their rapist fathers, see Gaca 2018a, 310–12; 2018b, 49.

[17]   On why *paides* refers strictly to girls in this fragment from the Peripatetic Clearchus, see Gaca 2014, esp. 324–31.

daytime" (*skēnopoiēsamenoi gymna pasi tēs hēmeras ta sōmata pareichon theōrein*). Then, in a manner strongly suggestive of predatory animals, each of the Tarentine soldiers "jumped as he wished" (*ho boulomenos parapēdōn*) on this "luckless herd" (*atychē agelēn*). Thereupon the Tarentine aggressors "sexually devoured the youthful beauty of their bodies [*sōmata*] that were rounded up" (*ethoinato tēn tōn athroisthentōn* [*sōmatōn*] *hōran*), stimulated as the forces were by their sexual desires (*tais epithymiais*; Clearchus frag. 48 in Ath. 12.522d–e).

Clearchus deplores the ravaging Tarentine sexual attacks on the preadolescent girls, early adolescent virgins, and grown women of Apulian Carbina. He too regards the Tarentine men in their sexual tyranny as men forcibly treating their victims as prostitutes. He refers to each Tarentine assailant as *ho boulomenos* in taking and sexually assaulting whichever of the naked female victims he wanted and doing what he wanted with them (Ath. 12.522e). This nominal participle *ho boulomenos* is common Greek wording for the prostitute's john,[18] but the name is especially fitting in the ravaging context of sexually degrading and subjugating captive women, girls, and virgins, where all that mattered were the libidinous and violent desires (*epithymiais*) of the armed assailants and where the exercise of their untrammeled will extended to being able to kill some of them as resisters, if they so chose (Hdt. 8.33; Paus. 10.22.4), and to leave other raped women behind likely to die (Isocrates, *Epist. Archidamus* 9.10).

No ancient sources expressly maintain that the ravaging of Aristotle's home city of Stagira helped provoke him and the Peripatetics to model and promote a more forthright biographical and historiographical discourse about ravaging warfare and rape therein. Yet it is hard to believe that this crisis would have played no role in making the Peripatetics much more outspoken in their *politeia* research about what enslavement sexually meant for ravaged war-captive girls and women, especially given the social import that Plato and Aristotle assigned to equitable heterosexual relations, procreation, and upbringing. The Peripatetics are standout voices in this regard because they refused to conceal these practices in their discourse—they set forth the dissolute and violent sexual aggression in ravaging warfare and indicated its adverse effects. This discursive stance had a wide-ranging influence on other ancient Greek moral historians and biographers such as Diodorus, the geographer Pausanias (10.22.2–4), and Plutarch (*De mul. vir.* 259f3–4 [in *Mor.*]), allowing them to venture to be more explicit about ravaging rape too, such as

---

[18] For example, Isae. 3.14–16: *hōs men hetaira ēn tōi boulomenōi kai ou gynē tou hēmeterou theiou*; Chrysippus, treatise 17, frag. 3 (in *SVF*, vol. 3, 196): *hai hetairai exemisthoun heautas tois boulomenois*.

Diodorus pointing out the defamation of the mother-daughter bond by aggressors raping young daughters in front of their mothers during the Carthaginian ravaging of Greek Selinous on Sicily in 409 BCE (Diod. Sic. 13.58.1–2).[19] Thanks to this Peripatetic-driven discursive shift granting greater openness and propriety to discuss ravaging rape in Greek historical and biographical narratives, this sexual aggression against targeted women and girls is sufficiently well documented in antiquity to see the ongoing connections in ravaging methods and aims still in modern times, such as in Bosnia.

5. Barriers to Justice in Procreation and Upbringing

To make social justice and equity attainable, consequently, Plato and Aristotle as leading Greek philosophers believed that the norms and conditions of heterosexual mating, procreation, childrearing, and education needed to be improved through judicious rational inquiry and ensuing social reform. In their distinct ways, they formulated reforms toward this end, because once the better norms were established and people followed them, the rest of society should develop rightly or in good order. This ethical principle has a larger focus on being biopolitical and gender-inclusive. It calls our attention to the sexual, and especially the reproductive, agency and treatment of girls and women, and brings to the fore that wrongs done here are harmful to society in pervasive ways across generations.

Plato, in particular, objected to women, girls, and boys being freeborn men's possessions, and the Peripatetics objected to one of the most ruthless ways they and their descendants became that way, through ravaging warfare. Both objections are valid, as we can see from the effects of both practices on Athens. Maternal figures conventionally took the early formative lead in childrearing, such as in wealthy Athenian households in Plato's day. In Athens, along with freeborn mothers, slave nurses and maids (*trophoi, therapainai*)—many of these slaves either themselves ravaged or born to ravaged and enslaved foremothers—imparted socially received ideas about virtues and vices to young children. The nurse maids indicated to them what counted in their day as "holy, just, and good and their opposites," administering

---

[19] This ravaging rape practice continues in recent and modern times. For instance, the forty-five-year-old Bosnian Muslim woman named Ziba, when asked about the aggression meted out to her, replied thus about her fourteen-year-old girl: "My daughter was raped along with me. First he [the aggressor] raped me, and then I had to watch while he raped my little girl." As the interviewer Alexandra Stiglmayer then sums up the rest of Ziba's testimony: for several ensuing months, "her daughter suffered from bleeding and infections" (Stiglmayer 1994, 119–20).

threats and beatings to children who proved recalcitrant to follow these lessons (Plato, *Prt.* 325c6–d5). In this way, the boys and girls started learning the received conventions of martial androcentrism in freeborn slaveholding houses and the custom of ravaging targeted enemies as war practices situated as though on the right and not the wrong side of holiness, justice, and goodness. The consequences of this sort of upbringing were at work, for instance, in state-sponsored Athenian forces ravaging resistant enemies like the Melian Greeks and enslaving and moving in with the women and girls kept alive from the massacred Melian men (Thuc. 5.116.2–4, pseudo-Andoc., *In Alcibiadem* 22).

However, an early formative development in reasoning and moral responsibility cannot be accomplished well or at all if the nurturers and children are objectified and enslaved or female and freeborn but still objectified, for from birth they are subjected to deprivations that preclude or discourage this development. Key deprivations include, for instance, receiving little or no education in developing an informed volition and mature moral reasoning, and being taught ravaging and other received doctrines that are narrow-minded and work against this moral maturity. Prominent among such debilitating norms has been the rule of retaliatory force as exercised in ravaging warfare, which made ravaging rape seem a normal way, one mandated as pious for the martial gods, to punish and gain at the expense of the attacked people labeled as insubordinate and, for this reason, also as enemies (Gaca 2016b; Gaca 2022, 168–70). Once the targeted men or men and boys were killed, the unenlightened gains took the form of slave maids, wives, and concubines being used as coerced reproductive vessels and as forced laborers for the men. A number of these women and their daughters and their daughters' daughters were put to raising freeborn children in Athens.

Ancient Mediterranean societies that were not themselves ravaged, such as Athens until Sulla had his Roman forces besiege and ravage the city in 87–6 BCE for going over to Mithridates, were consequently unjust as a result of being beneficiaries of ravaging in the form of having plunder-derived slave maids in their society—so many from Thrace that *Thrattai* became a nickname for them in Athens (see, for example, Plato, *Tht.* 174a5). As Plato and Aristotle understood, social justice cannot proceed when blocs of a populace are denied what it takes to become rational moral agents who know how to have a will of their own and the leeway and encouragement to act on it responsibly. Neither freeborn women nor slave-maid nurses were eligible to receive what freeborn families in Athens regarded as the best education in moral reasoning and effective communication that their sons could acquire—training from the likes of Protagoras. This denied freeborn mothers and slave nurses the opportunity to adapt and infuse their childrearing activities with Protagoras's valuable ideas. For instance, as disclosed by Plato in his dialogue about this sophist-educator, Protagoras showed an articulate resistance to the human habit of thinking in binary polarized opposites such as friend and enemy, Greek and barbarian, male and female. He insisted that the good was not for the gods to dictate, seeing that their very existence was open to doubt, and thus that the good was up to us as human beings to measure, determine, and agree upon by our best tested judgment. This challenges the martial devotion to war as war-god-approved and therefore pious. As Plato presents Protagoras saying, "There is a certain way in which white resembles black, and hard soft, and so on for all the polar opposites" (Plato, *Prt.* 331d2–5).

Further, agnosticism about the gods and an insistence that human beings have what it takes to formulate a good moral code are fundamental to Protagoras's outlook and education. As he is believed to have said in his own words, "I can neither affirm nor deny the existence of the gods." Given the gods' dubious status as existent moral arbiters, "The human being is the measure [*metron*] of all things" (Sextus, *Math.* 7.60). For human beings to become any good at being this sort of measure, however, no one should settle for less in the training they receive in moral reasoning. Second-rate training should not be available as a choice, even if it is the norm due to ingrained social inequities. Everyone should receive the best upbringing and education to rise and live up to being a sound moral measure. These were two ethical ideas that could have deterred ensuing generations of Greeks from continuing to be swayed by the martial ethos, which is based on intensifying the opposition between friends and enemies and insisting on helping friends or allies and harming enemies, and even on making friends in order to be more effective at harming enemies.

As a result, Athens substantively remained a backward and unfair place, even though this city by the fourth century was the renowned place to go in the Mediterranean for freeborn men and growing boys to learn ethics and political philosophy. Slave maids, slave nurses, and freeborn girls and women were largely left ignorant about high-quality moral reflections such as those of Protagoras, yet they were the ones mainly serving the nurturing roles of instilling the problematic received ethos into the next generation of boys and girls from infancy onward. What is more, slave maids and nurses had this childrearing work imposed on them as forced labor and they were required to carry it out. Being education-deprived and exploited in this way was hardly an optimal arrangement for them to raise the freeborn infants of their masters and mistresses to be mature and reflective moral agents.

Plato's biopolitical idea that sexuality, procreation, and early upbringing are a kind of first law that moves, via the customs at work, toward or away from social justice, is therefore persuasive. What each of us is raised to perceive as morality at work in our lives is shaped in its fundamentals by the customs of procreation, childrearing, and education of the women and men who have been in charge of nurturing and caring for us and thereby shaping our development from early childhood. How each of us has been raised to be moral agents historically depends on our luck of the draw in who these nurturing figures have been and in the social status, identity, and religious background that they bring to this work.

Thus, even though nurture starting in early childhood and the moral outlook it instills have deep historical roots that can be enlightening, we should not romanticize it as the warm and wonderful about love, moral intelligence, and creativity in childhood and parenting. Early childrearing and upbringing thereafter risk being a perpetuating ground of the deeply immoral and violent posing as that which is morally right and normal, such as the righteous martial posture that ravaging massacre, rape, and forced impregnation for the victors over their vanquished enemies are pious practices because they are war-god-approved. Norms of sexual copulation, procreation, and childrearing consequently merit serious investigation into their biopolitics, for historically, warfare, rape, and aggression have had a big hand in shaping these norms, especially among peoples turned into subordinate subjects of their warrior elite. Although this sort of position may initially seem self-evident and not in need of study, the opposite is the case. For example, Foucault on biopolitics has only spare comments about women's sexuality, procreation, and childrearing (Deutscher 2012; Mills 2017). Yet these practices are of key import to biopolitics, as Plato and Aristotle understood.

Hence sexual copulation, procreation, childrearing, and upbringing are historically and still today under the unexamined influence of misguided ideas being presented as the right way to think. This is substantively (though not only) because received morality historically has in its legacy a martially driven composite of harsh gendered inequities handed on across generations through an upbringing in religious violence that normalizes ravaging male massacre and female rape and enslavement as pious and just when meted out to peoples resistant or rebellious in response to being conquered and colonized as submissive collectives under the rule of force. This practice has produced the combatant and non-combatant subservient multitudes, many of them slaves, as persons seemingly good for forced labors but otherwise of negligible value, especially relative to the seemingly august worth of the warrior elite circles living off their multitudes and rivaling one another to exert a strong grip on state formation through conquest in and since antiquity. The martial legacy represses the human ability to respond judiciously to the Socratic question of how we ought to live, for subordinated male and female offspring in the martial hierarchy have had minimal choices for crafting a meaningful art of life in response to that question.[20] This discrepancy in life choices between the enslaved and the freeborn elite has made the producing and raising of children and what passes as morality and moral reasoning in grown men and women a significant vehicle for the gendered instatement and persistence of serious moral, sociopolitical, religious, and economic inequities deriving from martial conquest and colonialist aggression, starting with mass slaughter, rape, and enslavement.

6. Conclusion

It is no small achievement for Plato to have realized from his position of free-born Athenian male privilege that to be raised to conform to an unjust social hierarchy, and to use reinforcing oaths, myths, and violent rites for this purpose, is contrary to what an education in moral and political reasoning should do. This sort of education should be accessible to all and challenge us to excel at developing into responsible moral agents and to see through the fabrications that the powerful inflict on the young, impressionable, and disempowered, such as girls being given many signals that they and their education matter less than boys and their education. Childhood nurture by figures of parental authority who reinforce the status quo of power discrepancies can be the hardest to shake in the interest of justice, for society generally signals that parents are the adults their children should trust and obey. Plato accordingly sought to ameliorate the corruption in this status quo by insisting that the attainment of justice and equity needs to start with putting mothers on par with fathers and trying to make parental nurture of girls and boys communal, equitable, and enlightened. In this way, freeborn men could be made to step down from dominating the women and children they considered their familial and slave possessions, for in a just society, children and women should be persons in their own right and not continue to be slave and familial grades of possessions distributed among men and disadvantaged and oppressed by them.

Though Aristotle disagreed with Plato's communal sexual reforms for social justice, he fully supported Plato's insight that customary heterosexual

---

[20] On this central question in Socratic ethics, see Plato, *Resp.* 1.344d6–e3, 352d5–6; Williams 1985.

relations, reproduction, and upbringing of the offspring produced were key to making society proceed justly or unjustly. Taking their cue from Aristotle, whose home city of Stagira was ravaged, the Peripatetics in their *politeia* research included ravaging warfare as an extreme case of the precipitous violence and injustice that shows how society is made crooked through bad norms of sexual copulation, reproduction, and childrearing—ravaging rape, forced impregnation, compulsory procreation, and narrow-minded upbringing for girls and boys to mind their lowly gendered stations. In so doing, Aristotle and the Peripatetics transformed the discourse on ravaging rape, showing that this practice, though normalized among its male practitioners as a furious piety of war-god devotion, was ruthlessly anti-volitional for the women and girls and subjected them to a death-threat total whoring and total concubining when they were kept alive and enslaved rather than being killed off along with their male relatives.

References

Acropolites, George. 1978. *Georgii Acropolitae opera*. 2 vols. Edited by August Heisenberg, with corrections by Peter Wirth. Leipzig: Teubner.

Aelian (Claudius Aelianus). 1864. *Claudii Aeliani Varia historia*. Edited by Rudolf Hercher. Leipzig: Teubner.

Anaxandridas. 1954. In *Die Fragmente der griechischen Historiker*, vol. 3B, edited by Felix Jacoby, 298–300 [*FGrH* #404]. Leiden: Brill.

Andocides. 1966. *Andocide: Discours*. Edited by Georges Dalmeyda. Paris: Les Belles Lettres.

Appian. 2019. *Roman History*. Vol. 1. Translated by Brian McGing. Cambridge, MA: Harvard University Press.

Aristotle. 1954. *Aristotelis Politica*. Edited by William David Ross. Oxford: Clarendon Press.

Athenaeus. 2007–12. *The Learned Banqueters*. 8 vols. Edited and translated by S. Douglas Olson. Cambridge, MA: Harvard University Press.

Caesar (Gaius Julius Caesar). 1917. *The Gallic War*. Translated by Henry John Edwards. Cambridge, MA: Harvard University Press.

Chrysippus. 1903. *Stoicorum veterum fragmenta*. Vol. 3, *Chrysippi fragmenta moralia, Fragmenta successorum Chrysippi*. Edited by Hans von Arnim. Leipzig: Teubner.

Clearchus. 1969. *Klearchos*. In *Die Schule des Aristoteles*, vol. 3, 2nd ed., edited by Fritz Wehrli, 9–40. Basel: Schwabe.

De Sensi Sestito, Giovanna. 1999. "Schiave di guerra tra *dikaion* ed *ômotês*." In *Femmes-esclaves: Modèles d'interprétation anthropologique, économique, juridique:*

Atti del XXI Colloquio internazionale GIREA, Lacco Ameno-Ischia, 27–29 ottobre 1994, edited by Francesca Reduzzi Merola and Alfredina Storchi Marino, 111–28. Naples: Jovene.

Deutscher, Penelope. 2012. "Foucault's *History of Sexuality Volume I:* Re-reading its Reproduction." *Theory, Culture, and Society* 29: 119–37. https://doi.org/10.1177/0263276411423772.

Diels, Hermann, and Walther Kranz. 1996. *Die Fragmente der Vorsokratiker*. 18th ed. Vol. 2. Berlin: Weidmann.

Dio Chrysostom. 1946. *Discourses 37–60*. Translated by H. Lamar Crosby. Cambridge, MA: Harvard University Press.

Diodorus Siculus. 1964a. *Bibliotheca historica*. Vol. 3. Edited by Immanuel Bekker, Ludwig August Dindorf, and Friedrich Vogel. Stuttgart: Teubner.

Diodorus Siculus. 1964b. *Bibliotheca historica*. Vol. 4. Edited by Immanuel Bekker, Ludwig August Dindorf, and Curt Theodor Fischer. Stuttgart: Teubner.

Düring, Ingemar. 1957. *Aristotle in the Ancient Philosophical Tradition*. Gothenburg: Elanders.

Euripides. 1981. *Euripidis fabulae*. Vol. 2. Edited by James Diggle. Oxford: Clarendon Press.

Foucault, Michel. 1980. *The History of Sexuality*. Vol. 1, *An Introduction*. Translated by Robert Hurley. New York: Vintage Books.

Foucault, Michel. 2003. *"Society Must Be Defended": Lectures at the Collège de France 1975–1976*. Translated by David Macey. New York: Picador.

Gaca, Kathy L. 2003. *The Making of Fornication: Eros, Ethics, and Political Reform in Greek Philosophy and Early Christianity*. Berkeley: University of California Press.

Gaca, Kathy L. 2008. "Reinterpreting the Homeric Simile of *Iliad* 16.7–11: The Girl and Her Mother in Ancient Greek Warfare." *American Journal of Philology* 129 (2): 145–71. https://doi.org/10.1353/ajp.0.0001.

Gaca, Kathy L. 2010. "The Andrapodizing of War Captives in Greek Historical Memory." *Transactions of the American Philological Association* 140 (1): 116–71. https://doi.org/10.1353/apa.0.0051.

Gaca, Kathy L. 2011a. "Girls, Women, and the Significance of Sexual Violence in Ancient Warfare." In *Sexual Violence in Conflict Zones: From the Ancient World to the Era of Human Rights*, edited by Elizabeth Heineman, 73–88, 273–6. Philadelphia: University of Pennsylvania Press. https://doi.org/10.9783/9780812204346.73.

Gaca, Kathy L. 2011b. "Manhandled and 'Kicked Around': Reinterpreting the Etymology and Symbolism of *andrapoda*." *Indogermanische Forschungen* 116: 110–46. https://doi.org/10.1515/9783110239485.110.

Gaca, Kathy L. 2011c. "Telling the Girls from the Boys and Children: Interpreting *paides* in the Sexual Violence of Populace-Ravaging Ancient Warfare." *Illinois*

Classical Studies 35–6: 85–109. https://doi.org/10.5406/ILLICLASSTUD.35-36.0085.

Gaca, Kathy L. 2014. "Martial Rape, Pulsating Fear, and the Sexual Maltreatment of Girls (*paides*), Virgins (*parthenoi*), and Women (*gynaikes*) in Antiquity." *American Journal of Philology* 135 (3): 303–57. https://doi.org/10.1353/ajp.2014.0025.

Gaca, Kathy L. 2015. "Ancient Warfare and the Ravaging Martial Rape of Girls and Women: Evidence from Homeric Epic and Greek Drama." In *Sex in Antiquity: Exploring Gender and Sexuality in the Ancient World*, edited by Mark Masterson, Nancy Sorkin Rabinowitz, and James Robson, 278–97. London: Routledge. https://doi.org/10.4324/9781315747910.

Gaca, Kathy L. 2016a. "Continuities in Rape and Tyranny in Martially Run Society from Antiquity Onward." In *Women in Antiquity: Real Women Across the Ancient World*, edited by Stephanie Budin and Jean Macintosh Turfa, 1041–56. London: Routledge. https://doi.org/10.4324/9781315621425-109.

Gaca, Kathy L. 2016b. "Martial Religion, Ravaging Warfare, and Rape: Polytheistic Greek and Monotheistic Israelite Views." In *Feminism and Religion: How Faiths View Women and Their Rights*, edited by Michelle Paludi and J. Harold Ellens, 173–204. New York: Praeger, ABC-CLIO.

Gaca, Kathy L. 2018a. "The Martial Rape of Girls and Women in Antiquity and Modernity." In *The Oxford Handbook of Gender and Conflict*, edited by Fionnuala Ní Aoláin, Naomi Cahn, Dina Francesca Haynes, and Nahla Valji, 305–15. Oxford: Oxford University Press. https://doi.org/10.1093/oxfordhb/9780199300983.013.24.

Gaca, Kathy L. 2018b. "Ancient Warfare Beyond the Battle: Populace Ravaging and Heterosexual Rape." In *Civilians and Warfare in World History*, edited by Nicola Foote and Nadya Williams, 42–66. London: Routledge. https://doi.org/10.4324/9781315178844-4.

Gaca, Kathy L. 2022. "Procreative Genocide, Conquest, and Subservience." In *A Cultural History of Genocide in the Ancient World*, edited by Tristan Taylor, 154–78. London: Bloomsbury.

Grenfell, Bernard P., and Arthur S. Hunt. 1914. *The Oxyrhynchus Papyri*. Vol. 10. London: Egypt Exploration Society.

Herodotus. 1927. *Herodoti Historiae*. 3rd ed. 2 vols. Edited by Karl Hude. Oxford: Clarendon Press.

Hornblower, Simon. 2012. "Stagira." In *The Oxford Classical Dictionary*, 4th ed., edited by Simon Hornblower, Antony Spawforth, and Esther Eidinow, 1395. Oxford: Oxford University Press. https://doi.org/10.1093/acrefore/9780199381135.013.6055.

Isaeus. 1903. *Isaei Orationes cum deperditadum fragmentis*. Edited by Theodor Thalheim. Stuttgart: Teubner.

Isocrates. 1945. *Isocrates in Three Volumes*. Vol. 3. Edited and translated by Larue van Hook. Cambridge, MA: Harvard University Press.

Macey, David. 2008. "Some Reflections on Foucault's *Society Must Be Defended* and the Idea of 'Race.'" In *Foucault in an Age of Terror: Essays on Biopolitics and the Defence of Society*, edited by Stephen Morton and Stephen Bygrave, 118–32. New York: Palgrave Macmillan. https://doi.org/10.1057/9780230584334_7.

Mills, Catherine. 2017. "Biopolitics and Human Reproduction." In *The Routledge Handbook of Biopolitics*, edited by Sergei Prozorov and Simona Rentea, 281–94. London: Routledge. https://doi.org/10.4324/9781315612751-19.

Morton, Stephen, and Stephen Bygrave, eds. 2008. *Foucault in an Age of Terror: Essays on Biopolitics and the Defence of Society*. New York: Palgrave Macmillan.

Nicolaus of Damascus. 1926. In *Die Fragmente der griechischen Historiker*, vol. 2A, edited by Felix Jacoby, 324–430 [*FGrH* #90]. Leiden: Brill.

Ojakangas, Mika. 2016. *On the Greek Origins of Biopolitics: A Reinterpretation of the History of Biopower*. London: Routledge.

Pausanias. 1903. *Pausaniae Graeciae descriptio*. 3 vols. Edited by Friedrich Spiro. Leipzig: Teubner.

Plato. 1902. *Republic*. In *Platonis opera*, vol. 4. Edited by John Burnet. Oxford: Clarendon Press.

Plato. 1903. *Protagoras*. In *Platonis opera*, vol. 3. Edited by John Burnet. Oxford: Clarendon Press.

Plato. 1907. *Laws*. In *Platonis opera*, vol. 5. Edited by John Burnet. Oxford: Clarendon Press.

Plato. 1995. *Politicus*. In *Platonis opera*, vol. 1. Edited by E. A. Duke, W. F. Hicken, W. S. M. Nicoll, D. B. Robinson, and J. C. G. Strachan. Oxford: Clarendon Press.

Plato. 1995. *Theaetetus*. In *Platonis opera*, vol. 1. Edited by E. A. Duke, W. F. Hicken, W. S. M. Nicoll, D. B. Robinson, and J. C. G. Strachan. Oxford: Clarendon Press.

Plutarch. 1931. *Moralia*. Vol. 3. Translated by Frank Cole Babbitt. Cambridge, MA: Harvard University Press.

Plutarch. 1957–68. *Vitae parallelae*. 4 vols. Edited by Claes Lindskog and Konrat Ziegler. Leipzig: Teubner.

Polybius. 2010–14. *The Histories*. 6 vols. Translated by William Roger Paton, translation revised by Frank William Walbank and Christian Habicht. Cambridge, MA: Harvard University Press.

Sextus Empiricus. 1914–54. *Sexti Empirici opera*. Vols. 2 and 3. Edited by Hermann Mutschmann and Jürgen Mau. Leipzig: Teubner.

Stiglmayer, Alexandra. 1994. *Mass Rape: The War against Women in Bosnia-Herzegovina*. Translated by Marion Faber. Lincoln: University of Nebraska Press.

Strabo. 1866–67. *Strabonis Geographica*. 3 vols. Edited by August Meineke. Leipzig: Teubner.

Tacitus. 1975. *Cornelii Taciti Historiae*. Edited by Heinz Heubner. Leipzig: Teubner.

Theopompus. 1926. In *Die Fragmente der griechischen Historiker*, vol. 2B, edited by Felix Jacoby, 526–617 [*FGrH* #115]. Leiden: Brill.

Thucydides. 1942. *Thucydidis Historiae.* 2 vols. Edited by Henry Stuart Jones. Oxford: Clarendon Press.

Van Wees, Hans. 2016. "Genocide in Archaic and Classical Greece." In *Our Ancient Wars: Rethinking War through the Classics*, edited by Victor Caston and Sile-Maria Weineck, 19–37. Ann Arbor: University of Michigan Press. https://doi.org/10.3998/mpub.7652595.

William of Adam. 2012. *How to Defeat the Saracens.* Edited and translated by Giles Constable. Washington, DC: Dumbarton Oaks.

Williams, Bernard. 1985. "Socrates' Question." In *Ethics and the Limits of Philosophy*, 1–21. Cambridge, MA: Harvard University Press. https://doi.org/10.4324/9780203828281.

Xenophon. 1910a. *Anabasis.* In *Xenophontis opera omnia*, vol. 4, edited by Edgar Cardew Marchant. Oxford: Clarendon Press.

Xenophon. 1910b. *Cyropaedia.* In *Xenophontis opera omnia*, vol. 4, edited by Edgar Cardew Marchant. Oxford: Clarendon Press.

Xenophon. 1971. *Memorabilia.* In *Xenophontis opera omnia*, vol. 2, edited by Edgar Cardew Marchant. Oxford: Clarendon Press.

PART II
ANCIENT THOUGHT BEYOND BIOPOLITICS

4

Otherwise than (Bio)politics

Nature and the Sacred in Tragic Life

Kalliopi Nikolopoulou

1. Politics as Denaturalization

If, to follow Michel Foucault, the history of thought presents us not with solutions to our problems but with our anxieties about them, the current politicization of everything existing might be an index of our era's chief anxiety: the lack of a proper *polis* qua arena of meaningful interactions simultaneous with an explosion of global communication. Similarly, the quick reduction of every cultural issue to an analysis of power relations might appear progressive, but is more likely symptomatic. The prolific scholarship on, and the elaborate critiques of, biopolitics over the last two decades belong to this intense preoccupation with the political across many social and humanistic fields. Given the overwhelming preponderance of politics in current discussions, I wish today to shift away from politics proper and toward certain experiences that exceed, and even threaten, the political order, but also enrich it: nature and the sacred.

The present volume's focus on the question of biopolitics in antiquity permits me to attempt this shift by reconsidering some salient terms from contemporary political theory in light of ancient literature where these terms are animated quite differently. My specific choice of the tragic genre is emphatically deliberate: in tragedy, the experience of nature and the sacred, which is subordinated by biopolitical critique to the utilitarian project of improving politics, resonates more profoundly, albeit sometimes precariously. However, before discussing how specific tragedies offer a different model of being and (co)existence than political theory, I would first lay out some crucial notions and questions regarding biopolitics and its critique.

Kalliopi Nikolopoulou, *Otherwise than (Bio)politics: Nature and the Sacred in Tragic Life* In: *Biopolitics and Ancient Thought.*
Edited by: Jussi Backman and Antonio Cimino, Oxford University Press. © Oxford University Press 2022.
DOI: 10.1093/oso/9780192847102.003.0005

While the coinage of the term "biopolitics" is attributed to Swedish political scientist Rudolf Kjellén,[1] its recent currency owes to Foucault's theorization of biopower and its development in Giorgio Agamben's *Homo Sacer: Sovereign Power and Bare Life*. Agamben's study is not only a critique of what he considers the violence of biopolitical thought's naturalist and vitalist assumptions; it is also an attempt to reconstruct a longer philosophical history of biopolitics reaching back to Aristotle and Roman jurisprudence. As it turns out, biopolitics for Agamben serves a double historical function: (a) it charts a continuum between antiquity and modernity, both of whose conceptions of sovereignty ostensibly rely on biopolitical premises; and (b) it marks an epochal shift in which the moderns raise up the biopolitical state as a paradigm of unprecedented power, climaxing with the death camp. Thus, for Agamben, biopolitics is understood exclusively in negative terms.

To make the case for biopolitics in antiquity, Agamben argues that the underlying structure of biopolitics is to be found in a sharp binary Aristotle draws between *zōē* (bare life, the biological life-force) and *bios* (which Agamben chiefly interprets as the political institutions that separate humanity from animal life). As we will see shortly, this thesis is contentious, since Aristotle does not draw so impermeable a distinction between *zōē* and *bios*. Nonetheless, according to Agamben's interpretation, this binary produces a rigorous hierarchy between the higher *bios* and the lower *zōē*, and at the limit, this hierarchy leads to an outright exclusion of bare life from the realm of *bios*. Furthermore, Agamben maintains that this exclusion rests in a paradoxical structure of inclusion: *bios* and the legal contracts that protect it can only admit bare life by way of excluding it. For him, this exclusion is visible not only in places where bare life is so devalued as to be treated like debris—Auschwitz, refugee camps, the Tuskegee experiments—but also in moments where sovereign power sacralizes bare life so as to legitimize state violence.

Three important issues complicate this picture. The first concerns the limits of the critique of biopolitics insofar as this critique begs but does not address productively the more exhaustive question of the relation of nature to life, and to political life. The second involves Agamben's misreading of Aristotle to yield this binary. Thirdly, Agamben's repositioning of the sacred

---

[1] Markus Gunneflo traces the term to Kjellén's organicist theory of the state, while situating historically Kjellén's radical conservatism in relation to contemporary political theories, both of the left and right varieties. Gunneflo writes: "Because of the organicist analogies deployed by Kjellén, his biopolitical theory of the state is considered as a form of 'vitalism' or 'organicism' in the contemporary literature on biopolitics" (Gunneflo 2015, 24). See also Ojakangas (2016, 11), who traces the origins of the term to an article published in 1911 by G. W. Harris; my thanks to the editors of this volume for alerting me to this.

from the religious to the legal register, in his analysis of *homo sacer*, might serve well his critique of biopolitics, but elides the significant ways in which the sacred interrupts all politics as a utilitarian project.

Let me begin with the first issue. Given Agamben's concerns about the intense power that sovereignty exerts over mere life, one might think that his critique of state power would imply a positive reappraisal of *zōē*, but this is not the case. The vitalism of *zōē*—which, according to Agamben, biopolitics appropriates for insidious ends—must be equally subjected to critique. Biopolitical vitalism, as any organicist political theory, can inspire dangerous nationalist experiments: Nazism adopted major tenets of bio-political thought. Interestingly, while it is the modern catastrophe of Auschwitz that motivates Agamben's reflections on biopolitics, his critical project aims at uncovering a longer-standing complicity with biopolitics in the West.

However, his desire to locate the origin of biopolitical violence in Aristotle—a thinker immersed in a comprehensive study of nature and life activity—provokes a more expansive set of questions about nature and its relation to human life than those within the limited domain of already actualized political systems. Phrased differently, the necessary critique of Nazism's use of vitalism does not exhaust the pressing question of the status of nature in both political thought and the actual experience of living together. Must all appeals to nature be suspected because National Socialism used the discourse of nature toward atrocious ends? Does the thoroughly denaturalized politics toward which Western liberalism is advancing offer an inviolable guarantee for a conflict-free existence? Must a critical project exposing the contradictions and violences of liberalism's disavowal of nature inevitably raise fascism's specter?

The denaturalization of politics as the only admissible response to the dangers of fascism poses not only a theoretical problem—namely, the absolutism of claiming to be an exclusive answer—but also a practical one: simply put, *bios* requires embodiment, and embodiment reveals the pressures exerted by nature and mere life on our political norms and institutions. Bodies are sites of cultural inscription, but they are not that alone. Cultural inscription cannot write on a nonexistent surface: it needs a physical extension—that arrangement of cells we call a "body," the *ontic*, not the onto-logical, body—that is, the work of nature. No matter how we redefine nature, or reduce it to an effect of cultural attitudes, its ontic character can never be fully excised either from the concrete experience or from the theoretical dis-cussion of sociality. On the contrary, the coercive subordination of nature's thingliness to a cultural hermeneutic betrays an anthropocentrism hardly devoid of ethico-political violence.[2]

The danger of subordinating nature to politics is well illustrated in Sophocles' *Antigone*, our first, and rather brief, example from tragedy. For the critic of biopolitics, who requires that politics eschew reference to vitality, Antigone ought to emerge as a rather villainous character, unworthy of the high moral esteem she has commanded through the ages. But what does *Antigone* have to do with vitality? you might ask me. It is, after all, a tragedy about a corpse and it concludes with even more corpses. This is a fair objection, provided we add that the deaths result from her affirmation of the *natural* unit of the family. Antigone dies for the riveting bond of blood kinship, upholding precisely the aspect of natural vitality that makes the biopolitical critic uncomfortable. She explains her attachment to her brother in terms of having shared a common womb (*Ant.* 511). Because this irreducible familial intimacy appeals to natural rather than political categories, Antigone not only destabilizes the civic order but risks herself being aligned with perilous forms of nativism in the language of biopolitical critique.[3] The critique of biopolitics aims, in effect, at the inequality that results from the exclusive devotion to "one's own,"[4] because this sentiment threatens the infinite theoretical project of inclusion and universal siblinghood.

I now move to the second issue concerning Agamben's interpretation of Aristotle's binary distinction between bare life and *bios*. That Aristotle's zoology offers examples of *bios* in the animal world, and that Aristotle describes both human and animal life more dynamically than the two poles Agamben

---

[2] Because the subordination of nature to cultural construction serves the ever-expansive egalitarian project of liberal democracies, we tend not to focus on its anthropocentric basis, even though anthropocentrism is consistently critiqued by contemporary theory.

[3] It would be more convenient to interpret Antigone as a *femina sacra* and avoid the theoretical embarrassment of indicting a moral heroine to a fascist prototype. Yet tragedy should shake our "enlightened" theoretical comfort, and in this case, my reading of her along the lines of nature is supported by the text. The question is not whether she is on the side of nature, but whether the critic interprets this alliance negatively. All the same, her characterization as *femina sacra* would be amiss: Antigone is not exposed the way Agamben's *homo sacer* is, since she makes quite clear her own choices. For more on her as *femina sacra* or "proto-fascism," see also footnote 4.

[4] Antigone's use of "my own" (*Ant.* 48) demarcates the limit of Creon's power. Following the logic of biopolitical critique, one could argue that Creon's imposition of the death penalty via a special edict (a sovereign exception) illustrates the process of sovereign power acting upon Antigone's bare life, rendering her a *femina sacra*. This is partly true. It is also true, and more poignantly so, that Antigone's stance presents us with a risk—one that, as I already mentioned, biopolitical critique has identified in a thoroughgoing manner with fascism: the primacy of blood kinship over conventional community. It is not my purpose to examine this play in detail, but to point out the potentially strange inversions that emerge when biopolitical critique reduces every trace of nature to fascism. Perhaps I am too naive to think that others would be unsettled by this moral inversion of Antigone, or that someone would not propose an interpretation (theatrical or theoretical) of Antigone as a fascist instigator. That Jean Anouilh's version was (mis)interpreted by the Vichy regime to be collaborationist might, after all, provide appropriate fodder.

allows for, have been counterarguments raised by several scholars.[5] In Agamben's defense, it is arguable that his critique of biopolitics has merit even if Aristotle did not draw such a distinction, since a similar conceptual binary could be operative in other thinkers and, more likely, in actual political regimes. This is true, but Agamben's choice to situate the *origin* of what he considers a pernicious practice of sovereign power in Aristotle is not accidental. It is a question of method, and has profound moral and epistemic implications, not least of which involve Agamben's own "politics" of reading. I will postpone reflections on this issue and return to it in my conclusion.

Lastly, we arrive at the cardinal example Agamben submits to illustrate this binary: *homo sacer*, or the sacred man, was a legal category denoting a person who was considered impure to become a ritual sacrifice and at the same time unworthy of the protection of civic law. *Homo sacer* could be pursued and killed by anyone with impunity. By not holding his murderers accountable, the law that excluded the sacred man from its protection was also the law that sanctioned—thus included—his murder. Outside both religious and civic jurisdiction, and exposed to unaccountable violence, the fate of the sacred man demonstrates Agamben's biopolitical formula of sovereignty as inclusion-by-exclusion.

The transposition of the sacred away from religious and into juridical language constitutes a necessary *metaphor* for Agamben's critical project and for the kind of knowledge his critique wishes to yield. Indeed, if biopolitics is to be exposed for its vitalism, the sacred must first be detached from religion, wherein it was affirmed as the living presentation of nature's mysteries through rituals that gathered the community together. It must then be scaled down so that we can see not how it engenders the social bond but how it is itself *produced* as an effect of social regulations. The sacred is now shown to have been merely the profane; or, more aptly, it turns out to have always been imagined as a convenient site upon which the profane committed and justified its violence. This is key to understanding why Agamben (1998, 113) relegates Georges Bataille's call for a sacred sociology to yet another fascist myth, concurring in this with Walter Benjamin. Whereas the sacred appealed to Bataille for its inutility and its capacity to draw us out of the confines of quotidian rationality, Agamben needs to delimit the sacred within a legal, sociopolitical frame in order to carry out his critique of biopolitics.

---

[5] Finlayson (2010) takes Agamben to task for falsely attributing to Aristotle a strict binary distinction between mere life and the good life. Similarly, Brill (2018) argues that Aristotle's zoology contravenes Agamben's binary distinction; she does so by looking at Aristotle's example of the political life of bees. Brill (2020) elaborates this argument in a chapter in her book on Aristotle. See also chapter 1 by Brill in this volume. On the problems inherent in Agamben's notion of bare life and its attribution to Aristotle, see also chapters 5 and 9 by Adriel M. Trott and Antonio Cimino in this volume.

At the same time, Agamben's displacement of the sacred from religion to law relies on a peculiar equivalence, rather than a distinction, between religion and law: after denaturalizing and desacralizing the sacred in order to expose it as a cultural effect (an effect of *bios*), the sacred yields mere life yet again. In other words, law once produced *homines sacri* with religion as its handmaid, but now law unaided still produces *homines sacri*; except, this time, mere life returns more menacingly, since nature lacks the transcendent appeal that religion erstwhile had lent it. Agamben recognizes this epochal difference, but, unlike Bataille, refuses to discuss it in terms of the absence of religion. His refusal, expected now of political theory, is symptomatic of a more general anxiety about the types of knowledge we wish to pursue. Agamben stresses, for example, that the distinct violence of the modern biopolitical state is that its law is in force *without significance*: the death camp shows most formidably law's meaninglessness. Yet he refrains from discussing what agency would otherwise lend significance to the law, and, most crucially, what would *guarantee* that human beings recognize that significance as such and consent to it.

The elision of this discussion is understandable, since to imagine an ethical referent that both necessitates and guarantees common meaning would enmesh the theorist in the language of transcendence that is now taboo. While I am aware of the reasons behind this theoretical state of affairs, I submit that the notion of transcendence should still constitute a viable problem for us rather than a foregone solution. That Agamben's critique unfolds as an ever-increasing list of *homines sacri* produced during our time illustrates why transcendence (in its religious sense not least of all) should still concern us. Our next excursion into tragedy offers examples of an alternative mode of thinking, where topics now discussed solely in (bio)political terms—for instance, paternity, the foundation of a city, or exile—once resonated in another register. In other words, tragedy admits to and honors nature's imprint on human existence and political relations in a way that escapes the formalization and binarism of (bio)political discourse, thus also rendering moot the antinaturalist apologetics that characterizes the theoretical critique of biopolitics.

2. Ion and Oedipus: Paternity, City-Founding, and the Sovereign as *Homo Sacer*

The myths of Ion and Oedipus tell us that they became city-founders and sovereign leaders, but both were born as *homines sacri*. As infants, they were both abandoned to die of exposure: Ion in a cave, where his mother, Creusa, left him in shame of her dalliance with Apollo, Oedipus on a hillside where both his parents disposed of him, afraid of the prophecy he was bound to fulfill. Ion was metaphorically adopted by his natural father, since at Apollo's behest, Hermes brought him to Delphi, where he grew to be the head steward of the temple. Oedipus was rescued by a shepherd and given to the royal couple of Corinth who withheld from him his actual origin and raised him as a natural son. Arguably, Oedipus also died as a *homo sacer*, but I will comment on *Oedipus at Colonus* later. Euripides' *Ion* and Sophocles' *Oedipus Tyrannus* stand next to each other as reflections on familial origin.[6] Their differing models of paternity illustrate how tragedy understood the relation between nature and convention, blood tie and symbolic kinship. Since the story of Oedipus is well known, I will anchor my discussion and comparative remarks to the plot of the *Ion*, before engaging a particularly suggestive analysis of the same play by Karl Kerényi (1983).

Creusa, daughter of Athenian king Erechtheus, was seduced by Apollo in a cave, and the fruit of this union was Ion. With the god's help, she carried Ion in secret, but upon delivery, she returned him to the cave of his conception and left him to die. She placed him in a basket, with a necklace made of two golden snakes, in ritual commemoration of her ancestor, Erichthonius, whom Athena had entrusted as a baby to the daughters of King Cecrops, along with two guardian snakes. Creusa's ritual citation of the earth-born king and the chthonic nature of snakes point to Ion's divine destiny as ancestor of the Ionian people.[7] The birth of Erichthonius has other parallels to the birth of Ion. Erichthonius was the offspring of a failed attempt by Hephaestus to seduce Athena. In the struggle to subdue her, Hephaestus's semen fell onto her thigh, and Erichthonius was born from the woolen fabric with which Athena wiped off the seed and threw it on the earth, eliding her maternal function.[8] Ion and Erichthonius are both unwanted births. Like the mortal Creusa, Athena wished to conceal her part in the birth, but unlike Creusa, Athena took measures for the survival of Erichthonius just as Apollo ensured the survival of Ion.[9]

---

[6] All translations of the plays refer to the Grene and Lattimore editions unless otherwise noted; the Greek original of *Ion* is available at
http://www.perseus.tufts.edu/hopper/text?doc=Perseus%3Atext%3A1999.01.0109%3Acard%3D1.

[7] Cecrops is also portrayed as a snake, while the Pythian Apollo is a dragon-slayer. Erichthonius and Erechtheus were conflated in preclassical times but were separated in the classical era. Along with Cecrops, they are Athens's autochthonous kings, linked mythically to Athena, and their serpentine imagery symbolizes their relation to the earth.

[8] For *Ion*'s treatment of autochthony, and the elision of maternity and of female citizenship in foundation myths, see Loraux 1993.

[9] Contrary to the autochthonous Athenian tradition, the non-Athenian Xuthus will say to Ion that the earth does not bear children (*Ion* 542), when Ion jokingly suggests that his mother must be the earth, since Xuthus does not know with which woman he fathered him.

While Ion was growing up under Apollo's custody, Creusa married the foreign-born Xuthus, but the couple was childless and they come to Delphi to inquire about offspring. The oracle proclaims that the first person Xuthus sees upon exiting the sanctuary would be his son. Xuthus meets Ion and pronounces him his son,[10] but Ion is unclear whether Apollo has meant to give him to Xuthus again as an adopted son ("a gift") or has revealed him to be a natural son that Xuthus, unbeknownst to himself, had once produced. The god's plan of deliberately conflating natural reproduction and adoption is working, as a joyful Xuthus affirms his paternity of Ion with a seamless slippage between these two registers: "A gift and my own son" (*Ion* 537). As a good father wishing to ensure the welfare of his son, Apollo knew that it was the *fantasy* of nature that would enhance Xuthus's love for Ion. It is crucial here not to dismiss this fantasy as a lie, or as an atavism we must overcome through more "enlightened" forms of kinship. Instead, the play suggests that these nonbiological, symbolic forms of kinship are possible only because of their final reference to this fantasy; they rest in it as much as they arise from it, for—at bottom—this fantasy communicates the reality of how anything first comes to be (*physis*). The fantasy of the natural bond is constitutive of the exclusivity that gives meaning to any type of kinship, biological or otherwise. Consider, for example, this simple analogy we often make when we extol the affection of adoptive parents for their children: we say that they love them *as if* they were their natural children, but the analogy does not stand in reverse.

By no means am I suggesting that all natural parents love their children unfailingly; the myth of Oedipus is here to disabuse us of such certainty. Nonetheless, it is far too simple to read this myth as a dogmatic invalidation of the affection expected of natural parents toward their children. Oedipus's treatment by Laius and Jocasta is aberrant, and all the more so when juxtaposed to the care that his adoptive parents, Polybus and Merope, lavish on him. Still, we must also note that Sophocles extols Polybus's conduct *in that* it measures up to the natural standard: Polybus raised Oedipus as if he were his own flesh and blood (*OT* 1023). That Oedipus's destiny was to find his natural kin highlights the very topos we, the moderns, have been theoretically busy to dismantle: the irreducibility of nature in our self-definition. If we look at the myth unflinchingly, it tells us this: no matter how much we try to avoid our nature, we are bound to encounter it, and perhaps—like Oedipus—in the worst terms, because of having tried so assiduously to avoid it.

---

[10] David Kovacs's introduction to *Ion* emphasizes the priority of natural over conventional kinship by contrasting the natural affinity Ion has for Creusa when they first meet with the initial repulsion Ion feels for Xuthus (Kovacs 1994, 315–16).

Revealingly, where Oedipus's natural parents failed, their son succeeded precisely through his self-inflicted wounds, which show the pull that the natural bond exerts both immediately and symbolically. For Oedipus punishes himself not only because of the social disgrace he would incur but because—despite his parents' callousness—he was drawn by the blood tie and abhorred the way his crimes spoiled his own nature by spoiling his parents. Note his deep loyalty as he does not confront Jocasta with charges of abandonment, nor does he utter any accusations against the slain Laius. Oedipus's remorse at killing his father and defiling his mother, even though he committed these acts unknowingly, demonstrate a level of filial duty undeserved by parents such as his. Yet part of his noble stature owes exactly to this: he restores to nature (his parents) its proper dues, which these very parents had violated. Whether we look at Polybus's love, which is compared to that of a natural parent, or we look at Oedipus, who acted toward his delinquent natural parents with the filial duty expected of a natural son, the same point holds: when we speak of the intimacy of kinship—whether conventionally established or naturally begotten—our reference remains the natural bond.

Let us, however, return to Delphi and to Apollo's intention of handing Ion to Xuthus as a "gift," while making him believe that Ion was his natural son. Nietzsche famously aligned Apollo with illusion and its veils. We might thus say that the gift of Apollo to Xuthus is not merely the gift of the son, but the more salutary gift of the illusion of natural paternity. To secure for his natural son in Athens the care he had enjoyed at Delphi, it is urgent to convince the adoptive father that he is Ion's natural sire. On his part, Xuthus is eager to recall an earlier episode from his life that conveniently fits this narrative: Ion must have been conceived at a bacchanal near Delphi, and his lover probably left the baby at the temple steps (*Ion* 550–5).

This news hurts Creusa, who feels betrayed by Apollo's favor toward Xuthus. In despair, she confesses all she suffered as Apollo's mortal lover.[11] She plots to kill Ion but fails; hunted, she returns a suppliant to the altar where Ion confronts her. At this climax, the Pythia facilitates their recognition by presenting the cradle and amulets that Creusa had left with

---

[11] In *Fearless Speech*, Foucault (2001, 36–57) reads *Ion* for its two modes of *parrhēsia*: (a) the masculine type associated with the citizen and embodied by Ion; (b) the feminine, confessional type associated with Creusa. In *Discourse and Truth*, Foucault (2019, 81–99) reflects on emerging paradigms of truth by comparing *Ion* to *Oedipus Tyrannus*. For a psychoanalytic approach to *Ion* as a play about truth-telling, the quest for knowledge, and the practice of interpretation (thus in relation to Oedipus), see Voela 2017.

him in the cave.[12] Creusa lists the tokens accurately, and mother and son reunite. She then reveals to Ion that his birth father is Apollo, stressing the difference between nature and adoption that Xuthus had glossed over in his excitement: "Not born, but he gives you, born from himself" (*Ion* 1534–6).[13]

Perplexed, Ion wants confirmation from Apollo himself. The god of light and appearance, who has cared for his son all along, but without ever appearing to him, remains still hidden. Athena appears, instead, excusing his absence, but confirming Ion's natural parents to be the god and Creusa. She also corroborates Hermes regarding Apollo's providence for Ion: it was the divine plan to bring Creusa and Xuthus to Delphi so that Ion can be placed in a noble house and become the father of the Ionians. The secret of his divine origin was to be revealed in Athens, after Ion was safely installed on the throne, but accidental events necessitated an earlier disclosure in Delphi, introducing one more twist. Indeed, Athena departs with an order as enigmatic as the god she represents, casting a veil over, as much as sanctioning, the figure of the autochthonous king: she tells Creusa and Ion not to divulge the secret to Xuthus, but to let him think that he is Ion's father, which also means to hide that Ion is Creusa's son.[14]

We can read the mother's concealment as the myth's affirmation of the gender inequality that subtends a patriarchal *polis* and its religion, or we can see Creusa's loss and Xuthus's gain in terms of a sacred economy of power that signifies otherwise than the social distribution of power: because she knows that she is the natural parent, Creusa can afford "to lose" Ion symbolically; because he is not the natural parent, Xuthus needs the false assurance. Though it seems to require her marginalization, Creusa's secret comes from plenitude and guarantees the power of authentic knowledge: it carries in its darkness the disclosure that Apollo did not abandon her or her infant. Xuthus, on the other hand, is in need of the affirmation of his potency—not an enviable state to be in vis-à-vis his spouse and newfound son, especially in light of Athens's patriarchal values. Yet Apollo's charity lies in the fact that Xuthus does not know *that* he does not know. Xuthus may live in the blissful ignorance Jocasta failed to convince Oedipus to pursue at the crucial turning point of the *Tyrannus*.

---

[12] The juxtaposition of natural versus adoptive father here extends to the maternal function. Ion thanks the priestess for having performed a mother's role (*Ion* 1324).

[13] This translation is by Robert Potter; it appears in Oates and O'Neill (1938) and can also be found at http://www.perseus.tufts.edu/hopper/text?doc=Perseus%3Atext%3A1999.01.0110%3Acard%3D1510.

[14] On the dualities of *Ion* (human/divine spheres, inside/outside the *polis*), and the double hermeneutic frame into which it casts Apollo (a god beyond human moral judgment, or a culpable god, whose ambivalent oracles serve ulterior motives), see Kindt 2007. Kindt argues that the dramatic structure encourages us to assume both these hermeneutic stances—the sympathetic and the ironic—at once. See also Foucault 2019, where he argues that in *Ion*, Apollo's silence is deceitful (81).

Until now, I have underlined the primacy of the natural bond in kinship.
At this point, I will propose that nature—in Greek myth and tragedy at
least—was never "mere nature," but a placeholder of the sacred, and thus,
already spiritualized. Kerényi's (1983) monograph on Apollo begins with a
chapter titled "Apollo's Temple Servant." It is a commentary on Euripides' *Ion*
that highlights the *uncanny* passage between natural and adoptive—or "spiritual"—paternity. Unlike Loraux (1993), who focuses on political anthropology (gender roles and the politics of autochthony), Kerényi turns to religious
psychology. Instead of anthropologizing Apollo and secularizing myth,
Kerényi shows how the sacred engenders beyond utilitarian purposes. Myth
is not a *logos* of convenience that veils self-serving principles, but a venue for
the psyche to see the divine spark that, in turn, makes of human relationships
something more than mere transactions.

My analysis of Kerényi's notion of sacred paternity hinges on this term
"uncanny." This word is key to understanding the force that nature exerts on
symbolic kinship and that drives the play to reveal Ion's "adoptive" father as
also his natural one. It also shows that what is most "natural" about human
paternity is the custody a father assumes of his offspring, and not simply his
part in the reproductive process. Kerényi himself references the uncanny, but
more tangentially than I intend: he discusses it in terms of the prodigious-
ness of fire—solar and spiritual fire being the domains of Apollo.[15] However,
the uncanny applies chiefly to the temporality through which the symbolic
father is referred back to the natural process of generation and the duty this
process makes urgent: symbolic paternity is eventually returned and
grounded in natural paternity, yet this return is justified only because the
natural father (Apollo) had *first* manifested himself as care in adopting Ion.
The uncanniness consists in the fact that what makes nature's eventual revelation *as nature* both worthy and necessary is the fact that nature appeared
first not as begetting but as sheltering. In light of my earlier comments on
Antigone, it is worth citing Benardete (1999), who finds a similar structure in
Sophocles. Antigone, a proponent of natural kinship, does not take familial
intimacy for granted without proving herself worthy of it: "The love of her
own almost becomes a matter of choice. It is this to which Antigone partly
owes her awesome uncanniness," Benardete (1999, 13) writes. In reaching
her natural kin through service—not immediacy—she resembles Ion. Ion
too serves Apollo *as if* Apollo were his father, not knowing he *is* his father,

---

[15] Kerényi (1983, 4) cites Goethe's rhyming of fire (*Feuer*) with the prodigious or uncanny (*Ungeheuer*).
The rhyme reinforces the link between the prodigious (as both monstrous *and* miraculous) and divine
fire. The foreignness with which *Ion* confronts its modern translators (1–2) is another issue that could be
developed in terms of the uncanny, albeit Kerényi does not pursue it as such.

because he honors in Apollo the spiritual father who supported him. It is as if, in hindsight, Ion "deserved" to have Apollo as his natural father, and so was vindicated to learn this as a fact, having fulfilled his own filial duties.

Kerényi highlights the dialectic between nature and spirit through Ion's gratitude. He focuses on the ending of a hymn Ion offers to Phoebus, addressing him as his "father" before knowing the full resonance of this vocative: "In these last words, which in the mouth of a son sound so self-seeking, evidence is given that the essence of fatherhood is from something divine, not animal, from real fatherhood, to which Apollo was not unfaithful and which was on the contrary uniquely worthy to him" (Kerényi 1983, 7). Obeying the crude natural law, the dependent son might give thanks with the self-serving motive of expecting more favors his way. Yet this base natural expectation lets the sacred provenance of fatherhood shine through.

Sheltering and supporting are aspects of paternity that point beyond brute nature, but they themselves as moral *exigencies* best appear through the filter of nature, because nature is always exigency, because its every emergence is accompanied by a feeling of urgency. This is why in *Ion*, not only does nature disclose spirit, but spirit vindicates nature. Thus, Ion's gratitude—precisely in being directed toward him who is not yet known as the natural father—justifies the play's choice to reveal the adoptive/divine father as identical to the natural one. Natural fatherhood turns out to be the prize for the son who appreciated the "adoptive" father. The return home restores an aspect of uncanniness that we often underplay in favor of un-homeliness alone. In Freud, the uncanny's strangeness owes to excessive *familiarity*, which appears distorted due to mechanisms of repression. Delphi is not only the mark of foreignness that challenges Ion's claim to Athenian autochthony. Delphi—this stupendous place the Greeks imagined as the earth's navel—emerges as domicile and hearth, the humblest and most familiar of places. Kerényi captures this meeting of the stupendous with the ordinary in the image of Ion sweeping the temple's steps: "Does not, however, the most unpretentious and most domestic of all actions, sweeping, precisely because of its simplicity serve as an unrivaled symbol of the great plainness of the Greek idea of a 'pure and purifying god,' of Phoebus?" (Kerényi 1983, 6). Ancient custom required of women to preside over the *oikos* and of men to handle public affairs. The play subverts this distinction, as it is Ion's mother who abandons him, leaving the father—incidentally the most public of the Olympians, the sun shining over the citadel—to act as nurturer. This is why Goethe's rhyming of *Feuer* (fire) and *Ungeheuer* (uncanny) pertains to Kerényi's argument about the Delphic god as master of a domicile (4). In Delphi, the prodigious solar fire presides over something plain—the temple as home.

Correspondingly, the secret that links Apollo (the sun) to Ion (his son) could never be "ghastly" like that of Oedipus (6).

Oedipus and *Ion* are mirror tragedies on the meaning of paternity. Whereas mortal paternity fails, divine paternity shines eventually as an exemplar. Oedipus, like Ion, was a founder and civic father of sorts: in his wanderings, he had the sacred prerogative to curse or bless the cities he visited. At Colonus, the generous reception by King Theseus elicited Oedipus's blessing of Athens. Ion and Oedipus thus offer two different beginnings for Athens, two different civic myths that reflect respectively the models of familial parentage behind each hero. Athens could begin from the ghastly secret of Oedipus or from the luminous revelation of Apollo. The cantankerous Oedipus—who, in exile, had cursed his natural sons just as he himself was betrayed by his natural parents—is juxtaposed to Ion, the father of the Ionian race—who, as Kerényi (1983, 8) writes, found in Apollo's divine parentage a model for his own divine/civic parentage. Kerényi concludes thus: "The myth of the begetting of the father of the race through the race-god Apollo originates in a purely Ionian, fictitious, and futile invention in the quest for the spiritual reality of an experienceable divine parentage. Or was the myth already from the beginning *the myth of just that*?" (8, original italics). City-founding myths (and perhaps the foundation of all myth) are efforts to imagine the experience of sacred parentage collectively, to live a form of kinship where nature and convention depend on one another in a necessary and inevitable manner. In such a model, human solidarity is not a matter of political dicta alone but proceeds from an inner experience that enriches political life in affirming what the city often brackets—namely, the profound human need for an intimacy prior to any formal regulations.

I have thus far tried to locate this sacred experience in *Ion*'s model of paternity while contrasting it to *Oedipus Tyrannus*. Yet the *Tyrannus* also ends by evoking the sacred: the self-wounded Oedipus rises as a sacred figure both in the juridical sense of Agamben's *homo sacer*, and in the religious sense further developed in *Oedipus at Colonus*. I will address this facet of Oedipus in order to show, contra Agamben, how the sacred speaks otherwise than politics.[16] In Agamben's binary opposition, bare life—a synonym for sacred life—is exposed to the whims of sovereign power, a power thoroughly inaccessible to the bearer of bare life. The conclusion of *Oedipus Tyrannus*, however, neutralizes this bipolarity, since the sovereign voluntarily imposes upon himself the predicament of *homo sacer*. Bypassing proper trial in his

---

[16] On the correspondence between the Theban plague in the *Tyrannus* as a reflection of the epidemic that devastated Athens during the Peloponnesian War, see Knox 1994.

homeland, polluted and unprotected, Oedipus throws himself into exile—a pariah whom anyone can kill with impunity. The strangeness of the *Tyrannus* does not consist in the fact that an erstwhile sovereign ends up as a *homo sacer*; history is rife with fallen rulers. Instead, it rests with the king's voluntary choice to become a *homo sacer*. Oedipus's decision renders him a sovereign in the ontological sense well after he has crossed the legal threshold of the *homo sacer*. He is a sovereign closer to Bataille's definition of this term: someone who wills his own destruction in a sacred expenditure that opposes the political ruler's goal of power accumulation.[17]

This ontological sovereignty is on exhibit everywhere in *Oedipus at Colonus*: the old man's imperious posture is noted by the Athenian chorus, and Karl Reinhardt rightly reads this tragedy as a sacred phenomenology, where the gods are heard to summon this beleaguered but upright being to their arms (Reinhardt 1979, 223). Such a stance sets Oedipus apart from ordinary refugees, and from the legal discourse of rights surrounding their plight. The play rejects the language of rights, as it is not concerned with the ameliorative project of "settling into a better life"—this being the focus of politics. Oedipus comes to Colonus to die, and no one can be *granted* by anyone the right to die. His insistence on the locality of Colonus bespeaks not a formal demand for a right but the sacred duty to fulfill the prophecy that saw his death at the grove of the Eumenides there. Death involves the language of the taboo, which is a religious, not a secular, prohibition. As such, it opens beyond the juridical discourse of rights, and the equally juridical criticism of them. In a Nietzschean vein, I dare say that the manner of Oedipus ennobles the figure of the refugee but remains irreducibly foreign to the secular-political parameters through which the displaced person is currently understood.

3. Ancients and Moderns: Tragedy and *Assujettissement*

Agamben's *Homo Sacer* proceeds from two modern philosophical sources, which it aspires to bring into contact: Michel Foucault's theorization of biopower and Hannah Arendt's reflections on totalitarianism. Agamben's Arendtian legacy is clearly visible in his choice of the death camp as *the* biopolitical paradigm of modernity. Foucault, on the other hand, focused on carceral technologies of biopower, but did not discuss at length the Holocaust. Samuel Kessler (2014) views Foucault's silence about the death camp as structurally necessary to his theory of history, which proposes that

---

[17] See Bataille 2001, especially p. 188.

current power formations derive from the epistemic shift of the eighteenth century. For Kessler, the resort to the eighteenth century cannot explain the rise of the death camp, which he—like Agamben—sees as a unique departure from previous techniques of biopower.

The question of whether the liminality of the camp exceeds Foucault's view of history is itself worthy of further treatment. Here, I only submit a modest point: if the absence of the death camp points to an immanent limit in Foucault's theory of modern biopower, it also allows for thinking of biopower in its productive possibilities. In fact, not only can biopower work productively, but it is impossible to imagine complex societies without some form of population management. Public health, demographic control, crime and its curtailment are issues germane to embodied existence, and they require regulation. Foucault is aware of this urgency, when he states: "My point is not that everything is bad, but that everything is dangerous, which is not exactly the same as bad" (Foucault 1984, 343). In other words, there is nothing transparently terrible about a concept such as "biopower" or "biopolitics"; rather, Foucault suggests that we remain alert to the dangers that arise as practices and institutions appeal to, exercise, modify, and eventually abuse these concepts in the name of a "rational" end—population management. Simply put, a critique of the health system does not mean that we can or should do away with the hospital. It is beyond my purpose here to assess the merits or demerits of historicism, or to offer a definitive opinion on Foucault's particular method. Rather, I wish to stress how Agamben's and Foucault's respective citations of antiquity reveal our own anxieties in reading the ancients, as we ascribe to them certain origins of our condition, all the while declaring ruptures so severe that they could not be legible against any historical backdrop.

To recall our introduction, Agamben situates the philosophical origin of biopolitics in Aristotle. Hence, even though he identifies the camp as a singularly modern example of the biopolitical state, he also draws a continuous arc from the classical era to modernity. One could cite even more ancient texts that describe forms of population control—the Old Testament, for example[18]—but perhaps Agamben intends a disciplinary distinction between philosophy and other types of narrative. Still, that Greco-Roman antiquity provides the philosophical origin and the main figure (*homo sacer*) through which the most horrific example of modern biopolitics unfolds, is not so neutral an interpretive choice. Agamben's genealogy is indicative of a

---

[18] Ritual dietary laws, the divine commands to kill preexisting "heathen" populations, or the prohibition of intermarriage with non-Jews all appeal to theological truth, but historical Biblical scholarship detects techniques of regulating health, reproduction, demographics, and so on. Other sacred texts can also be read as manuals for the physical (and spiritual) survival of their intended communities.

symptomatic paradox that underlies much of contemporary thought: while Western modernity proclaims its discontinuity from the Greeks, particularly regarding claims of "progress," it often discovers conveniently a "Greek origin" for its own ills. The political utilitarianism of this gesture notwithstanding, it presents us with at least as skewed a view of history as Foucault's. For if the death camp presents a catastrophic caesura from any previous episteme, on what epistemic ground can Agamben reinscribe it at the end (the telos, in fact) of a genealogy starting with Aristotle and Roman law? Modernity, Agamben suggests, is different in its horror, but also in its progress—a progress tacitly affirmed through the very critique of biopolitics *as a critique of progress* he himself advances; at the same time, modernity, and especially its horrors, are quite legibly translatable back into antiquity via the "classical" gesture of discovering distant origins.

Foucault's keen insights on this epochal translation between ancients and moderns come not from his analysis of biopower, but from his later work, which shifted from eighteenth-century episteme to the thought of antiquity, and from questions of power to questions of ethics and the care of the self.[19] It is from these later reflections that a fruitful examination may begin of whether biopolitics (and its critique) even constitute proper concepts in the antique context, and it is for this reason that I briefly turn to these reflections in the closing remarks of my chapter.

The very term "ethics" signifies for Foucault the mode of *assujettissement* (subjectivation) through which the self is fashioned in various epochs. Of the Greek ethical mode, Foucault says that it was mainly aesthetic. The care of the self was a problem of personal choice, reserved for an elite constituency, and thus, it did not yield a culture of normalization (Foucault 1984, 341). It was motivated by "the will to live a beautiful life, and to leave to others memories of a beautiful existence" (341). This aestheticized ethics conforms with Foucault's notion that the Greeks did not derive their morality from religion. Rather than asking religious questions, they pursued self-relation and the relation to others. Yet such relations cannot be described as "social," "institutional," or even "legal" (343), Foucault adds; in short, they were not formalized. To better understand what this "aesthetics of existence" looks like, the example of Greek restraint can help: Greek restraint does not refer to the humility before a God who exacts abstinence for salvation. Instead, it shows the subject's ability to voluntarily control itself, because mastery and discipline are valued as nobler than weakness and self-indulgence. Though Foucault does not use this term explicitly, this austere

---

[19] On the relation between Foucault's studies of biopower and his work on the ancient techniques of the self, see chapter 8 by Sergei Prozorov in this volume.

posture corresponds to the ethos we encounter in tragic heroes. Tragedy shows us ethics as an aesthetics of existence. I submit that it is precisely this aesthetic dimension of tragedy—a dimension connected to vitalism by the very appeal to *aisthēsis*, if nothing else—that runs counter to the recent theoretical project of the critique of biopolitics. Yet, as I have also suggested in the introduction, it is because of this aesthetic dimension that tragedy affords us a rich vocabulary with which to think through the inevitable pressures of nature upon our individual and social existence—a vocabulary, however, that cannot be reduced to a formal political theory such as biopolitics.

How, then, does this Greek mode of aesthetic subjectivation relate to our self-fashioning? Foucault (1984, 343) sees a moment of contact between the two epochs: insofar as we no longer derive our ethics from religion, we face with the ancients the same problem of subjectivation. Nonetheless, as a modern historicist, he rejects any "return" to the Greeks, not only because history is never an exact repetition but because the Greek mode of subjectivation was not a "solution" even for the Greeks themselves; it was the expression of a problem. In Foucault's rejection of the Greek mode, we thus hear his version of the gap between ancients and moderns. On the other hand, his diagnosis of the common problem we face in constructing a moral code in the absence of religious authority is more far-reaching than even Foucault himself may have realized.

A brief glance at our global culture—a culture of celebrity and hypermediatization that deifies youth despite its mandatory lip service to ageism—suffices to show that we too practice a form of aesthetic subjectivation. The problem, however—as with everything we "continue" from the past—is that it is translated, and with translation come not only gains but losses. Thus, the aesthetic mode of subjectivation, which led the Greeks to restraint, in our era appears as vapid consumerism and self-absorption, and it does so exactly in its pretense to be "more" than image, to be morally engaged. Hence, the narcissistic celebrity selfie is always at the service of advancing world equality, body positivity, inclusiveness, and the like. In other words, it is in being *normalized* through the advent of technology that our aesthetic mode is unlike its Greek counterpart, which—involving fewer persons—cultivated a deeper relation to self and others.

Can our aesthetic propensity, no matter how differently expressed, link us substantively to the Greeks, or is the resemblance superficial? If the link is substantive, how may we evaluate the modulations between these two versions of aesthetic subjectivation so that we can see whether the moderns can "learn" something from this difference? Does it even matter to speak of evaluation and historical learning anymore? Perhaps none of these questions proves helpful right now. There is, however, one small phrase that has escaped proper questioning, a phrase that regularly concludes all discussions on the relation of ancients and moderns, thus posing as a "solution" when it could be the problem: "we cannot return." Virtually all modern and postmodern thinkers (up and including Foucault) have been murmuring this to us in different versions: we cannot return home, to the past, to the self, to anything. This insistence, however, betrays that the statement is not a simple declaration, but itself a site of anxiety, to use Foucault's own symptomatic logic. Why indeed does the word "return" produce such an immediate discomfort as to mobilize numerous theoretical apparatuses against it? Exemplified by the absurdist demand of the French Revolution's Terror to erase the past, modernity's project has been to ban the concept of return, to ridicule nostalgia, and to eliminate any sense of historical gratitude—a project justified by holding the past morally culpable for all of modernity's ills. This could be one way of reading Agamben's exaggeration of Aristotle to supply an "origin" for the formal theoretical binary that led to the death camp: thus, the story goes, antiquity begat modernity's violence over and above modernity's valiant efforts to deconstruct it. At the risk of overdetermining the context of paternity and filiation developed in this paper, let me conclude by saying that it may be time to pay attention to the gratitude of Ion as much as to the rebellion of Oedipus.

References

Agamben, Giorgio. 1998. *Homo Sacer: Sovereign Power and Bare Life*. Translated by Daniel Heller-Roazen. Stanford, CA: Stanford University Press.

Bataille, Georges. 2001. "The Sovereign." In *The Unfinished System of Nonknowledge*, translated by Michelle Kendall and Stuart Kendall, edited by Stuart Kendall, 185–95. Minneapolis: University of Minnesota Press.

Benardete, Seth. 1999. *Sacred Transgressions: A Reading of Sophocles' Antigone*. South Bend, IN: St. Augustine's Press.

Brill, Sara. 2018. "Unlivable Life: Aristotle after Agamben." Paper presented at the Department of Comparative Literature, University at Buffalo, Buffalo, NY, October 4.

Brill, Sara. 2020. *Aristotle on the Concept of Shared Life*. Oxford: Oxford University Press.

Euripides. 1958. *Ion*. Translated by Ronald Frederick Willetts. In *The Complete Greek Tragedies*, vol. 4, edited by David Grene and Richmond Lattimore, 9–79. Chicago: University of Chicago Press.

Finlayson, James Gordon. 2010. "'Bare Life' and Politics in Agamben's Reading of Aristotle." *The Review of Politics* 72 (1): 97–126. https://doi.org/10.1017/S0034670509990982.

Foucault, Michel. 1984. "On the Genealogy of Ethics: An Overview of Work in Progress." In *The Foucault Reader*, edited by Paul Rabinow, 340–72. New York: Pantheon.

Foucault, Michel. 2001. *Fearless Speech*. Edited by Joseph Pearson. Los Angeles: Semiotext(e).

Foucault, Michel. 2019. *"Discourse and Truth" and "Parrēsia."* Edited by Henri-Paul Fruchaud and Daniele Lorenzini. Translated by Nancy Luxon. Chicago: University of Chicago Press.

Grene, David, and Richmond Lattimore, eds. 1959. *The Complete Greek Tragedies*. 4 vols. Chicago: University of Chicago Press.

Gunneflo, Markus. 2015. "Rudolf Kjellén: Nordic Biopolitics Before the Welfare State." *Retfærd: Nordisk Juridisk Tidskrift* 38 (3/150): 24–39.

Kerényi, Karl. 1983. *Apollo: The Wind, the Spirit, and the God: Four Studies*. Dallas, TX: Spring Publications.

Kessler, Samuel Joseph. 2014. "Foucault and the Holocaust: Epistemic Shift, Liminality and the Death Camps." *Dapim: Studies on the Holocaust* 28 (3): 139–54. https://doi.org/10.1080/23256249.2014.941155.

Kindt, Julia. 2007. "Apollo's Oracle in Euripides' *Ion*: Ambiguous Identities in Fifth-Century Athens." *Ancient Narrative* 6: 1–30.

Knox, Bernard. 1994. *Oedipus at Thebes: Sophocles' Tragic Hero and His Time*. New Haven, CT: Yale University Press.

Kovacs, David. 1994. Introduction to *Ion*. In *Trojan Women, Iphigenia among the Taurians, Ion*, by Euripides, 315–19. Cambridge, MA: Harvard University Press.

Loraux, Nicole. 1993. *The Children of Athena: Athenian Ideas about Citizenship and the Division between the Sexes*. Translated by Caroline Levine. Princeton, NJ: Princeton University Press.

Oates, Whitney J., and Eugene O'Neill, Jr., eds. 1938. *The Complete Greek Drama*. Translated by Robert Potter. New York: Random House.

Ojakangas, Mika. 2016. *On the Greek Origins of Biopolitics: A Reinterpretation of the History of Biopower*. London: Routledge.

Reinhardt, Karl. 1979. *Sophocles*. Translated by Hazel Harvey and David Harvey. New York: Barnes and Noble.

Sophocles. 1959a. *Antigone*. Translated by Elizabeth Wyckoff. In *The Complete Greek Tragedies*, vol. 2, edited by David Grene and Richmond Lattimore, 159–204. Chicago: University of Chicago Press.

Sophocles. 1959b. *Oedipus at Colonus*. Translated by Robert Fitzgerald. In *The Complete Greek Tragedies*, vol. 2, edited by David Grene and Richmond Lattimore, 79–155. Chicago: University of Chicago Press.

Sophocles. 1959c. *Oedipus the King*. Translated by David Grene. In *The Complete Greek Tragedies*, vol. 2, edited by David Grene and Richmond Lattimore, 11–76. Chicago: University of Chicago Press.

Voela, Angie. 2017. *Psychoanalysis, Philosophy and Myth in Contemporary Culture: After Oedipus*. London: Palgrave Macmillan.

5

Beyond Biopolitics and Juridico-Institutional Politics

Aristotle on the Nature of Politics

Adriel M. Trott

Two opposing strains of commentary among those concerned with the role of nature and life in ancient Greek political theory have emerged in the last half-century. Broadly speaking, some think that ancient Greek politics aimed to cordon off the natural from the political, while others find that Greek politics centrally concerned itself with the biological. Hannah Arendt and Giorgio Agamben could be said to fall into the first group. While Arendt sees Greek politics as transcending our more natural existence (see Arendt 1998; Trott 2017), Agamben argues that Aristotle's division between biological and political life depends on policing the biological. For Agamben, this investment in managing and limiting the biological makes Aristotle's view biopolitical.[1] Mika Ojakangas falls in the second group. From references to population and territory in Plato's and Aristotle's work, Ojakangas argues that their political theories organize and ground political life in the biological, rather than in a continued effort to break from it. Ojakangas follows Foucault's account of biopolitics as "a politics the aim of which is to optimize and multiply life by subjecting it to precise controls and comprehensive regulations," a political practice that went "hand in hand with the decline of the juridico-institutional discourse and practice of politics" (Ojakangas 2016, 4). He locates the rise of biopolitics and the decline of juridico-institutional practice of politics in ancient Greek philosophers. Ojakangas criticizes Foucault for viewing biopolitics as an exclusively modern idea, while relying on Foucault's conception of biopolitics to make his case for finding it in

---

[1] Agamben maintains that Aristotle's perfect community "results from the articulation of two communities: a community of the simply living and a political community" (Agamben 2015, 197). Agamben argues that Aristotle's political theory allows for a kind of life that is able to reach biological self-sufficiency but not able to become part of the political community and thus that "through the concept of autarchy, the Aristotelian political community preserves a biological character" (198). In support of this reading of Aristotle's *Politics*, see Rasmussen 2018.

Adriel M. Trott, *Beyond Biopolitics and Juridico-Institutional Politics: Aristotle on the Nature of Politics* In: *Biopolitics and Ancient Thought*. Edited by: Jussi Backman and Antonio Cimino, Oxford University Press. © Oxford University Press 2022.
DOI: 10.1093/oso/9780192847102.003.0006

ancient political practice and theory (1–4). For the purposes of this essay, I will thus follow Ojakangas's use of biopolitics and juridico-institutional politics, which he draws from Foucault (Foucault 1978, 85, 89, 136–44; see Miller 2020 for a defense of Foucault's biopolitics against Agamben's critique).

If biopolitics understands nature as life processes that politics aim to foster, juridico-institutional politics treats nature as what can and must be overcome in order to form and recognize a subject beyond nature. What Agamben's analysis has shown is that any politics concerned to separate itself from biological life, by virtue of its negative definition of itself vis-à-vis life, requires careful attention to the restriction of life from politics' center. This focus on bracketing life from political concerns paradoxically centers biological concerns, which makes the political project biopolitical because politics becomes invested in controlling, managing, and monitoring biological life, even though it develops this focus in order to restrict the role of biological concerns in the political domain (Agamben 1998, 2–6). Thus neither biopolitics nor juridico-politics escapes the problem of a politics that concerns itself with considering and controlling the biological capacities and powers of its members.

I argue in this chapter that Aristotle neither invites a sharp break from the biological nor places the biological at the heart of politics. My point of departure is that Aristotle's conception of nature as the internal source of movement and rest makes the most sense of his claim that political life is natural and that human beings are naturally political (Trott 2014). I argue that Aristotle's natural politics on this account is neither biopolitical in Foucault's sense (focused on managing life) nor juridico-institutional (focused on including life only for the sake of superseding it). Aristotle does not reduce nature and human nature to biological processes. He neither reduces human existence to mere life processes to serve state ends nor represses the biological in order to distinguish between recognizable citizens and more natural (and less political) beings. Aristotle offers a third alternative, an emergent sense of politics in activity, based on a conception of nature that neither aims to separate human and political life from the biological nor focuses centrally on the biological to the exclusion of other aspects of human and political life. Aristotle's concern with the biological aspects of life is part of an effort to foster the flourishing of life without excluding concerns for benefit, justice, and the good life.

While considerable work has been done to challenge the strict division of the biological from the political in Aristotle's political theory (most recently Brill 2020, and see also chapter 1 by Brill in this volume; Miller 2020), the view that Aristotle's politics springs forth from the biological requires further attention. The first half of this chapter counters that argument by scrutinizing the four ways in which, according to Ojakangas, Aristotle's politics is biopolitical. The second half responds to two ways of understanding concerns with the body in Aristotle to suggest that Aristotle neither considers the body in order to transcend it following certain strains of biopolitics as well as juridico-institutional politics, nor makes the body the center and ground of political life. Against those who would separate the body from the soul, or the nutritive and the perceptive and appetitive part of the soul from the *logos*-possessing part, I submit that Aristotle's psychology separates neither body from soul nor the nutritive soul's work from the soul as a whole. The concerns with the living human body are therefore never merely biological, and the concerns with living well are never separable from the body.

1. Arguments for Aristotle's Politics as Biopolitical

This section builds the case against the view that Aristotle's politics is biopolitical through a critique of the four kinds of claims Ojakangas makes to support that view.

1.1 Biopolitics as Focus on Population

Ojakangas's principal argument is that Aristotle views the community's central concerns as biopolitical because the main means of achieving the happiness of individuals in a *polis* is through managing the quantity or quality of the population (Ojakangas 2016, 38–9). Ojakangas offers support from the directives in *Politics* 7 that involve maintaining a certain size and kind of population and territory. His strongest argument in this vein is that Aristotle's concern for virtue is a concern for the quality of the population (45). Ojakangas adds to this point that the association of *hexis* with physical states in the Hippocratic corpus indicates that, while Aristotle's allusions to medicine and health are metaphors and not literal, Aristotle is thinking about the biological and medical existence of human beings (105–6).

Much of Aristotle's *Nicomachean Ethics* and *Politics* could be said to be about developing the quality of people and communities. Aristotle discusses the quality and quantity that make up a *polis* in *Politics* 4.12, where quality specifically means that which the people think gives them a right to rule (wealth in an oligarchy, good birth in an aristocracy, freedom in a democracy; *Pol.* 4.12.1296b15–19). The defining characteristic of the regime in each case is not a matter of biological life. Aristotle wants to foster virtue through reasoned concern for how one lives. Focusing on virtue and flourishing changes the way people are. If aiming to improve people is what is meant by having a concern for the quality of the population, then Aristotle does hold this position. But if all concerns of quality are biopolitical, then biopolitics includes any concern with forms of life, not just the concern for fostering biological life.

Ojakangas recognizes that "there is no such thing as unqualified life for Aristotle," and yet understands qualified life as biological (Ojakangas 2016, 18). For Ojakangas, unqualified life would seem to mean the genus of animal, and qualified life would be the specific form of living of each kind of animal. But Aristotle's qualified life is not just the way of being an animal, but the way of being *good* at being a specific animal, namely, the human animal (*Pol.* 1.2.1252b28–9).

1.2 Biopolitics Views Naturalness as Biological

Second, Ojakangas's reading depends on viewing Aristotle's claims about naturalness in biological terms. Aristotle describes the ways political life addresses the nature of the soul and compensates for nature's deficiencies. Ojakangas concludes from these references that the fulfillment of the city and the citizens is achieved through "the scientific inquiry of human nature," which he concludes is a biopolitical conception of politics (Ojakangas 2016, 39). Ojakangas suggests that Aristotle focuses on life to foster the good life *"by developing the immanent potentialities of natural life and to bring these potentialities to fruition"* (Ojakangas's italics), and as a result, to unleash "the hidden potentiality of this animality" (17). This argument takes what Aristotle calls natural and reduces it to the biological in order to ground the claim that Aristotle's focus on the natural is biopolitical. Ojakangas maintains that the definition of the human being as a political animal—as the living being for whom it is natural to live with others—is evidence of Aristotle's biopolitical approach because such a being is not a juridical subject (7). This argument depends on viewing juridico-institutional and biopolitical approaches as the only possible approaches to politics.

1.3 Biopolitics as Focus on the Economic

Third, Ojakangas argues rightly and contra Agamben that Aristotle is concerned with economic and household issues in political life (on this, see Finlayson 2010). But from this concern, Ojakangas concludes that Aristotle views the primary concern of political life as economic. Particularly strange in a discussion of Aristotle is Ojakangas's claim that "the end of politics has almost always been the continuous increase of wealth" (Ojakangas 2016, 47). Leaving the historical evaluation of that claim aside, Aristotle argues for a limit to wealth acquisition in the household and accuses those who pursue wealth as if that were the end of life of mistaking living large for living well. As Aristotle writes,

> [T]hey are preoccupied with living, not with living well. And since their appetite for life is unlimited, they also want an unlimited amount of what sustains it. And those who do aim at living well seek what promotes physical gratification. So, since this too seems to depend on having property, they spend their time acquiring wealth.   (*Pol.* 1.9.1257b41–1258a5)

Aristotle argues that pursuing wealth without end continues a narrow focus on living, which is not sufficient for achieving human flourishing. Rather, a concern that takes one beyond the means needed for living to living well is required. Elsewhere Aristotle is critical of regimes that aim toward wealth (*Pol.* 2.9.1269b21–3). He does think the city needs to consider how it distributes goods and how it allows for wealth acquisition, not because these are the goals of the city, but because these too are matters of justice. Factions develop when great distance exists between the wealthy and the poor, but even greater divisions exist when there is a great distance between the virtuous and the vicious (5.3.1303b14–16, 5.4.1304a38–b5).

Ojakangas argues that the *polis* is like an extended household and its way of being governed is administrative. He points to the many offices that are involved in administrative tasks, such as those who manage contracts in the marketplace (Ojakangas 2016, 48), and argues further that while Aristotle distinguishes between the household and the political community, he considers them a unit, referencing a passage in the *Politics* in which Aristotle contends that they are less of a unity than Socrates makes them (*Pol.* 2.5.1263b30–1). Ojakangas draws attention to the use of words related to *oikonomia* to describe the administration of the city (Ojakangas 2016, 53–4). This treatment ignores the opening gambit of the *Politics*, where Aristotle chides those who suppose that political and household rule only differs in the number of subjects on the basis of the view "that there is no difference between a large household and a small city-state" (*Pol.* 1.1.1252a10–11). Aristotle says of this position, "But these claims are not true" (1252a16–17), and then launches into a discussion of the naturalness of political life and of the various parts of household rule, and one might say, into the rest of the book. Sara Brill argues that Aristotle's admonition to limit acquisition is rooted in what she calls an "anti-natalist" anxiety about reproduction without limit, which is to say an anxiety about the biological becoming the focus of politics (Brill 2020, 220). Brill warns against the danger of Aristotle's view, which seems to circumscribe the biological, and with it the maternal, as what is required for, but ultimately excluded from, political life (223–5). While I argue below that Aristotle makes the case for how the management of reproduction becomes a concern for political life without reducing political life to biopolitics, Brill complicates the sense in which Aristotle's concern for the biological could be understood as the central focus of political life.

1.4 Biopolitics as Focus on Social Norms

Fourth and finally, Ojakangas argues, following Foucault, that one of the indicators of a biopolitical approach to politics is that not law but social norms organize and discipline the community (Ojakangas 2016, 54–5). Since law is a mere means of administration of the city-state for Aristotle and the Greeks, Ojakangas concludes that Greek thinkers including Aristotle relegate the law to the status of social norms. Even though Aristotle describes the law as a source of habituation to produce the good character of the citizens, he still treats the laws as general principles, not merely as mechanisms of discipline that reach into individual lives to control their behavior as social norms do for Foucault. Foucault's argument that distinguishes biopolitics from other politics by distinguishing law from social norms would make little sense if all laws only ever operated at the level of social norms. Thus, I argue that Foucault's case regarding social norms implies a break from a period in which law, not social norms, organize communal life.

Moreover, when Foucault speaks of social norms, he means them in the sense of behavioral norms, the result of the kinds of distributed disciplinary forces that subjectify individuals, both in the sense that individuals become subject to them and become subjects through them (Foucault 1977; on behavior replacing action, see also Arendt 1998, 40–1). Aristotle recommends using the law to habituate people to become certain kinds of characters able to engage in political life (*Eth. Nic.* 10.9.1180a1–5) and counsels the legislator and the citizens to put the law to work to improve the citizens and the city in order to achieve the good life (*Pol.* 7.2.1325a7–10, 7.14.1333b34–8). Yet the law functions differently for Aristotle than Foucault's social norm does. While the social norm works through the disciplinary power circulating through everyone in the community, aiming to produce a kind of normalized behavior, Aristotle's law works to institute the deliberations of the citizens regarding what should constitute their goals as a community and how they should achieve it, which is to say, the law puts their deliberations into action. Such law is not to be found at the microlevel of power that Foucault describes at work in the social norms of biopolitics. Moreover, while it is true that *nomos* means "custom" in fifth-century BCE Greece, Foucault distinguishes between the work that law does and the work that norms do in the nineteenth century:

> And if it is true that the juridical system was useful for representing, albeit in a nonexhaustive way, a power that was centered primarily around deduction [*prélèvement*] and death, it is utterly incongruous with the new methods of power whose operation is not ensured by right but by technique, not by law but by normalization, not by punishment but by control, methods that are employed on all levels and in forms that go beyond the state and its apparatus. We have been engaged for centuries in a type of society in which the juridical is increasingly incapable of coding power, of serving as its system of representation.
>
> (Foucault 1978, 89)

Foucault opposes biopolitical power to law because the law cannot achieve the kind of control that biopolitical methods can. Aristotle similarly describes the broad sense of law as universal reason, where asking "law to rule would seem to be asking god and the understanding alone to rule" (*Pol.* 3.16.1287a28–9); by contrast, whoever asks a human being to rule "asks a wild beast as well" (1287a30). Aristotle offers a dialectical rather than an oppositional view of the relation of law to human rule, since he recognizes that laws are formed by human beings and that human beings need to deliberate and make judgments about which law is applicable in which situation and laws, being general rules, do not always capture the specifics of particular cases (1287b16–21, 4.4.1292a33–4).

Ojakangas argues, following Foucault, that a sign of biopolitical rule is that the law is no longer the reference point of governing. While Aristotle does speak of the constitution as the law, the Greeks' equation of the constitution with the political community, Ojakangas argues, shows that the constitution is not law but the order of the community (Ojakangas 2016, 55). Ojakangas argues that the constitution is a mode of life around which one's life must be organized (55), and thus that the constitution is a source of biopolitical organization replacing the law as the "primary reference point in governance" (54).

Another way to understand the constitution is that it is the juncture between the citizens and the goal around which they organize the community. The goal serves to determine who should be included based on who contributes to the goal (*Pol.* 3.6.1278b8–10, 3.16.1287a17–18). When Aristotle associates the constitution with law and with the citizenry, he offers a view of political life that involves the community in political activity, an activity in which they are fully actualized (see Trott 2014, 2018). Aristotle associates the constitution with the community to show that government is not a separate entity imposing law and requiring a certain kind of subject who alone can be recognized by the law, as in a juridico-institutional model. Nor is the constitution a set of plans for controlling human behavior on a biopolitical model. The constitution is the people who participate in political life. The constitution is the organization of the community, and this organization is law (*Pol.* 3.1.1274b37, 3.6.1278b8–10, 3.16.1287a18). Constitutions are defined both by who is included in the rule and by the goal of that rule: whether it aims to serve those who rule or the whole community (3.6.1279a16–19). Laws institute the deliberative engagements of citizens, and in this sense serve the ends of the constitution (3.12.1282b12, 4.2.1289a13–17). While it is the case that the constitution does not exist to enable people to choose their mode of life (a classically liberal view of the constitution), and thus that the constitution *is* the way of life of the political community, as Ojakangas (2016, 56) concludes this section, the constitution is the way of life that citizens have determined as best realizing living well (wealth, virtue, or freedom; *Pol.* 4.12.1296b15–19). The implication is not that the constitution merely prescribes life and is thus biopolitical. Aristotle's human being is not a biological instrument of the state, both because the human being is not solely a biological being and because the interests of the community are not at odds with the flourishing of the human being.

Ojakangas importantly gets right the sense in which Aristotle's politics cannot be captured by a juridico-institutional model, which requires all of its subjects to be transformed from biological subjects into deliberating citizens in order to be recognized by the sovereign. He recognizes that Aristotle's city does not bar concerns for life in order for the community to be political, but these are not the community's sole concerns. In contrast to Agamben's biopolitics, wherein political life focuses on life by excluding it from political space, and Foucault's biopolitics, wherein life is the central concern of politics, Aristotle offers a different model. This view is made possible by a conception of nature that is neither separate from nor reducible to biological life.

2. Nature beyond Biology

The conception of nature as that which moves from within itself to fulfill itself leads to a view of nature wherein the forces of life make the living thing what it is. The human being and the *polis* are natural because the activity that characterizes them and is their end is also the activity that brings them into their actuality. Political activity is deliberative activity about the end that constitutes living well, the end toward which one should organize her life and the means to achieve it. These activities, rather than biological projects or the institution and maintenance of laws and institutions alone, define Aristotle's politics.

Here I extend this argument in two ways. First, I argue that the unity of body and soul in Aristotle's anthropology shows that what seem like bodily concerns in Aristotle's political theory are concerns for the whole human. Second, I argue that the activity of engaging in *logos* requires the nutritive soul and the sensitive and appetitive soul to be active in their functions in order to show that these aspects of the soul are not eclipsed in an included excluded structure as Agamben suggests (1998); nor does attention to the nutritive soul or the sensitive and appetitive soul suggest a sole concern for the biological because these aspects of the soul ultimately serve the good of the human being as a whole, insofar as their flourishing contributes to the flourishing of the rational soul.[2] The nutritive and the appetitive are not so much conditions for the rational soul, in which case the concomitant concerns of the three types of the soul would be divided between the more or less natural and the more or less rational, but are rather co-determinative with the rational soul. Understanding the human as a unity of body and soul and a unity of the parts of the soul shows that Aristotle's advice to legislators and citizens regarding the management of material and biological necessities treats them as matters of justice, even though they are not the only elements with which justice is concerned.

Arguments about the biopolitical nature of ancient Greek politics come in response to those who argue that the Greeks are the origin of the political project that enables private inequality for the sake of political equality by eliminating the concerns for the body from political activity, which is most proper to being human, as Arendt suggests in *The Human Condition* (Arendt 1998, 24–33). Recovering the concern for the biological and for household affairs in which the biological takes precedent would seem to be an antidote to this structure, while also showing how nutritive and reproductive concerns between human beings are matters of justice. But in the process of salvaging the passages that address biological and household concerns, a new danger arises. In turning toward the biological, the human being gets

---

[2] Agamben develops this structure as that between the *hypokeimenon* or *suppositum*—what is put under—and essence (Agamben 2015, 115–34).

stripped down to the biological contribution, whether for the sake of reproduction, for labor, or for war. Signs of this "stripping down" can be found in readings of Aristotle's *Politics* that argue that this stripping down of some becomes the condition of becoming more than biological beings for others, as certain readings of Aristotle's treatment of women and slaves suggest (see, among others, Brown 1988; Okin 1979). One interesting effect of Ojakangas's reading is that it puts all human beings on the level of the biological, rather than dividing between those beings with biological concerns and those with loftier concerns. Yet this equality is won by construing all human beings as solely biological, and the state's power as focused on controlling the body, instead of showing how the human being is always both biological and political, and communal life is always concerned with the good life.

2.1 Unity of Body and Soul

Treating the human being as a biological being would require separating, if not in fact, at least in focus, the body from the soul and the nutritive and appetitive parts of the soul from the rational soul. Aristotle presents an integrated model for the relation of the rational soul to the appetitive and nutritive soul and of the soul to the body. On this model, the actualizing of the rational soul does not require separating and distinguishing from the activity of the nutritive and appetitive parts of the soul, as an Agambenian reading that views the biological as included only in order to be excluded (sometimes called an "included excluded" structure) would suggest (Agamben 2004, 13–16, 37–8; 2007, 3–6).[3]

In *Nicomachean Ethics* 1.13, Aristotle describes the excellence of the soul that is required for happiness. He writes, "By human excellence we mean not that of the body but that of the soul; and happiness also we call an activity of soul" (*Eth. Nic.* 1.13.1102a16–17). He continues with an analogy: just as the student of the eyes must know the whole body, so must the student of politics know the soul in order to achieve the excellence of the human being (see also Plato's *Charmides* 156b–157a). The implication here is that the soul is not a part of the human opposed to the body, but in some sense the whole that must be made healthy in order for the body to be healthy, which is to say that the soul is the whole of which the body is a part. This view is borne out by Aristotle's treatment of the work of the soul in *De anima* 2.

---

[3] On the problems inherent in Agamben's concept of "bare life" and the "included excluded" structure, see also chapter 9 by Antonio Cimino in this volume.

In *De anima* 2.1, Aristotle first defines the body as "the subject or matter," which might suggest an easy division of roles between the soul and body, where the soul is form and the body is the matter (*De an.* 2.1.412a19). Aristotle proceeds to define the soul as the "substance in the sense of form of a natural body having life potentially within it" (412a20–1), which suggests that the soul is the form of a body that is potentially alive, again implying a determinate distinction in natural living beings between soul and body. Charlotte Witt argues that even when we recognize that natural things are composed of fully integrated soul and body and form and matter, Aristotle's hylomorphic metaphysics still establishes soul and form as normative and everything else (body and matter) as measured on the terms that value soul and form as more actual and more complete, making matter and body *for* the form and soul (Witt 1998). That hierarchy depends on being able to determine a distinction at some level—even if only a conceptual one and even if every natural form is always enmattered. Many scholars still maintain a kind of ontological separability when they defend the view that Aristotle's natural form most exists at the species level, an account that involves form being externally imposed on matter following a *technē* model of nature, rather than individual forms causing a natural substance together with the material (*inter alia* Whiting 1986, 1991; Woods 1968; Gelber 2010; Connell 2016, 319; contra Balme 1980; Frede and Patzig 1988; Witt 1987). If form exists at the species level, the individual form that is enmattered is not as much causal form as the species form is, so its integration with matter and body does not really point to integration of form and matter in Aristotle's account. Such positions contribute to a view that makes the body exist for the sake of the soul, rather than seeing a mutual interdependence. From that perspective, the problem with biopolitics is that it is overly concerned with the body. Juridico-institutional politics is superior because it aims to overcome concerns with the body to focus on the good life, but in so doing privileges the concerns of the soul over the body in a way that excludes those more concerned with the body.[4]

What follows in *De anima* 2.1 challenges the notion that the body and the soul are easily distinguishable and separable. Aristotle introduces the next sentence with a "but" (*de*). Rather than distinguishing between some material thing and the form that works on it, Aristotle explains, "But substance is actuality [*hē d' ousia entelecheia*], and thus soul is the actuality of a body as above characterized" (*De an.* 2.1.412a21–2). The soul is substance as the

---

[4] See the critiques of Pateman (1988, 48–60) and Winnubst (2006, 40–8) on the exclusionary implications of efforts that aim to diminish bodily nature for the sake of the more rational political life.

actuality of the body that is potentially alive. The soul is this kind of actuality: "an actuality of the first kind of a natural body having life potentially in it" (412a29). Such a body is one that Aristotle tells us is organized. The parts of the living thing, such as a plant, work to actualize the plant's aim of living and are what they are by being organized by the soul that actualizes the plant as living (412a29–b5). This example of the plant leads Aristotle to make quick work of the question of whether the soul and the body are one. As he concludes this argument, "Unity has many senses (as many as 'is' has), but the proper one is that of actuality" (412b8–9).

The examples that follow clarify the sense in which the soul just is the organization of a body potentially alive so that the body might fulfill its end of living. These examples—the axe and the eye—show that the body appears as a natural body potentially alive due to the animating work of soul, which organizes the body to be so animated (*De an.* 2.1.412b12–15; see Gill 1991, 200). If the axe were a natural thing, it would be so because it could move itself to do what axes do and would be what it is on account of its soul. As an artefact, the axe must be moved by a user. The natural being having a soul is moved by itself.

Aristotle shifts the example to a part of the living body—the eye. If the eye were an animal, its soul would be sight, since sight is the actuality of the eye, and as the actuality, it is the account and substance of the eye (*De an.* 2.1.412b18–20). The soul just is the power to organize the body so that it might fulfill its end. If the eye were a natural being, the soul would be what organizes it to have the shape and material by which it can see. The soul is what makes the body show up as the body it is, which, in the case of the human, is a living, perceiving, and thinking body.

When Aristotle argues in *De anima* 2.2 that "the soul cannot be without a body, while it cannot be a body; it is not a body but something relative to a body," he is not making a case to distinguish what appears as body from some other thing as soul (*De an.* 2.2.414a19–21). Rather, he explains that the soul is the source that causes the body to be both alive and organized in a way that enables it to fulfill the actuality of the soul that characterizes it. In *De anima* 2.4, describing the soul as "the cause or source of the living body" that is also "the essence of the whole living body" (2.4.415b9–11), Aristotle points to the integrated unity of the body with the soul, thereby showing how the soul is the whole that makes the body and the living substance what it is. Objects of artifice are not unified in the way that natural living beings are because the material of the artificial thing can be separated from its form, as the beam can be a beam and separable from its form as threshold. This separability is why Antiphon thinks artifice best exemplifies nature and that the material elements are the most stable, because they are what remain through change. Antiphon sees nature as material because he sees the natural substance's relation of form to matter and soul to body as an incidental one rather than a unity. This view makes of form just the arrangement, *rhythmos*, of matter, not the internal source that organizes and continues to work on making the natural being what it is (see Heidegger 1998, 205–9; Brogan 2005, 59–62). In contrast to the threshold, wherein the beam is only a threshold by being put in the proper place, the horse's body cannot be separated from the horse's soul that animates it by organizing it (Kosman 1987, 373–7). The being alive of the horse and the being able to do horse-like things coincide in the horse's soul and body, though we might say that the soul is the source of the former and the body of the latter.

The Agambenian structure of included excluded where the body is included only for the sake of focusing on its exclusion as the rational soul actualizes the human being requires a clear distinction between the body and the soul. Yet Aristotle argues for a sense of body that is organized as body to fulfill the being that the soul is. Any focus on the body to the exclusion of the soul would have no purchase on Aristotle's account. When Aristotle describes the human excellence as excellence of the soul and not of the body in *Nicomachean Ethics* 1.13, he is not speaking of the excellence of the soul to the exclusion of the body, but as the whole and actuality of the body as the analogy that follows suggests (*Eth. Nic.* 1.13.1102a14–17).

On this account, a person who is as far from another as the body is from the soul, as Aristotle suggests the slave would have to be to justify enslavement (*Eth. Nic.* 1.6.1254b16–20), would seem to make no sense of Aristotle's account of the soul as the whole of the human being in which the body is integrated and indistinguishable (contra Agamben 2015, 5). Some conclude from Aristotle's description of the slave as the body to the master's soul that the slave is the excluded human that makes true human flourishing possible (Agamben 1998, 20). Another way of reading this account is that the notion that there can be a human who is excluded from properly human life depends on a view of the relation of the soul to the body that Aristotle does not hold. Such a reading shows how the account of the slave requires denying that a natural slave exists and that no pure biopolitics that focuses only on the body is possible because there is no human as body (Trott 2014, 178–87). Notably, it seems like not even plants, on Aristotle's account, could be understood to have bodies that are separate from their souls. To be living is already to be integrated with a body and a soul. A focus on the soul is always in some sense also a focus on the body. The focus on the body requires a concern for the flourishing of the soul.

2.2 The Unity of the Nutritive, Sensitive, and Thinking Parts of the Soul

Someone might argue that biopolitics is not so much a focus on the body to the exclusion of the soul as a focus on the nutritive soul to the exclusion of the sensitive and the thinking soul, while juridico-institutional politics is a focus on the rational soul that requires a sublation of the nutritive and perceptive activity of the soul.[5] Ojakangas's case suggests that Aristotle's focus on the biological is akin to a focus on the nutritive soul. But in *De anima* and *Nicomachean Ethics*, the treatment of the nutritive soul might be understood to involve more of the sublation model.

In *Nicomachean Ethics* 1.13, Aristotle describes the nutritive as that which is shared by other living things and so "has no share in human excellence" (*Eth. Nic.* 1.13.1102b11–12; see also 1.7.1098a1–2), and the appetitive as the part of the soul that shares in a rational principle but is capable of resisting it (1.13.1102b23–4), and therefore needs to be properly habituated in order to follow reason. These claims make it quite clear that Aristotle is not advocating for an exclusive focus on the nutritive soul for the sake of the flourishing of the rational, but they expose Aristotle to the criticism that the nutritive and sensitive soul cease to be the concern of those whose work is in and with *logos*.

Against the argument that Aristotle's conception of the human soul requires bracketing or sublating the living and perceptive soul, I argue in this section that all activities of the soul are at work at once. The body of the one with a thinking soul does not cease to be perceiving and sensing and self-nurturing when it is thinking. The nutritive and the appetitive are part of the efforts to cultivate our political engagement over questions of living well, an activity that involves active engagement with *logos*.

After treating the way the soul organizes and actualizes the body and the way the body contributes to the fulfillment of the actuality of the soul, Aristotle turns, in the rest of *De anima*, to describe the different powers of the soul: the nutritive soul, which is responsible for nutrition and reproduction (*De an.* 2.4.416a19), the sensitive soul which is responsible for locomotion, affect (2.5.416b33–4), and imagination (3.3.428a21), and the thinking soul.

---

[5] Agamben maintains that by making *logos* political activity Aristotle posits politics as that which "allows one to treat a human life as if in it sensitive and intellectual life were separable from vegetative life—and thus, since it is impossible in mortals, of legitimately putting it to death," a division which is performed by the juridical law or sovereign in *The Use of Bodies* (Agamben 2015, 204). On this account, our ability to speak about these capacities of the soul as distinct would seem to both make and justify their distinction.

The thinking soul might be considered distinct from the body, not because it does not cause the body of those with a rational soul, but because it does not exist except in the activity of thinking and so is not really blended with the body (3.4.429a24–5). Even when it does think, it is always thinking with images, which are dependent on embodied senses, and is, in this sense, reliant upon a body (3.7.431a15–16). In the *Nicomachean Ethics*, Aristotle dedicates much of the text to describing how the excellences of the appetitive soul—having the right relation to pleasure and pain—must be fostered for the human being to live a life according to reason (*Eth. Nic.* 2.3.1104b10–11, 21–4, 27–8, 1105a4–6, 10–16). Legislators aim to make citizens good by forming good habits in them, a work that occurs on the appetitive soul (2.1.1103b3–5). Taking the right kind of pleasure in one's action as well as the action of a friend prepares a person to contemplate what is most true and unchanging (8.3.1156b14–16, 8.5.1157b32–3). Finally, the person who seems to think for the sake of thinking itself and not for the sake of action nonetheless remains concerned with having a healthy body (10.8.1178b34), and, having a sensible body, with the passions, and thus with excellences of character (1178a14–22; see Richardson 1992; Richardson Lear 2004). While contemplation is the most self-sufficient activity for a human being, it still requires concern for cultivating the excellences of both the nutritive and appetitive parts of the soul, since the human is not so self-sufficient as to exist without a body (*Eth. Nic.* 10.8.1178b34).

This point about the ongoing work of the nutritive and appetitive in the context of the contemplative life is beyond the scope of this argument, since what matters for our case is that the use of *logos* in practical life involves the continued concern for the excellences of character and the thriving of the nutritive soul for the sake of the flourishing of the human being and the community. Aristotle supports that case by connecting practical wisdom to excellence of character through *Nicomachean Ethics*, but specifically in 10.8, when he writes, "Prudence too is yoked to the virtue of one's character, and it to prudence. . . . These virtues, moreover, in being knit together with the passions, would be concerned with what is composite [*syntheton*] in us, and the virtues of this composite thing [*tou synthetou*] are characteristically human" (*Eth. Nic.* 10.8.1178a15–22).

Similarly, in *Politics* 1.2, Aristotle argues that the human being is more political than other animals because the human has speech. While voice is for designating the pleasant and the painful, speech is for figuring out together what is beneficial or harmful, just and unjust (*Pol.* 1.2.1253b9–15). Having language, human beings are better able to engage with one another to organize a world that allows them to live well. In this explanation, having speech requires voice but is more than voice. Against the view that voice disappears in the use of speech, which Derrida locates in Husserl (Derrida 1973, 77–8; Agamben 1991, 195–213), Aristotle's account shows how voice also indicates meaning. As Aristotle explains in *Metaphysics* 4, all one must do to show she accepts the bar on contradiction is to say something that means (*sēmainein*) something to oneself and another (*Metaph.* 4.4.1006a21–2). Aristotle uses the same term for "mean" here that he uses to describe what animals do with voice (*sēmeion*) at *Politics* 1.2 (1253a11). Animals indicate something meaningful and thereby accept the first principle of being, the principle barring contradiction. The human is more political because speech organizes the meaning the voice indicates, but the animal and the human are engaged in parallel pursuits: both perceive the world, make judgments about it by taking the world as something for them, and signal that meaning to someone else. The human being engaging with others in a process of coming to see what is just does not cease to feel pleasure or pain or cease to be capable of signaling pleasure and pain, but is also able to organize the world to determine that some pains are worth withstanding and some pleasures to be avoided.

Earlier in the same chapter, Aristotle explains that the *polis* comes into existence for the sake of living (*Pol.* 1.2.1252b28). Even human living is never merely nutritive, but always also sensitive and discursive. The *polis* continues to exist for the sake of living well, at which point it achieves self-sufficiency (1252b27), which Aristotle later says is organized around all things involved in being fully human together—eating, using tools, defending ourselves, acquiring necessary means, honoring the gods, and judging what is beneficial (7.8.1328b5–22). Even if we understand that the nutritive, appetitive, and the rational cannot be divided, Agamben's challenge is that by dividing a kind of substratum for life—living and perceiving—from a formed way of living (*bios*)—a life of *logos*—the substratum is a concern only in order to see it be superseded by the higher form of life (Agamben 2015). The household would seem to be the substratum for life that the formed way of living of the *polis* supersedes. Against Agamben's reading, I argue that Aristotle's *polis* is the end of the first community because in it, all the concerns of the first community are finally secured (*Pol.* 1.2.1252b29–30). By saying that the *polis* is the end of the household, Aristotle suggests that the coming-to-be of the household is fulfilled in the *polis* (1252b30–3). Those in the first communities are not solely nutritive souls but already have as their end the fully self-sufficient political community. Contra Ojakangas, focusing on the needs of the first community alone would not achieve the ends of the political community. But focusing on these needs does not make the community concerned with them either non-political or biopolitical, as if focusing on these needs is irrelevant to questions of justice and the good life. Aristotle discusses the need to form the household for the end of the *polis* because what happens in the household cannot be kept apart from what happens in the city (1.13.1260b15–19). What happens in private reproductive and nutritive life we know very well is a matter of justice. These practices, like the distribution of rule in the community, can be organized around contested conceptions of what is beneficial, good, and just. The capacity for *logos* and the ability to manage these aspects of life involve seeing these aspects as already formed life, as ways of organizing various capacities that have an effect on life outside the household. Aristotle acknowledges as much when he notes that the education of the children in the household will affect those who become citizens. The habituation toward equality and sharing rule in the household is required to motivate those kinds of capacities in political life. In *Politics* 7.15, Aristotle repeats his claim that "reason and understanding constitute our natural end," and as such "they are the ends that procreation and the training of our habits should be organized to promote" (7.15.1334b14–16). As Aristotle explains, the earlier concerns are not set aside in political life, but "supervision of desire should be for the sake of understanding, and that of the body for the sake of the soul" (1334b26–7). The focus on the body remains a concern for the soul in ways that are inextricable from and yet irreducible to concerns for the soul.

3. Conclusion

In order to overcome the twin horns of the biopolitical and juridico-institutional dilemma, political life must acknowledge the biological being of the human and make these issues matters of justice without reducing all political concerns to these matters. Such a view would recognize that biological processes affect our being in the world but are themselves organized by human beings around a conception of what it means to live well. Such a view would refuse to divide the world between those more or less affected by biological processes. It would refuse to make political life a space that requires a passage beyond these processes. It involves a more robust notion of nature than what is biological, one that includes more than the biological without excluding the biological as beyond the concern of justice and collective consideration. Such a view, I argue, can be found in Aristotle.

Aristotle's account of the unity of the body and the soul and the dependence and inseparability of the nutritive and perceptive soul from the rational soul points to a model of the form-of-life, "life unsegregatable from its form," that Agamben argues "must become the guiding concept and the unitary center of coming politics" (Agamben 2015, 213). Without suggesting that Aristotle's account carries with it all the implications of Agamben's sense of the term, this reading finds in Aristotle something like what Agamben calls form-of-life in which "a life that cannot be separated from its form is a life for which, in its mode of life, its very living is at stake, and, in its living, what is at stake is first of all its mode of life" (207).

This account of politics has several factors: (a) it is marked by an activity that actualizes the human and the political community; (b) by considering political life natural, it offers a normative framework for fostering and affirming political life as the site in which human beings flourish; and (c) it invites a sense of nature that is inclusive of concern for all ways of living. This last point is the most important for the purposes of responding to charges of biopolitics in Aristotle. Aristotle's sense of nature asks how to organize and enable the biological—the work required to eat and to reproduce—because it is relevant for political life. A tension arises in excluding those who work because they do not have time for political life (*Pol.* 3.5.1278a2–12, 7.9.1329a19–20) while defining what it means to be human as having the capacity to organize the world according to what one judges to be best. Insofar as the purpose of the *polis* is to fulfill the being of the human (1.2.1253a8–18), politics would be a matter of addressing those circumstances that produce the exclusion of some rather than a project of maintaining the exclusion.

References

Agamben, Giorgio. 1991. *Language and Death: The Place of Negativity*. Translated by Karen E. Pinkus and Michael Hardt. Minneapolis: University of Minnesota Press.

Agamben, Giorgio. 1998. *Homo Sacer: Sovereign Power and Bare Life*. Translated by Daniel Heller-Roazen. Stanford, CA: Stanford University Press.

Agamben, Giorgio. 2004. *The Open: Man and Animal*. Translated by Kevin Attell. Stanford, CA: Stanford University Press.

Agamben, Giorgio. 2007. "The Work of Man." Translated by Kevin Attell. In *Giorgio Agamben: Sovereignty and Life*, edited by Matthew Calarco and Steven DeCaroli, 1–10. Stanford, CA: Stanford University Press.

Agamben, Giorgio. 2015. *The Use of Bodies*. Translated by Adam Kotsko. Stanford, CA: Stanford University Press.

Arendt, Hannah. 1998. *The Human Condition*. Chicago: University of Chicago Press.

Aristotle. 1984. *De Anima*. Translated by John Alexander Smith. In *The Complete Works of Aristotle: The Revised Oxford Edition*, edited by Jonathan Barnes, 641–92. Princeton, NJ: Princeton University Press.

Aristotle. 1998. *Politics*. Translated by C. D. C. Reeve. Indianapolis, IN: Hackett.

Aristotle. 2011. *Aristotle's Nicomachean Ethics*. Translated by Robert C. Bartlett and Susan D. Collins. Chicago: University of Chicago Press.

Balme, D. M. 1980. "Aristotle's Biology Was Not Essentialist." *Archiv für Geschichte der Philosophie* 62 (1): 1–12. https://doi.org/10.1515/agph.1980.62.1.1.

Brill, Sara. 2020. *Aristotle on the Concept of Shared Life*. Oxford: Oxford University Press.

Brogan, Walter. 2005. *Heidegger and Aristotle: The Twofoldness of Being*. Albany: State University of New York Press.

Brown, Wendy. 1988. *Manhood and Politics: A Feminist Reading in Political Theory*. Lanham, MD: Rowman and Littlefield.

Connell, Sophia M. 2016. *Aristotle on Female Animals*. Cambridge: Cambridge University Press.

Derrida, Jacques. 1973. *Speech and Phenomena and Other Essays on Husserl's Theory of Signs*. Translated by David B. Allison. Evanston, IL: Northwestern University Press.

Finlayson, James Gordon. 2010. "'Bare Life' and Politics in Agamben's Reading of Aristotle." *The Review of Politics* 72 (1): 97–126. https://doi.org/10.1017/S0034670509990982.

Foucault, Michel. 1977. *Discipline and Punish*. Translated by Alan Sheridan. New York: Vintage Books.

Foucault, Michel. 1978. *The History of Sexuality*. Vol. 1, *An Introduction*. Translated by Robert Hurley. New York: Vintage Books.

Frede, Michael, and Günther Patzig. 1988. "Sind Formen allgemein oder individuell?" In *Aristoteles Metaphysik Z: Text, Übersetzung und Kommentar*, vol. 1, edited and translated by Michael Frede and Günther Patzig, 48–57. Munich: Beck.

Gelber, Jessica. 2010. "Form and Inheritance in Aristotle's Embryology." *Oxford Studies in Ancient Philosophy* 39: 183–212.

Gill, Mary Louise. 1991. *Aristotle on Substance: The Paradox of Unity*. Princeton, NJ: Princeton University Press.

Heidegger, Martin. 1998. "On the Essence and Concept of *physis* in Aristotle's *Physics* B1." Translated by Thomas Sheehan. In *Pathmarks*, edited by William McNeill, 183–230. Cambridge: Cambridge University Press.

Kosman, L. Aryeh. 1987. "Animals and Other Beings in Aristotle." In *Philosophical Issues in Aristotle's Biology*, edited by Allan Gotthelf and James G. Lennox, 360–91. Cambridge: Cambridge University Press. https://doi.org/10.1017/CBO9780511552564.020.

Miller, Paul Allen. 2020. "Against Agamben, Or Living Your Life, *Zōē* versus *Bios* in the Late Foucault." In *Biotheory: Life and Death under Capitalism*, edited by Jeffrey R. Di Leo and Peter Hitchcock, 23–41. New York: Routledge. https://doi.org/10.4324/9781003021506-3.

Ojakangas, Mika. 2016. *On the Greek Origins of Biopolitics: A Reinterpretation of the History of Biopower*. New York: Routledge.

Okin, Susan Moller, 1979. *Women in Western Political Thought*. Princeton, NJ: Princeton University Press.

Pateman, Carole. 1988. *The Sexual Contract*. Stanford, CA: Stanford University Press.

Rasmussen, Esben Korsgaard. 2018. "Aristotle and the Constitution of the Political Community." *Epoché: A Journal of the History of Philosophy* 23 (1): 19–46. https://doi.org/10.5840/epoche2018718118.

Richardson, Henry S. 1992. "Degrees of Finality and the Highest Good in Aristotle." *Journal of the History of Philosophy* 30 (3): 327–52. https://doi.org/10.1353/hph.1992.0060.

Richardson Lear, Gabriel. 2004. *Happy Lives and Highest Good*. Princeton, NJ: Princeton University Press.

Trott, Adriel M. 2014. *Aristotle on the Nature of Community*. Cambridge: Cambridge University Press.

Trott, Adriel M. 2017. "Nature, Action, and Politics: A Critique of Arendt's Reading of Aristotle." *Ancient Philosophy* 37 (1): 113–28. https://doi.org/10.5840/ancientphil20173716.

Trott, Adriel M. 2018. "'Not Slavery, But Salvation': Aristotle on Constitution and Government." *Polis: The Journal for Ancient Greek and Roman Political Thought* 34 (1): 115–35. https://doi.org/10.1163/20512996-12340120.

Whiting, Jennifer E. 1986. "Form and Individuation in Aristotle." *History of Philosophy Quarterly* 3 (4): 359–77.

Whiting, Jennifer E. 1991. "Metasubstance: Critical Notice of Frede-Patzig and Furth." *The Philosophical Review* 100 (4): 607–39. https://doi.org/10.2307/2185176.

Winnubst, Shannon. 2006. *Queering Freedom*. Bloomington: Indiana University Press.

Witt, Charlotte. 1987. *Substance and Essence in Aristotle: An Interpretation of Metaphysics VII–IX*. Ithaca, NY: Cornell University Press.

Witt, Charlotte. 1998. "Form, Normativity, and Gender in Aristotle: A Feminist Perspective." In *Feminist Interpretations of Aristotle*, edited by Cynthia A. Freeland, 118–37. University Park: Pennsylvania State University Press.

Woods, Michael J. 1968. "Problems in *Metaphysics* Z, Chapter 13." In *Aristotle: A Collection of Critical Essays*, edited by Julius Moravcsik, 215–38. Notre Dame, IN: University of Notre Dame Press. https://doi.org/10.1007/978-1-349-15267-4_11.

6

Bene vivere politice

On the (Meta)biopolitics of "Happiness"

Jussi Backman

1. Introduction: Foucault, Ojakangas, and the Biopolitics of Antiquity

In his Collège de France lecture courses *"Society Must Be Defended"* (1975–6) and *Security, Territory, Population* (1977–8), Michel Foucault develops his newly introduced concept of biopolitics, understood as the wielding of biopower, that is, techniques of government aimed at biological human populations as collective subjects (Foucault 1997, 213–35; 2003, 239–64; 2004, 3–118; 2009, 1–114).[1] Biopower is seen by Foucault as a sequel and complement to the disciplinary control and normalization of individual bodies studied in *Discipline and Punish* (1975) and the lecture courses of the early 1970s; disciplinary power had, in turn, evolved from the sovereign power of the absolutist early modern state, which had primarily addressed its subjects as moral agents in the form of commands and punishments.[2] In the first volume of *The History of Sexuality* (1976), Foucault singles out the disciplinary "anatomo-politics of the human body"—the administration of individual bodies—and the regulatory "bio-politics of the population"—the management of species-life—as the two central aspects of the new technology of power associated with nascent modern capitalism (Foucault 1976, 177–91; 1978, 135–45).

   In Foucault's narrative, the idea of the biopolitical management of life gradually emerges in the second half of the eighteenth century; he traces its

---

[1] I thank Antonio Cimino and Ville Suuronen warmly for excellent comments on earlier versions of this chapter. This work was supported financially from my Academy of Finland project *Creation, Genius, Innovation: Towards a Conceptual Genealogy of Western Creativity* (project number 317276).
[2] On the distinction between sovereign power, disciplinary power, and biopower, see Lilja and Vinthagen 2014.

Jussi Backman, Bene vivere politice: *On the (Meta)biopolitics of "Happiness"* In: *Biopolitics and Ancient Thought.* Edited by: Jussi Backman and Antonio Cimino, Oxford University Press. © Oxford University Press 2022. DOI: 10.1093/oso/9780192847102.003.0007

roots back to the Christian notion of the pastoral government of human beings, modeled on the manner in which a shepherd governs a flock of sheep. The notion of pastoral political power, Foucault maintains, remained fundamentally foreign to Greek antiquity (Foucault 2004, 139–51; 2009, 135–47). The herder, such as a keeper of horses or cows (*hippophorbos, bouphorbos*), and herding (*agelaiotrophia*) as metaphors for a political ruler and political rule are taken up and analyzed by Plato in the *Statesman* (261d–277a) but, according to Foucault's interpretation, are ultimately discredited there. Defining political rule as caring for the human flock does not, Plato's Socrates notes, allow us to distinguish between the statesman and other providers, such as merchants and physicians (*Plt.* 267e–268a), or between the political ruler and the divine shepherd (*poimēn*) who allegedly provided for humankind in the mythical age of Cronus (274e–275c). The ruler is not an uncontested superior who cares for the needs of inferiors, as a herdsman is to his flock, but rather a human being among humans, and the art of the ruler must thus be distinguished from arts related to the management of herds (*agelas*; 287b4–6). The art of ruling, Socrates concludes, should rather be compared to the art of weaving (*hyphantikē*) a unitary texture out of separate and contrasting elements (279a–283b, 305e–311c; Foucault 2004, 144–50; 2009, 140–7).[3] Foucault claims that classical antiquity generally rejected the very idea of political "government" in the modern sense.

> [I]t seems that for Greek and Roman societies the exercise of political power entailed neither the right nor the possibility of "government" understood as an activity that undertakes to conduct individuals throughout their lives by putting them under the authority of a guide who is responsible for what they do and for what happens to them.   (Foucault 2004, 373; 2009, 363)

It is during the Christian centuries of ecclesiastical pastorate, Foucault maintains, that the Western human being has been gradually penetrated by

---

[3] This reading is challenged by Ojakangas (2016b, 3–4, 79–83, 134), who argues that the model of the herdsman is in fact not rejected in the *Statesman*, but that herdsmanship and weaving are rather mutually complementary paradigms in a Platonic pastoral model of political governance as "selective breeding." Ojakangas notes that in the *Laws* (5.734e–736a), the analogy between political rule and herdsmanship is reintroduced side by side with the analogy of weaving, and the civic "purges" performed by the lawgiver (*nomothetēs*), especially the one who is also a tyrant (*tyrannos*), are compared to the selective breeding performed by the shepherd (*poimēn*) or the cowherd (*boukolos*). On this reading of the *Statesman* and the *Laws*, see also chapter 2 by Ojakangas in this volume. A similar critique of Foucault's reading of the *Statesman* can be found in Naas (2018, 72–96). Lane (1998, 57–8) offers an interpretive compromise: "[T]he revision of the name of the herding art so as to embrace what the statesman actually does . . . makes the notion of 'caring' for a herd sufficiently general to purge it of any special reference to herds at all. The language of 'caring for' [*therapeuein*] is emptied of its pastoral references and made available to weaving as to statecraft."

"governmentality" and has "learned to see himself as a sheep in a flock, something that assuredly no Greek would have been prepared to accept" (Foucault 2004, 134, see also 151–93, 374; 2009, 130, see also 147–90, 364). The development leading from the pastoral administration of human herds to the subsequent biopolitical management of human populations is thus decisively set apart from the political thought and practices of Greek antiquity. While, in the Aristotelian paradigm, the human being was "a living animal with the additional capacity for a political existence," in the biopolitical matrix of modernity, (s)he becomes "an animal whose politics places his existence as a living being in question" (Foucault 1976, 188; 1978, 143).

In *On the Greek Origins of Biopolitics: A Reinterpretation of the History of Biopower* (2016), Mika Ojakangas challenges this view of biopolitics and bio-power as distinctively modern phenomena in the history of Western political theory and political technology. According to Ojakangas's main thesis,

> the conception of politics as the regulation of the living in the name of the security and happiness of the state is as old as Western political thought itself: the politico-philosophical categories of classical thought, particularly those of Plato and Aristotle, were already biopolitical categories.
>
> (Ojakangas 2016b, 6; see also Ojakangas 2012, 2016a)

In the alternative narrative offered by Ojakangas, the Christian pastorate was not a prologue to modern governmentality, but rather "a rupture in the historical process that had started in classical Greece and continued in early modern Europe....It is not the Judeo-Christian pastorate, but the Renaissance of classical culture and literature…that is the true prelude to modern governmentality and biopolitics" (Ojakangas 2016b, 142).

Among the specific aspects of the Foucauldian narrative that Ojakangas criticizes is the notion he attributes to Foucault that it was only the emergence of the seventeenth- and eighteenth-century theories of the "police," in the sense of early welfare policies or management techniques designed to enhance the vital forces of the state (see Foucault 2004, 320–1; 2009, 312–14), that "made the happiness of individuals relevant for government for the first time in the history of Western societies" (Ojakangas 2016b, 31). Against this view, Ojakangas maintains that "the aim of the Platonic-Aristotelian biopolitics was exactly the same as in the modern biopolitics, that is to say, the security (*asphaleia*) and well-being (*eudaimonia*) of the city-state and its inhabitants" (9). Citing Aristotle's premise in the *Politics* (7.2.1324a23–6, 7.9.1328b33–6, 7.13.1332a3–7), according to which the optimal polity (*politeia*) is the one that provides maximal "prosperity" (*eudaimonia*) and a "blessed life" (*zōē makaria*) to its citizens, Ojakangas points out that, already for Aristotle, "the ultimate aim of the art of government is to promote the happiness of the city-state and the felicity of its inhabitants" (Ojakangas 2016b, 38–9). Since Aristotle starts his discussions of the material framework of the *polis* by considering the quantity and quality of its multitude of people (*plēthos tōn anthrōpōn*) as its most basic prerequisite (*Pol.* 7.4.1326a5–7), Ojakangas goes on to claim that "the main means for achieving this end" is "the regulation of the quality and quantity of population according to the immanent norms of life known through the scientific inquiry of human nature" (Ojakangas 2016b, 39).

That Aristotle's ethics and political thought indeed revolve around *eudaimonia*, happiness, prosperity, or human fulfillment, is certainly undeniable. Foucault, too, is fully aware how focused the entire Western tradition of political thought has been on happiness as the aim of political government—the Aristotelian tradition culminating in Thomas Aquinas, in particular (Foucault 2004, 239; 2009, 233). If concern with the happiness of the civic community is taken as a defining feature of biopolitics, "biopolitics" would indeed be practically coextensive with political theory since antiquity. However, there is a decisive distinction to be made between the classical and the modern forms of this concern. Foucault maintains that it is only with the modern conception of the "reason of state" or "national interest" (*raison d'État*) that this happiness and felicity, the ultimate instance of which Aristotle and Aquinas had situated beyond the political realm and, to a certain extent, beyond ordinary "terrestrial" human life itself, becomes fully immanent to the life of the state.

> Royal government [for Aquinas] did indeed fall under a particular terrestrial art, but its final objective was to ensure that on leaving their terrestrial status, and freed from this human republic, men can arrive at eternal bliss [*félicité*] and the enjoyment [*jouissance*] of God. This means that, in the end, the art of governing or ruling in Saint Thomas was always organized for this extraterrestrial, extra-state…purpose…and, in the last and final instance, it was for this end that the *res publica* had to be organized…. The end of *raison d'État* is the state itself, and if there is something like perfection, happiness [*bonheur*], or felicity [*félicité*], it will only ever be the perfection, happiness, or felicity of the state itself.
>
> (Foucault 2004, 264; 2009, 258)

What, for Foucault, is specific to the modern "police" or "policy" state is the "connection between strengthening and increasing the powers of the state, making good use of the forces of the state, and procuring the happiness of its subjects"—this happiness being now understood as the "well-being" (*bien-être*) or welfare of individuals that constitutes the strength of the state (Foucault 2004, 335; 2009, 327–8). In other words, while for Aristotle and Aquinas the political realm is ultimately an instrument for making possible the supreme individual felicity, for modern state reason, civic well-being becomes an instrument for enhancing the forces of the state.

Foucault's distinction gives us a useful tool for comparing and contrasting the Aristotelian-Thomistic understanding of the kind of fulfillment that is the ultimate aim of polities with the notion of happiness inherent in modern "governmentality," in which, for Foucault, political power for the first time assumes a genuinely biopolitical form. In what follows, I will briefly sketch out such a contrast and suggest that the Aristotelian *eudaimonia* and the Thomistic *beatitudo* are inherently "*meta*-biopolitical" ideals, in the sense that they are situated above and beyond the realm of "human affairs"— beyond human life in its ordinary biological and terrestrial form and beyond politics as the intersubjective realm in which human affairs are played out. Finally, I will point to the Hobbesian theory of the commonwealth as a distinctive turn to a modern, truly "biopolitical," and immanent understanding of civic happiness as essentially consisting in the preservation of life itself and the optimization of its inherent (subjective, material, biological) quality. In the modern liberal and utilitarian paradigm, life itself is promoted, according to Hannah Arendt, to the position of the "highest good," the *summum bonum*.

2. Aristotle and Aquinas: The Transcendence of the Blessed Life

The basic premise of Aristotle's *Politics*, stated at the very outset of book 1 (*Pol.* 1.1.1252a1–7), is that all human communities (*koinōniai*) are constituted for the sake of some good (*agathon*); accordingly, as the supreme (*kyriōtatē*) and most comprehensive (*periechousa*) type of community, the *polis* aims at the supreme good. The *polis* grows out of more primitive types of community that address immediate or long-term biological and economic necessities: households (*oikiai*), which are unions of husband and wife for the purpose of producing offspring, and of master and slaves for the organization of necessary labor, and villages (*kōmai*), which are conglomerations of households. The *polis*, however, is more than the sum of these constituent parts, more than an extended household or village: it exists not simply in order to guarantee mere staying alive (*zēn monon*), but for the sake of a specific, qualified kind of being-alive, "living well" (*eu zēn*; 1.2.1252a26–b30; 3.9.1280a31–2).[4]

The supreme good that is the purpose of the political community is a certain kind of good life within a civic framework, a form of *bene vivere politice*, as Aristotle's *kalōs politeuesthai* (*Pol.* 2.9.1269a34–5) was rendered in the Latin translation of William of Moerbeke.[5] This good life involves a "happiness" (*eudaimonia*) consisting in a life that is freely chosen (*zēn kata proairesin*) for its own sake, and for that reason, a community of unfree beings, such as slaves or nonhuman animals, can never qualify as a *polis* (3.9.1280a32–4). The fact that civic happiness is based on choice rather than necessity means that it cannot be defined by mere material interests: the *polis* is not primarily an economic cooperative for the purpose of protecting and accumulating property or advancing trade, nor does it exist simply for the sake of military organization or simply in order to guarantee the judicial rights of its citizens (1280a25–31, 34–b33). Aristotle explicitly rejects the idea that the political community could be based on a mere extrinsic contract or covenant (*synthēkē*) between individuals, without a qualitative transformation of the life of these individuals qua citizens (1280b10–12). Rather, it is only by becoming citizens that the members of households and families gain access to a life characterized by completeness and self-sufficiency (*zōē teleia kai autarkēs*), which is what living happily and appropriately (*zēn eudaimonōs kai kalōs*) fundamentally means (1280b33–5, 40–1281a2).

What this complete and self-sufficient life of happiness consists in precisely is not really specified by Aristotle in the *Politics*. This is because politics is subservient to ethics. In the *Politics*, Aristotle simply posits that there is one mode of life (*bios*) that is maximally fulfilling and maximally "happy" for all human beings, taken either as individuals or as members of a political community (*Pol.* 7.3.1325b30–2), and it is ultimately the task of ethics to determine the nature of this absolutely supreme mode. Political science is an instrumental study whose task is to elaborate what type of political order (*taxis*) optimally allows any given individual to pursue the most blissful (*makarios*) way of life (7.2.1324a23–5). This instrumental role makes Aristotelian political theory, as Ojakangas (2016b, 12) notes, a largely technical inquiry into the organization of political life involving large amounts of

---

[4] As I have argued elsewhere (Backman 2017), this Aristotelian distinction between *zēn monon* and *eu zēn*, "merely living" and "living well," is the most appropriate rendering of what Agamben (1995, 3–4; 1998, 1–2) designates as the allegedly Aristotelian distinction between *zōē* and *bios*. On the problematic nature of Agamben's distinction, see also Finlayson 2010; Miller 2020; and chapters 5 and 9 by Adriel M. Trott and Antonio Cimino in this volume.

[5] On *bene vivere politice*, see Albertus Magnus, *Politicorum libri VIII* 2.7.b; Thomas Aquinas, *Sententia libri Politicorum* 2.13.2.

empirical material, rather than a true "political philosophy" oriented to fundamental rational principles. The principal domain of this inquiry includes questions related to the material and institutional organization of the *polis*—geographical location, the physical structure of the settlement, political constitution, political institutions and offices, customs, norms, and laws. Political science inevitably also involves extensive considerations encroaching upon the domain of the household, *oikos*, as the biological and economic foundation and infrastructure of the *polis*; these include the quantity and quality of the population with its implications for the management of sexual relations, marriage, reproduction, and education as well as the role of women, slaves, and children, and the distribution of wealth and labor. On the technical level of means, Aristotelian political science thus certainly has an important "biopolitical" dimension, even though its focus is not biological life as such.

The question concerning the supreme *bios* is touched upon in the *Politics* only to the extent to which it involves participation in public affairs, as the ethical role of public life naturally has implications for the optimal organization of the *polis* (*Pol.* 7.2.1324a13–23). It is argued by Aristotle that true fulfillment cannot consist in the possession of any external good or in any bodily state but must rather be based on the ability to exercise a certain virtue or excellence (*aretē*) of the soul (7.1.1323a21–b36). This leaves us with two main candidates for the best mode of life: the life of political participation and action (*bios politikos kai praktikos*), based on the virtue of practical prudence (*phronēsis*), and the contemplative life (*bios theōrētikos*) of the philosopher, based on the virtue of theoretical wisdom (*sophia*; 7.2.1324a25–35; see also *Eth. Nic.* 6.5.1140a24–b11, 6.7.1141a20–b8, 6.8.1141b23–1142a10). Aristotle agrees with those who favor the political life that the best mode of life cannot be an inactive one; flourishing necessarily involves action in the sense of the exercise of a virtuous capacity (*Pol.* 7.3.1325a16–b16). Yet the life of action, Aristotle emphasizes, is not necessarily a *public* life of *political* action, as many of his contemporaries would have been inclined to suppose. Action, *praxis*, is defined by Aristotle as an activity that does not aim beyond itself but is rather itself its own end. Applying this definition of action, the most perfect and complete form of action is precisely the most self-sufficient and self-immanent one: "The life of action is not necessarily oriented to others, as some believe, nor are only those thoughts active [*praktikas*] that concern the external results of acting; much more active are the contemplations [*theōrias*] and acts of thinking that are their own ends [*autoteleis*] and take place for their own sake" (7.3.1325b16–21; my translation). Aristotle has thus implicitly answered the question concerning the happiest *bios*: it is the life of self-referential contemplation, the *bios theōrētikos*, which, according to Aristotle's definition of *praxis*, is also the most "active" or "action-related," *praktikos* (on this, see also Backman 2010).

This answer is explicitly given and elaborated in the *Nicomachean Ethics*. Aristotle enumerates three main modes of life that are freely chosen for their own sake: the life of enjoyment (*bios apolaustikos*), the life of political partic-ipation (*bios politikos*), and the life of contemplation (*bios theōrētikos*). Of these, the first, despite its popularity, is instantly dismissed by Aristotle as a life "fit for cattle"; but even the second, focused on the quest for recognition through public activity, is not truly self-sufficient, since honor or recognition (*timē*) is dependent also on those who recognize, not only on the one who is recognized (*Eth. Nic.* 1.5.1095b17–26). We are thus left with contemplation (*theōrein*), which is the active exercise of wisdom (*sophia*) or comprehensive understanding, one of the principal intellectual virtues of the human soul (6.7.1141a16–22, 6.13.1145a6–11). The contemplative beholding of reality as a whole in the light of its fundamental, necessary, and permanent intuitive metaphysical principles is the most self-sufficient, enjoyable, and carefree activity, one that elevates the one who contemplates above the concerns and vicissitudes of communal human affairs (10.7.1177a12–b26). As such, the life of contemplation constitutes the supreme human fulfillment, *eudaimonia*. Yet, Aristotle points out, as the closest approximation of the human being to the perfect activity of the metaphysical divinity, consisting in an immediate and complete reflective awareness of being-aware (*noēsis noēseōs*; *Metaph.* 12.9.1074b34–5), contemplation is in fact something more than human, something superhuman:

> Such a [contemplative] mode of life [*bios*] would be superior to the human mode of life; for one will not pass one's life [*biōsetai*] in this manner to the extent that one is human, but rather to the extent that there is something divine [*theion*] present in oneself....If the intellect [*nous*] is indeed divine with respect to the human being, the mode of life according to the intellect is divine with respect to the human mode of life. One must not heed those who demand that one must con-sider human things, being a human, or mortal things since one is a mortal; rather, one must be immortal [*athanatizein*] to the extent that this is possible and do everything in order to live according to that which is supreme in oneself.
> (*Eth. Nic.* 10.7.1177b26–8, 30–4; my translation)

Since the human being is not the supreme being in the cosmic order—there are many far more divine, that is, intransient, necessary, and self-sufficient, things (*Eth. Nic.* 6.7.1141a20–b2)—the supreme human life, in which the human being maximally approximates the perfect and permanent life of the divinity, is not truly "human" but rather divine. The ultimate end of the *polis* is to make possible the life of contemplation—the activity of the philosopher—by providing the necessary institutional background framework of security, freedom, and leisure. The task of political science is to establish how this framework is to be organized and what kind of material, biological, and economic infrastructure is needed to support it. Politics is subservient to ethics and ethics is subservient to metaphysical theology. Politics must be based on biopolitics, on the proper administration of biological life and natural necessity, but the true end of politics is ethical and, literally, *meta*-biopolitical: the political realm serves a mode of life, a *bios*, that transcends the ordinary concerns of the situated, embodied, and temporal human *bios*.

This was the fundamental premise of Aristotelian political philosophy, a tradition that remained without much consequence or relevance during the Hellenistic and Roman periods, in classical Arabic philosophy, and in the early Middle Ages, but was reappropriated at the height of scholasticism by Albertus Magnus and Thomas Aquinas and transposed into the Christian monarchical framework.[6] *De regno* (On Kingship), an unfinished treatise traditionally attributed to Aquinas—apparently originally intended as a gift to King Hugh II of Cyprus and later completed by Bartholomew (Tolomeo, Ptolemy) of Lucca under the title *De regimine principum* (On the Government of Rulers; see Dyson 2002, xix)—reiterates the basic premise of Aristotle's *Politics*. Human beings gather into a civic community in order to live well together (*ut simul bene vivant*), and the good life (*bona vita*) is life in accordance with virtue (*secundum virtutem*); thus, a true civic multitude (*multitudo*) is one that is directed by the same laws and the same government (*regimen*) to live virtuously (*De regno* 2.3.58–73 [1.15]).[7] However, for Aquinas, in contrast to Aristotle, supreme fulfillment does not consist in the exercise of a virtue; rather, virtuous temporal life is only a means for attaining the ultimate end (*ultimus finis*) common to the individual and the community, namely, the eternal enjoyment of God (*fruitio divina, fruitio Dei*) in

---

[6] Aristotelian political theory was to a certain extent studied and developed within the original Peripatetic school, but access to the text of the *Politics* was severely limited during the Hellenistic period and late antiquity; the only Greek commentary on the *Politics* was a twelfth-century work by Michael of Ephesus of which fragments have been preserved in the manuscript scholia published in the 1909 Immisch edition of Aristotle's *Politics* (see Immisch 1909, xv–xx). On this reception history of the *Politics*, see Horn 2008; O'Meara 2008. No Arabic translation of the *Politics* has been discovered, and it only became relevant for medieval philosophy with the appearance of the Latin translation of William of Moerbeke (ca. 1260) and the subsequent Latin commentaries by Albertus Magnus (ca. 1264–7) and Thomas Aquinas (ca. 1269–72); see Söder 2008.

[7] There are two different main ways of dividing *De regno* into books and chapters. I use here the division adopted in volume 42 the Leonine edition of Aquinas's *Opera omnia*; the alternative division is given in brackets.

the hereafter, which is also the ultimate happiness or beatitude (*ultima beati-tudo*; 2.3.32–8, 74–80 [1.15]). In the *Summa theologica* (1a.2ae.q3), Aquinas demonstrates, closely following the reasoning of the *Nicomachean Ethics*, that ultimate and perfect beatitude consists in the perfect activity of the contemplative or speculative intellect (*intellectus speculativus*)—more specifically, in an active contemplation (*contemplatio*) or vision (*visio*) of God's essence. This contemplative vision is delight (*delectatio*) or enjoyment (*fruitio*) insofar as it is not merely "intellectual" but also an attainment of the final end of the human will (*voluntas*). Ultimate beatitude is not attainable by human virtue alone, but also requires divine grace (*gratia*) and is thus dependent on divine government (*De regno* 2.3.94–8 [1.15]); nonetheless, the basic function (*officium*) of the temporal government of the king is to "promote the good life of the multitude in such a way as to make it suitable for the attainment of heavenly beatitude" (2.4.22–4 [1.16]; my translation). For Aquinas, in an even more radical sense than for Aristotle, the happiness that is the final end of civic government is thus entirely "meta-bio-political"— situated not only beyond communal and public life but beyond temporal and this-worldly human life in general. But even for Aquinas, as Ojakangas points out, optimal governmental technique involves not only moral but also "biopolitical" considerations of and interventions in the material and biological infrastructure of the human political community, such as climate, physical surroundings, food supply, health, and trade (2.5–8 [2.1–4]; Ojakangas 2016b, 130–1).

3. Hobbes and Modernity: The Life-Immanence of Happiness

We thus see that on the level of political technique, biopolitical considerations have indeed been an integral aspect of political theory since antiquity. Interventions into the material—biological and economic—domain of human life, which constitutes the infrastructure of the political domain, were deemed necessary by the Aristotelian-Thomistic tradition in order to organize the optimal political framework most conducive to the ultimate end of individual and communal human life: perfect happiness. Yet this end itself was seen by the tradition as metabiopolitical, transcendent to the biological and communal levels of human existence. Political thought thus arguably became truly and completely biopolitical only at the point at which this transcendence was abandoned and the ultimate end and aim of politics was itself made immanent to the biological and the political. As Roberto Esposito

(2008, 17, 46–7, 57–9, 149), among others, has shown, this happens most clearly at the threshold of modern political thought, in the work of Thomas Hobbes.[8]

Hobbes begins the second part of his *Leviathan* (1651), "Of Commonwealth," by stating the fundamental aim of the commonwealth:

> The finall Cause, End, or Designe of men...in the introduction of that restraint upon themselves, (in which wee see them live in Common-wealths,) is the foresight of their own preservation, and of a more contented life thereby; that is to say, of getting themselves out from that miserable condition of Warre, which is necessarily consequent...to the naturall Passions of men.
>
> (Hobbes, *Leviathan* 2.17.85)

The final end of life in a political community is the "contentment" afforded by the preservation of life, which, in the prepolitical state of nature—for Hobbes, inherently a state of war consisting in the famous "warre of every man against every man" (*Leviathan* 1.13.63)—is constantly under threat of violent death due to the "natural passions" of human beings, such as lust for honor and dignity, pride, envy, hatred, and vengefulness. Peace and preservation are brought about only through the fusion of conflicting individual wills into a common will under civil government; this is by no means a natural process, but indeed contrary to the human being's natural inclinations and based purely on an artificial covenant (2.17.87). It follows from this artificial character of the commonwealth that it can have no "natural" end, as in Aristotelian teleology, apart from the purpose for which human beings decide to enter into a civil covenant—that is, their desire to leave the state of war in order to preserve their lives. Moreover, Hobbes explicitly rejects the Aristotelian doctrine of an ultimate end of human life as such in the sense of a final object of all desire; desire is rather by nature an endless pursuit of transient and changing objects.

> [W]e are to consider, that the Felicity of this life, consisteth not in the repose of a mind satisfied. For there is no such *Finis ultimus*, (utmost ayme), nor *Summum Bonum*, (greatest Good,) as is spoken of in the Books of the old Morall Philosophers. Nor can a man any more live, whose Desires are at an end, than he,

---

[8] On biopolitics in Hobbes, see also Hull 2009, 14, 137–46; Piasentier and Tarizzo 2016. For Arendt's reading of Hobbes as *the* philosopher of the bourgeoisie and its interest in private acquisition, see Arendt 1979, 139–47; 1998, 31.

whose Senses and Imaginations are at a stand. Felicity is a continuall progresse of the desire, from one object to another.   (*Leviathan* 1.11.47)[9]

The "Felicity of this life"—as opposed to the Thomistic beatific vision and other joys of the hereafter, which Hobbes considers incomprehensible from our viewpoint in the here and now—consists in "continuall prospering," that is, "[c]ontinuall *successe* in obtaining those things which a man from time to time desireth.…For there is no such thing as perpetuall Tranquillity of mind, while we live here" (*Leviathan* 1.6.29).

By contrast, there is a *summum malum*, a universal greatest evil: violent death, the fear of which is the greatest fear for all humans (Hobbes, *De cive* ep. ded. 10, 1.2.18). It is the fear of death, together with the "Desire of such things as are necessary to commodious living; and a Hope by their Industry to obtain them," that motivates humans to establish a commonwealth under a sovereign power for the sake of peace (*Leviathan* 1.13.63). The "ultimate end" of the commonwealth is thus primarily negative: avoidance of violent death and preservation of life in order to allow individuals to pursue the ful-fillment of their various, shifting, and unending desires by seeking "commo-dious living" through private industry.

In *De cive* (On the Citizen, 1642), Hobbes elaborates that civic "safety" (*salus*) does not mean simply the preservation of life in whatever condition (*vitae qualitercunque conservatio*) but rather the safeguarding of "happy life" (*vita beata*), of the possibility to live "in a maximally pleasurable way" (*iucundissime vivere*) to the extent that this is allowed by the human condi-tion (*conditio humana*). Therefore, rulers are expected to provide their sub-jects with the means of sustaining not only "mere life" (*vita modo*) but also delight (*delectatio*), that is, with things that will enable the citizens to grow "strong" (*fortes*; *De cive* 2.13.4). But it turns out that this happy, delightful, pleasurable, and reinforced life amounts to nothing more than the "commo-dious" life of material prosperity acquired through work. Hobbes does take into consideration the Thomistic notion that it is the ultimate task of rulers to guide their subjects toward eternal salvation (*salutem aeternam*), noting that the princes themselves generally believe this to be their duty, and that there is no reason why they should not heed their conscience (*conscientiam*) in this matter (2.13.5). However, insofar as *this* (temporal) life is considered (*quae hanc tantum vitam spectant*), there are four main concrete benefits (*commoda*) that sovereign government holds out to its subject: protection

---

[9] On the early modern transformations in the philosophical concept of happiness and the break with the Aristotelian *eudaimonia* and the Christian *beatitudo*, see Spaemann 1974a, 1974b. On Hobbes on hap-piness, see also Kitanov 2011; Foisneau 2014; Hamilton 2016; Airaksinen 2019, 163–80.

from external enemies, preservation of internal peace, private enrichment to the extent that is allowed by public security, and enjoyment of a liberty harmless to others. "Even the supreme commanders [*imperatores*] can contribute no more to civic happiness [*faelicitatem civilem*] than that, preserved from external and civil war, they [the citizens] may enjoy [*frui*] the works of their industry" (2.13.6; my translation). Here, then, in stark contrast to the Thomistic ideal of eternal salvation and the enjoyment of God—which, for Hobbes, has become a matter of faith and conscience—we find the modern liberal paradigm of civic happiness: preservation of life for the pursuit of maximal private enjoyment and contentment, primarily in the form of private acquisition and wealth.

4. Arendt on Life as the Greatest Good and the Possibility of Public Happiness

It is the post-Hobbesian liberal ideal of happiness as "commodious" living that is at stake in Arendt's (1998, 133–4, 308–11) interpretation of the modern utilitarian principle of the "greatest happiness for all" and of the ubiquitous demand for happiness in the contemporary consumer society of the *animal laborans*, the late modern human being whose principal activities are labor and consumption, in other words, the sustainment and enjoyment of biological life. Happiness, in the modern sense, is simply the fundamental subjective quality of the biological life-process, the "quality of life" that modern consumer societies ceaselessly seek to enhance; it is the presence of the feeling of pleasure in the largely negative sense of the absence of pain (112–15). Arendt points out that the Aristotelian *eudaimonia* or the Thomistic *beatitudo* do not mean "happiness" at all in this modern subjective sense but rather "blessedness," fulfillment of one's inherent potential (192–3). Once the Aristotelian-Christian aspiration for salvation in an immortal blessed life of contemplation loses its orienting meaning, the only "highest good" left to Western political thought is life *as such*, the bare biological life-process, and the optimization of its inherent quality, that is, happiness (313–20).[10] Late modernity has succumbed to

> the persistent demands of the *animal laborans* to obtain a happiness which can be achieved only where life's processes of exhaustion and regeneration, of pain and release from pain, strike a perfect balance....For only the *animal laborans*,

[10] On Arendt's analysis of life as the "highest good" for the *animal laborans*, see also chapter 7 by Ville Suuronen in this volume.

and neither the craftsman nor the man of action, has ever demanded to be "happy" or thought that mortal men could be happy. (Arendt 1998, 134)

This understanding of the post-Hobbesian promotion of the intertwining ideals of life and happiness or "quality of life" is, as Giorgio Agamben (1995, 6; 1998, 3–4) and Esposito (2008, 149–50) point out, Arendt's account of the birth of modern "biopolitics"—an account that, even though it operates without the terms "biopolitics" and "biopower," comes quite close to Foucault's interpretation of the maximization of civic happiness through emerging modern welfare policies as a maximization of the vital forces of the state (see Braun 2007; Blencowe 2010; Diprose and Ziarek 2018; Suuronen 2018, and chapter 7 by Suuronen in this volume). Like Foucault, Arendt, too, finds the roots of biopolitics in this sense in Christianity—in the Christian belief in the sacredness of life as such that "has survived, and has even remained completely unshaken by, secularization and the general decline of the Christian faith" (Arendt 1998, 314). As we have seen, the "immanent" biopolitics of modernity in the sense proposed in this chapter emerges from the medieval metabiopolitics of Aquinas precisely at the point where, due to the process of increasing secularization, the ideal of life loses its transcendent, spiritual, speculative, and beatific status, and its sanctity is bequeathed to our material, biological, and organic life here and now, transforming temporal government from a preparation for salvation into a "government of the living." It is only in this sense that the Christian belief in personal immortality ultimately gives life on earth the status of the "highest good of man" (316).

With the modern turn to life's biological immanence, the great aversion of the Church Fathers to certain types of biopolitical interventions—cited by Ojakangas as the main reason for the "decline and eventually…the end of Greco-Roman biopolitical rationality in the medieval Christian world" (Ojakangas 2016b, 125)—also begins to fade, but now in the light of a completely new rationality that was as such unknown to classical antiquity. While the ancient ideas of the necessity of "purging" life deemed degenerate, described by Ojakangas as a central facet of ancient biopolitics, were always geared to the interests of the *polis* and its metabiopolitical ends, the modern focus on the inherent and immanent quality of the biological life-process as an end in itself ultimately gives rise to the notion of "life unworthy of being lived" (*lebensunwertes Leben*) so infamously exploited by Nazi and proto-Nazi eugenicists.[11] As soon as the maximization of the quality of (biological)

---

[11] The concept was popularized by a 1920 pamphlet published by the jurist Karl Binding and the psychiatrist Alfred Hoche, bearing the ominous title *Die Freigabe der Vernichtung lebensunwerten Lebens*

life—of "happiness" in the genuinely biopolitical sense—is accepted as a political end, the elimination of life regarded as biologically inferior readily offers itself as a means to this end.

Without disputing the presence of biopolitical techniques in Plato's and Aristotle's political thought, I have tried to show that the underlying rationale for these measures—the overall understanding of the ends of politics and the *polis*—is most appropriately characterized as metabiopolitical in the context of ancient and medieval Aristotelian political theory. For Aristotle and Aquinas, the final end of politics is neither mere preservation of life nor "happiness" in the sense of the optimal subjective quality of the life-process, but rather fulfillment in the form of an extraordinary mode of life beyond involvement in ordinary communal human affairs, even beyond temporal and biological life as such. Moreover, in Arendt we find a narrative that complements and supports Foucault's notion of the Christian roots of modern biopolitics: the post-Hobbesian focus of political theory on the preservation and enhancement of life as such is grounded in the Christian concept of the sanctity of life.

In closing, we should note that we also discover in Arendt an alternative to the metabiopolitical Aristotelian ideal of *eudaimonia/beatitudo* as well as the biopolitical Hobbesian quality-of-life ideal of happiness as "commodious living": a genuinely *political* ideal of "public happiness," consisting in political participation in public affairs, in having access to the public realm and a share in public power (Arendt 1990, 119, 123, 126–38, 255, 269, 279). This ideal, Arendt emphasizes, was promoted by the founders of the American Revolution, particularly John Adams, for whom the desire for public esteem was itself a "principal end" as well as a "principal means" of government (Adams 2000, 313; Arendt 2018, 213).[12] As Arendt points out, while both the Aristotelian and Hobbesian models instrumentalize politics as a means to an end found outside the political sphere, the ideal of public happiness sees political activity as an end in itself: "In this definition of the 'end of government,' means and end obviously coincide; the moment one puts the notion of 'public happiness' in the place of private rights and personal interests, the very question: What is the end of government? loses its sense" (Arendt 2018, 213). Between the transcendent beatitude of the contemplative life and the immanent happiness of optimized biological life, we find the public happiness of participating in a shared political space of visibility, so manifestly neglected by the Western tradition of political theory.

(trans. *Allowing the Destruction of Life Unworthy of Life*). See Agamben 1995, 150–9; 1998, 136–43; Esposito 2008, 194.

[12] Soni (2010) challenges Arendt's notion of public happiness, maintaining that the idea of happiness espoused by the American revolutionaries was an essentially private one.

References

Adams, John. 2000. *The Political Writings of John Adams*. Edited by George W. Carey. Washington, DC: Regnery.

Agamben, Giorgio. 1995. *Homo sacer: Il potere sovrano e la nuda vita*. Turin: Einaudi.

Agamben, Giorgio. 1998. *Homo Sacer: Sovereign Power and Bare Life*. Translated by Daniel Heller-Roazen. Stanford, CA: Stanford University Press.

Airaksinen, Timo. 2019. *Vagaries of Desire: A Collection of Philosophical Essays*. Leiden: Brill.

Albertus Magnus. 1891. *Opera omnia*. Vol. 8, *Politicorum libri VIII*. Edited by Auguste Borgnet. Paris: Vivès.

Arendt, Hannah. 1979. *The Origins of Totalitarianism*. 2nd ed. San Diego, CA: Harcourt Brace & Co. First published 1951.

Arendt, Hannah. 1990. *On Revolution*. London: Penguin. First published 1963.

Arendt, Hannah. 1998. *The Human Condition*. 2nd ed. Chicago: University of Chicago Press. First published 1958.

Arendt, Hannah. 2018. *Thinking without a Banister: Essays in Understanding 1953–1975*. Edited by Jerome Kohn. New York: Schocken Books.

Aristotle. 1872. *Politicorum libri octo*. Translated into Latin by William of Moerbeke, edited by Franz Susemihl. Leipzig: Teubner.

Aristotle. 1894. *Ethica Nicomachea*. Edited by Ingram Bywater . Oxford: Clarendon Press.

Aristotle. 1909. *Politica*. Edited by Otto Immisch. Leipzig: Teubner.

Aristotle. 1924. *Metaphysics*. 2 vols. Edited by David Ross. Oxford: Clarendon Press.

Aristotle. 1957. *Politica*. Edited by David Ross. Oxford: Clarendon Press.

Backman, Jussi. 2010. "The End of Action: An Arendtian Critique of Aristotle's Concept of Praxis." In *COLLeGIUM: Studies across Disciplines in the Humanities and Social Sciences*, vol. 8, *Hannah Arendt: Practice, Thought and Judgment*, edited by Mika Ojakangas, 28–47. Helsinki: Helsinki Collegium for Advanced Studies. http://hdl.handle.net/10138/25817.

Backman, Jussi. 2017. "Aristotle." In *Agamben's Philosophical Lineage*, edited by Adam Kotsko and Carlo Salzani, 15–26. Edinburgh: Edinburgh University Press. https://doi.org/10.3366/edinburgh/9781474423632.003.0002.

Binding, Karl, and Alfred Hoche. 1922. *Die Freigabe der Vernichtung lebensunwerten Lebens: Ihr Maß und ihre Form*. 2nd ed. Leipzig: Meiner. First published 1920.

Binding, Karl, and Alfred Hoche. 2012. *Allowing the Destruction of Life Unworthy of Life: Its Measure and Form*. Translated by Cristina Modak. Greenwood, WI: Suzeteo Enterprises.

Blencowe, Claire. 2010. "Foucault's and Arendt's 'Insider View' of Biopolitics: A Critique of Agamben." *History of the Human Sciences* 23 (5): 113–30. https://doi.org/10.1177/0952695110375762.

Braun, Kathrin. 2007. "Biopolitics and Temporality in Arendt and Foucault." *Time &* *Society* 16 (1): 5–23. https://doi.org/10.1177/0961463X07074099.

Diprose, Rosalyn, and Ewa Plonowska Ziarek. 2018. *Arendt, Natality and Biopolitics: Toward Democratic Plurality and Reproductive Justice.* Edinburgh: Edinburgh University Press.

Dyson, R. W. 2002. Introduction to *Political Writings,* by Thomas Aquinas, edited by R. W. Dyson, xvii–xxxvi. Cambridge: Cambridge University Press. https://doi.org/10.1017/CBO9780511801952.002.

Esposito, Roberto. 2008. *Bíos: Biopolitics and Philosophy.* Translated by Timothy Campbell. Minneapolis: University of Minnesota Press.

Finlayson, James Gordon. 2010. "'Bare Life' and Politics in Agamben's Reading of Aristotle." *The Review of Politics* 72 (1): 97–126. https://doi.org/10.1017/S0034670509990982.

Foisneau, Luc. 2014. "Hobbes on Desire and Happiness." *Homo oeconomicus* 31 (4): 479–89.

Foucault, Michel. 1976. *Histoire de la sexualité.* Vol. 1, *La volonté de savoir.* Paris: Gallimard.

Foucault, Michel. 1978. *The History of Sexuality.* Vol. 1, *An Introduction.* Translated by Robert Hurley. New York: Pantheon.

Foucault, Michel. 1997. *"Il faut défendre la société": Cours au Collège de France (1975–1976).* Edited by Mauro Bertani and Alessandro Fontana. Paris: Gallimard; Seuil.

Foucault, Michel. 2003. *"Society Must Be Defended": Lectures at the Collège de France, 1975–76.* Translated by David Macey. New York: Picador.

Foucault, Michel. 2004. *Sécurité, territoire, population: Cours au Collège de France (1977–1978).* Edited by Michel Senellart. Paris: Gallimard; Seuil.

Foucault, Michel. 2009. *Security, Territory, Population: Lectures at the Collège de France, 1977–78.* Translated by Graham Burchell. Basingstoke: Palgrave Macmillan.

Hamilton, James J. 2016. "Hobbes on Felicity: Aristotle, Bacon and *eudaimonia.*" *Hobbes Studies* 29 (2): 129–47. https://doi.org/10.1163/18750257-02902002.

Hobbes, Thomas. 1983. *De Cive: The Latin Version.* Edited by Howard Warrender. Oxford: Clarendon Press. First published 1642.

Hobbes, Thomas. 1996. *Leviathan.* Edited by Richard Tuck. Cambridge: Cambridge University Press. First published 1651.

Horn, Christoph. 2008. "Hellenismus und frühe Kaiserzeit: Der Peripatos." In *Politischer Aristotelismus: Die Rezeption der aristotelischen "Politik" von der Antike bis zum 19. Jahrhundert,* edited by Christoph Horn and Ada Neschke-Hentschke, 20–41. Stuttgart: Metzler. https://doi.org/10.1007/978-3-476-00106-1_2.

Hull, Gordon. 2009. *Hobbes and the Making of Modern Political Thought.* London: Continuum.

Immisch, Otto. 1909. Preface to *Politica*, by Aristotle, edited by Otto Immisch, v–xxxix. Leipzig: Teubner.

Kitanov, Severin V. 2011. "Happiness in a Mechanistic Universe: Thomas Hobbes on the Nature and Attainability of Happiness." *Hobbes Studies* 24 (2): 117–36. https://doi.org/10.1163/187502511X597667.

Lane, Melissa S. 1998. *Method and Politics in Plato's Statesman*. Cambridge: Cambridge University Press.

Lilja, Mona, and Stellan Vinthagen. 2014. "Sovereign Power, Disciplinary Power and Biopower: Resisting What Power with What Resistance?" *Journal of Political Power* 7 (1): 107–26. https://doi.org/10.1080/2158379X.2014.889403.

Michael of Ephesus. 1909. Scholia and glosses to *Politica*, by Aristotle, edited by Otto Immisch, 293–329. Leipzig: Teubner.

Miller, Paul Allen. 2020. "Against Agamben: Or Living your Life, *Zōē* versus *Bios* in the Late Foucault." In *Biotheory: Life and Death under Capitalism*, edited by Jeffrey R. Di Leo and Peter Hitchcock, 23–41. New York: Routledge. https://doi.org/10.4324/9781003021506-3.

Naas, Michael. 2018. *Plato and the Invention of Life*. New York: Fordham University Press.

Ojakangas, Mika. 2012. "Michel Foucault and the Enigmatic Origins of Bio-politics and Governmentality." *History of the Human Sciences* 25 (1): 1–14. https://doi.org/10.1177/0952695111426654.

Ojakangas, Mika. 2016a. "Biopolitics in the Political Thought of Classical Greece." In *The Routledge Handbook of Biopolitics*, edited by Sergei Prozorov and Simona Rentea, 23–35. London: Routledge. https://doi.org/10.4324/9781315612751-2.

Ojakangas, Mika. 2016b. *On the Greek Origins of Biopolitics: A Reinterpretation of the History of Biopower*. London: Routledge.

O'Meara, Dominic J. 2008. "Spätantike und Byzanz: Neuplatonische Rezeption—Michael von Ephesos." In *Politischer Aristotelismus: Die Rezeption der aristotelischen "Politik" von der Antike bis zum 19. Jahrhundert*, edited by Christoph Horn and Ada Neschke-Hentschke, 42–52. Stuttgart: Metzler. https://doi.org/10.1007/978-3-476-00106-1_3.

Piasentier, Marco, and Davide Tarizzo. 2016. "'The Government of a Multitude': Hobbes on Political Subjectification." In *The Routledge Handbook of Biopolitics*, edited by Sergei Prozorov and Simona Rentea, 36–49. London: Routledge. https://doi.org/10.4324/9781315612751-3.

Plato. 1900. *Platonis opera*. Vol. 1. Edited by John Burnet. Oxford: Clarendon Press.

Plato. 1907. *Platonis opera*. Vol. 7. Edited by John Blurnet. Oxford: Clarendon Press.

Söder, Joachim R. 2008. "Hochmittelalter: Die Wiedergewinnung des Politischen." In *Politischer Aristotelismus: Die Rezeption der aristotelischen "Politik" von der Antike bis zum 19. Jahrhundert*, edited by Christoph Horn and Ada Neschke-Hentschke, 53–76. Stuttgart: Metzler. https://doi.org/10.1007/978-3-476-00106-1_4.

Soni, Vivasvan. 2010. "A Classical Politics without Happiness? Hannah Arendt and the American Revolution." *Cultural Critique* 74: 32–47. https://doi.org/10.1353/cul.0.0057.

Spaemann, Robert. 1974a. "Glück, Glückseligkeit III." In *Historisches Wörterbuch der Philosophie*, vol. 3, edited by Joachim Ritter, 697–707. Basel: Schwabe. https://doi.org/10.24894/HWPh.5161.

Spaemann, Robert. 1974b. "Gut, höchstes." In *Historisches Wörterbuch der Philosophie*, vol. 3, edited by Joachim Ritter, 973–6. Basel: Schwabe. https://doi.org/10.24894/HWPh.1467.

Suuronen, Ville. 2018. "Resisting Biopolitics: Hannah Arendt as a Thinker of Automation, Social Rights, and Basic Income." *Alternatives: Global, Local, Political* 43 (1): 35–53. https://doi.org/10.1177/0304375418789722.

Thomas Aquinas. 1891. *Opera omnia.* Vol. 6, *Summa theologiae, Ia IIae, qq. 1–70.* Rome: Typographia poliglotta S. C. de Propaganda Fide.

Thomas Aquinas. 1971. *Opera omnia.* Vol. 48, Sententia libri Politicorum, Tabula libri Ethicorum. Rome: Ad Sanctae Sabinae.

Thomas Aquinas. 1979. *Opera omnia.* Vol. 42. Rome: Editori di San Tommaso.

PART III

BIOPOLITICAL INTERPRETATIONS OF ANCIENT THOUGHT

7

Hannah Arendt's Genealogy of Biopolitics

From Greek Materialism to Modern Human Superfluity

Ville Suuronen

1. Introduction: Arendt's Presumed Devaluation of Biological Life

The accusations that Hannah Arendt's political thinking somehow depreciates or devalues biological life and that it is defined by a problematic dose of nostalgic Grecophilia have become widely accepted clichés[1] (see, for example, Pitkin 1998; Euben 2000; Wolin 2003; Schaap 2010; Ojakangas 2016). When confronted with these accusations, Arendt (2007, 332n3) herself once noted: "I do not think that I am hostile to life. Life is a magnificent thing, but it is not the highest good. Whenever life is assessed as the highest good, life is just as soon whisked away." What did Arendt mean with these rather cryptic comments?

To answer these questions, this chapter aims to tease out a historical genealogy of biological life from Arendt's thinking. While several studies have provided more nuanced readings of the complex role of labor and "the social" in Arendt (see, for example, Villa 1996; Tsao 2002; Gündogdu 2015; Suuronen 2018), a systematic genealogical treatment of biological life in her works is still missing. In attempting to provide such a reading, I draw new insights from Arendt's lesser-known and recently published works (Arendt 2002, 2018a, 2018b), which complement her well-known historical narratives and arguments presented most famously in *The Human Condition* (1958).

Mapping this genealogy of biological life also serves another purpose. I argue that Arendt's thinking offers an original take on the history of biopolitics, that

---

[1] This research was funded by the Centre of Excellence in Law, Identity and the European Narratives, University of Helsinki, Academy of Finland funding decision number 312154.

Ville Suuronen, *Hannah Arendt's Genealogy of Biopolitics: From Greek Materialism to Modern Human Superfluity* In: *Biopolitics and Ancient Thought*. Edited by: Jussi Backman and Antonio Cimino, Oxford University Press. © Oxford University Press 2022.
DOI: 10.1093/oso/9780192847102.003.0008

is, on the way human life as a biological fact appears as an object of political and statistical manipulations, strategies, and interventions during different eras in history.[2] Although several recent studies have offered readings of Arendt as one of the early thinkers of biopolitics (Duarte 2005; Vatter 2006; Braun 2007; Blencowe 2010; Oksala 2010; Suuronen 2018), previous literature focuses almost exclusively on Arendt's reflections concerning the modern age and treats her genealogical narrative of biological life as a mere sidenote. To amend this lack of attention, I will contrast Arendt's historical narrative with Michel Foucault's famous reflections concerning the birth of biopower in modernity and its origins in the Christian pastorate, and also with Mika Ojakangas's recent reinterpretation of the history of biopolitics according to which this phenomenon has its roots in the ancient Greek world. I argue that Arendt's genealogy of biological life locates the intellectual roots of modern biopolitics in both Greek philosophy and Christian theology, which reappropriates the Greek heritage in a different form.

I begin by reinterpreting Arendt's arguments concerning the *oikos/polis* distinction and the way the Greeks considered it necessary to exclude labor and biological life from the realm of freedom. I argue that Arendt offers a reading of Western intellectual history and its Greek beginning as ridden with what Arendt characterizes as a profound "materialism." Arendt argues that this materialism is born in the philosophies of Plato and Aristotle, the first Western thinkers to subordinate politics to the commands of contemplation from whose perspective political action appears as an activity that deals with the necessities of life in order to make the *bios theōrētikos* of the philosophers possible. As we will see, Arendt also maintains that this is where the modern concept of sovereignty has its shady historical roots: in the *oikonomic* domination of the necessities of life, originally institutionalized in the Greek slave economy, from which this model then gradually spreads to the realm of politics itself. For Arendt, all of Western history up until the modern age appears like a set of variations and repercussions on the axiomatic and originally Greek themes of materialism and (proto-)sovereignty, on this compelling necessity to exclude labor and biological life from the realm of true freedom and on the equally necessary counterpart of this exclusion, the introduction of this model of sovereign rule as *the* model of politics.

After analyzing the foundational role of the Greeks, the subsequent sections of this chapter will move chronologically, first analyzing the way Arendt understands the rise of Christianity as a subterranean affirmation of worldly life in the name of an afterlife, laying the intellectual groundwork for what

---

[2] On biopolitics, see Lemke 2011.

Arendt (2007, 332n3) referred to as the "enormous overestimation of life" that defines the modern era. We then examine how the modern era renounces all such teleological-theological ideals, which had thus far served as the ontological basis for the exclusion of biological life. In turning around the Greek metaphysical hierarchy—a turn most clearly indicated in the works of Karl Marx and Charles Darwin—modernity begins to value life itself (or, in Arendt's terminology, labor) as the highest human activity. In the realm of the social, the politicized life-process now occupies the realm of human action in its totality. Finally, trying to formulate an answer to Arendt's problem of why life is "whisked away" precisely when it is seen as the "highest good," I conclude by exploring how the victory of the *animal laborans* constituted the metaphysical framework in which it suddenly became possible to introduce distinctions within the realm of biological life itself. Analyzing how *human superfluity* began to emerge precisely at the moment when all human activities were understood as laboring activities, I reflect on the complex ways in which Arendt understood totalitarianism as a rootless and completely unprecedented phenomenon, which was, nevertheless, also partially enabled by the profound "materialism" of the Western tradition itself.

2. The Birth of Materialism and the Prefiguration of Sovereignty in Plato and Aristotle

In *The Human Condition*, Arendt famously maintains that the prephilosophical Greek world was defined by a distinction between two spheres of life: the *oikos* and the *polis*. Referring to Werner Jaeger's *Paideia* (Jaeger 1947, 111), Arendt argues that "the rise of the city-state meant that man received besides his private life a sort of second life, his *bios politikos*. Now every citizen belongs to two orders of existence; and there is a sharp distinction in his life between what is his own (*idion*) and what is communal (*koinon*)" (Arendt 1998, 24). According to Arendt, the new freedom of the *polis* was based on an exclusion of biological life and necessity, which were relegated to the sphere of the household, the *oikos*. While the *polis* was the realm of equals based on freedom from necessity, the *oikos* was a realm of absolute inequality in which "necessity ruled over all activities performed in it." Only those who were free from the tasks of the *oikos*, the free male citizens of Athens, could rise to the realm of equality in the *polis* in which freedom meant "neither to rule nor to be ruled" (30, 32, 72).

On the one hand, the *polis* was supposed to make it possible for every citizen to distinguish themselves and to attain immortal fame by offering an institutionalized realm for the constant *aiei aristeuein* of the rivalling citizens. On the other hand, in functioning as "a kind of organized remembrance," the *polis* also offered a solution to what Arendt calls the "frailty of human affairs." By creating a lasting space of appearance and action, it endowed human deeds with a place where their meaning could last and inspire future genera-tions (Arendt 1998, 41, 197–8; see also Canovan 1992, 137–8). According to Arendt, who cites Aristotle very freely here, both of these functions corre-sponded to the general Greek estimate that what made it "worthwhile for men to live together (*syzen*)" was, as Aristotle once puts it, precisely the *logōn kai pragmatōn koinōnein*, the "sharing of words and deeds" (Aristotle, *Eth. Nic.* 4.6.1126b; Arendt 1998, 196–7). In this short moment in history in Periclean Athens, "conducting all public matters through <u>peithein</u>, persuasion with words," became a self-evident fact (Arendt 2018a, 270). For Arendt, Athens was nothing less than the "first permanent organized community in which freedom was being realized" (449), the first historical moment in which "freedom in its essential sense is: *logon echōn*" (Arendt 2002, 425; my translation).

In a recent study, Mika Ojakangas calls Arendt's interpretation into ques-tion and argues that the *oikos/polis* distinction was, in fact, "far from being as clear-cut in classical *poleis*" as Arendt suggests. Referring to Carl Schmitt, Ojakangas argues that the classical *polis* was nothing less than a "total state" that mercilessly intervened in all spheres of life.[3] Contrary to what Arendt thought, biological life and the sphere of the *oikos* were not excluded from the Greek realm of politics, but actually constituted the main target of its administration (Ojakangas 2016, 17, 49).

However, Ojakangas's criticism of Arendt as the paragon of a thinker who misunderstands the nature of the classical *poleis* assumes that Arendt draws her interpretation of the *oikos/polis* distinction directly from Aristotle's *Politics*. Although this assumption is characteristic of the studies that focus on Arendt's reading of the Greeks, it is, in fact, very problematic. Arendt always argued that it was decisive that Plato's and Aristotle's political philoso-phy was born as a counterreaction to the decay of the *polis*, symbolized above all by the death sentence of Socrates (Arendt 1978, 176; 1994, 428; 1998, 17–18; 2002, 414, 423, 457; 2005, 6–7, 36, 81, 130; 2006, 17; 2018b, 84, 230). Although Arendt clearly locates the beginning of philosophy in Plato and Aristotle in the experience of *thaumazein* (see Plato, *Tht.* 155d; Aristotle,

---

[3] This clearly runs against Schmitt's own theory, which defines the state as a "concrete concept bound to a historical epoch"—the epoch of modernity. See Schmitt 1958. On Schmitt's political uses of ancient history, which form interesting parallels with Arendt, see Suuronen 2020.

Metaph. 1.2.982b; Arendt 1998, 302n67), she also emphasizes, in a more specific sense, that "not the philosophy, but the political philosophy of Plato and Aristotle grew out of the decline of the *polis*" (Arendt 1978, 152). For Arendt, it was crucial to emphasize that both Plato and Aristotle lived and thought "in the fourth century, under the full impact of a politically decaying society and under conditions where philosophy quite consciously either deserted the political realm altogether or claimed to rule it like a tyrant" (Arendt 2018a, 279; see also 2002, 423).

All of this is crucial if one wants to grasp what Arendt means with her *oikos/polis* distinction. In order to illustrate in what sense Arendt used Plato and Aristotle as historical sources, it is fruitful to draw an analogy to the way Plato would use Socrates in his own dialogues. Just as Plato, in some of his dialogues, appropriated his own teacher as "the spokesman for theories and doctrines that were entirely un-Socratic . . . this by no means signifies that the same dialogue does not give fully authentic information about the real Socrates" (Arendt 1978, 168). This was precisely how Arendt read Plato and Aristotle: although the political philosophy of both, to different extents, was decisively influenced, burdened, and clouded by the decaying *polis*, the works of both nevertheless also obviously contained factual information about what politics *had been* like during its democratic heyday under Pericles. Arendt maintains that while Pericles' Funeral Oration, handed down to us by Thucydides, still "corresponded and articulated the innermost convictions of the people of Athens" (Arendt 1998, 205), if one wanted to dilute this same political experience from the works of Plato and Aristotle, it was necessary to read their statements against the grain in order to come to terms with their metaphysical prejudices against politics and action. It is for this reason that Arendt wonders in her *Denktagebuch* "[h]ow a philosophy of politics would have looked a hundred years before Plato" (Arendt 2002, 414; my translation).

While Arendt indeed argued that prephilosophical *polis* life was defined by its strict separation from the *oikos*, she also maintained that already by the time of Plato, these conditions were in full decay. As Arendt emphasizes, Pericles' famous words "were spoken at the beginning of the end" and the era of politics "had already come to an end when the first political philosophies were formulated" (Arendt 1998, 205). If we read *The Human Condition* carefully, we find that Arendt clearly maintains that the *oikos/polis* distinction is, in fact, no longer present in the works of Plato and Aristotle in its original, prephilosophical form. Rather, it is only "quite manifest in Plato's and Aristotle's political philosophies" (37). It is, in fact, in distinction to the Periclean age that, increasingly, the borderline between household and *polis* is occasionally blurred, especially in Plato who, probably following Socrates, began to draw his examples and illustrations for the polis from everyday experiences in private life, but also in Aristotle when he, following Plato, tentatively assumed that at least the historical origin of the polis must be connected with the necessities of life and that only its content or inherent aim (*telos*) transcends life in the "good life."   (Arendt 1998, 37)

It is Plato's utopian vision, in particular, that not only "foresaw the abolition of private property" but even imagined "an extension of the public sphere to the point of annihilating private life altogether," as Arendt highlights in *The Human Condition* (Arendt 1998, 30). The reason one could still discern the distinction between the *oikos* and the *polis* in Plato's and Aristotle's thinking was because "the background of actual political experience . . . remained so strong that the distinction between the spheres of household and political life was never doubted" (37). This is precisely what Arendt means when she notes that "Greek political philosophy still follows the order laid down by the *polis* even when it turns against it" (301). On one especially interesting occasion, Arendt describes this process of blurring of the two realms of life in Plato as follows:

Politics . . . begins already in Plato to comprehend more than politeuesthai, more than those activities which are characteristic of the Greek polis and for which the mere fulfillment of the needs and necessities of life were a pre-political condition; it begins, as it were, to expand its realm downward to the necessities of life themselves, so that to the philosophers' scorn for the perishable affairs of mortals was added the specifically Greek contempt for everything that is necessary for mere life and survival.   (Arendt 2018a, 294)

The essential fact in Plato's reaction against *polis* life is to be found in the fact that politics now expands "its realm downward to the necessities of life," that is, politics itself becomes one of those necessities that no longer has a *telos* in itself but is rather perceived as a mere precondition for the activity of contemplation. The central point here is, of course, that the prioritization of *theōria* over every other form of human activity corresponds to the relegation of action into a mere necessity.

While Arendt always thought that in Plato's political philosophy this "enormous superiority of contemplation over activity of any kind" was a rather self-evident given, more interestingly, she also argues that Aristotle's articulation of the three different *bioi*—those of enjoyment, politics, and contemplation—as explicated in his *Nichomachean Ethics* (1.5.1095b) and

Eudemian Ethics (1.4.1215a–b), was "clearly guided by the ideal of contemplation" and thus also by the corresponding relegation of politics to a mere necessity of life (Arendt 1998, 14). Citing the *Politics* (7.13.1333a), Arendt (1998, 15) argues that Aristotle makes a decisive distinction between all imaginable forms of "external physical movement," which are now described with the distinctionless and all-comprehensive concept of *a-scholia* (literally, "un-quiet"), and between the perfect stillness and quiet of contemplation. In making this argument, Arendt is, of course, fully aware that Aristotle regarded *theōria* and *nous* as the highest forms of actuality and of "action" (206n36), and her point is not to deny this but rather to argue that Aristotle is the first thinker to offer a more systematic interpretation of thinking as the highest form of action.[4] By confusing worldly action with the non-worldly solitude of contemplation and then praising the latter as the highest form of the former, Aristotle denies worldly action its autotelic ontological significance, and in doing so, offers the model through which the Western tradition will see in action a mere subsidiary of *theōria*.[5]

Here we begin to see more clearly another typical feature of Arendt's interpretation of the Greeks: she always took for granted that the contradiction between "eternity" and "immortality," between philosophy and politics, was more profound in Plato than in Aristotle. Arendt, in fact, always thought that, in a sense, Aristotle tried to "alleviate" (*mildern*; Arendt 2002, 414) Plato's hostile reaction to the death of Socrates and the *polis*. While Plato's thinking offered a mere "feeble echo of the prephilosophical Greek experience of action and speech as sheer actuality" because it instrumentalized action under the commands of *theōria*, Aristotle was "still well aware of what is at stake in politics," namely, that the *eu zēn* of the citizen lies in its "sheer actuality" and thus "outside the category of means and ends" (Arendt 1998, 206–7, also 193; see also Backman 2010, 36). While Arendt, then, portrays Plato as the "inventor" of Western metaphysics, Aristotle is depicted as his partially unwilling and unconscious follower, who, precisely through his attempts to "alleviate" Plato's reaction against the *polis*, nevertheless formulates a more systematic theory of what Plato had already, ontologically speaking, presupposed in a less articulate form. It is in this sense that Arendt sometimes refers to the "eventual prevailing of the Aristotelian tradition . . . over the purely Platonian [sic]" (Arendt 2018a, 262).[6]

---

[4] However, while Arendt does clearly note that *theōria* and *nous* constitute the highest form of *praxis*, she does not fully recognize all of the implications that this definition entails, especially the way contemplation is also situated within the framework of means and ends. See Backman 2010.

[5] On the ideal of the contemplative life in Aristotle, see also chapter 6 by Jussi Backman in this volume.

[6] Thus, Villa (1996, 50) is too hasty in claiming that Aristotle would occupy, for Arendt, "a position structurally similar to that which Plato occupies for Heidegger."

In a series of interesting reflections, Arendt describes the attitude of the philosophers toward politics with two labels: "materialism" and "idealism." Arendt maintains that our tradition of *thought* is "materialistic" to the bone in the sense that action is seen as only one of the materialistic preconditions for something higher. On the other hand, this tradition is equally "idealistic" in the sense that only *theōria* or some other and higher *telos* can justify the existence of action:

> This materialism, the conviction that all action is basically motivated by material needs, has as much remained a continuous feature of our traditional political thought as the corresponding idealism which deems that a higher ideal another, higher type of life is necessary to justify political action altogether.
>
> (Arendt 2018a, 263; see also 295)

Once again, in Arendt's reading, the birth of this "materialist" attitude has its beginning in Plato and its end in Aristotle. While Plato, in his relentless opposition to the *polis*, opens the path to seeing action as mere subsidiary of *theōria*, it is in Aristotle's political philosophy that we find "the first systematic theory of material interests" that, in a more refined manner, relegated "all political activity to the strictly material sphere of life" (Arendt 2018a, 263).

It is thus quite clear that Arendt does not offer a reading of Aristotle according to which "the politics of the *polis* did not concern things necessary to the sustenance of life related to bodily needs," as Ojakangas (2016, 49) claims.[7] Ironically, Ojakangas actually agrees with Arendt that "the affairs of the *oikos* were the primary target of Aristotelian state administration" (17), even if Ojakangas indeed clearly emphasizes this aspect of Greek thinking much more heavily than Arendt does.

---

[7] Arendt's position comes very close to the historical judgment expressed by Cornelius Castoriadis, who was himself influenced by Arendt:

"The Greece that matters is the Greece extending from the eight to the fifth century B.C.E. This is the phase during which the polis created, instituted, and, in approximately half the cases, transformed itself more or less into the democratic polis. This phase came to a close with the end of the fifth century; important things still happened in the fourth century and even afterward, notably the enormous paradox that two of the greatest philosophers who ever existed, Plato and Aristotle, were philosophers of the fourth century but were not philosophers of the Greek democratic creation. . . . [I]t follows immediately that, when we are reflecting on Greek politics, our sources cannot be the philosophers of the fourth century and, in any case, certainly not Plato, who was imbued with an ineradicable hatred of the democracy and of the demos. One is quite often grieved to see modern scholars, who have otherwise contributed much to our knowledge of Greece, searching for Greece's political thought in Plato. It is as if one were to seek the political thought of the French Revolution in a reactionary like Charles Maurras." (Castoriadis 1997, 88)

This of course raises the question: What, then, should be our sources in understanding the Greek reality? Castoriadis answers this question by asserting that one needs to look at "the reality of the polis, the reality expressed in its laws" that allows one to find "a form of political thought" in the very "practice of the polis, in its spirit." In this genealogical task, the historians "Herodotus and especially Thucydides . . . are infinitely more important . . . than Plato or others" (89).

After Aristotle, Arendt continues, all of Western thinking gradually becomes "materialistic" by taking for granted the antipolitical presuppositions of Greek philosophy:

> In the apolitical time of the fourth century, *politeuein* transforms into *philosophein*. Only now politics becomes identified with rule over others [*Herrschaft*] and is therewith moved to a lower realm of life, namely, the realm in which only the fulfillment of the necessities of life was originally situated. From this point onward politics becomes "materialistic."   (Arendt 2002, 424; my translation)

By adding politics among the necessities of life, the philosophers begin to prefigure a wholly negative understanding of human worldliness according to which one must now be equally hostile toward any kind of worldly activity—that is, one must be equally hostile toward action as toward the necessity of labor, which both appear as nothing more than distinctionless *ascholia* (Arendt 1998, 85). There is thus a curious similarity between Ojakangas's (2016, 141) argument that "a biopolitical understanding of politics is as old a phenomenon as Western political thought itself" and Arendt's claim that the "materialism" of Western thinking "is . . . as old as our history of political theory" (Arendt 1998, 183). However, the crucial difference is that while Ojakangas argues that this relegation of action to an activity that is occupied almost exclusively with biological life allows us to discover the roots of "biopolitics" in classical Greece, Arendt maintains that the Greek "materialism" was never concerned with biological life for the sake of life as such, but rather for the sake of making the *bios theōrētikos* possible. From an Arendtian perspective, the notion of "biopower" becomes intelligible only at the moment when this pole of "idealism" becomes meaningless—that is, at the dawn of modernity.

But what is the reason for this simultaneous idealization of *theōria* and the denigration of *praxis*? Can such an important transformation really be explained solely by the death of Socrates and the decaying *polis*, or are there other reasons for these historically important changes? In one of her *Denktagebuch* entries, Arendt suggests that the roots of the invasion of necessity to the realm of politics lie in the Greek slave economy. After and during the decay of the *polis*, it was precisely in the domination of slaves that the model of "the rule of <u>one</u> over many" became widely accepted and institutionalized (Arendt 2002, 367). Arendt writes:

> The revenge of slavery consists in the fact that it has transformed all political questions into problems of ruling over others [*Herrschaftsprobleme*]. Because of

the fact that one could only become the master of *anankaia* by ruling over other [*beherrschte*] human beings, that is, by beginning to rule [*herrschen*], all political relations between human beings were transformed into a matter of ruling [*Herrschen*] or being ruled [*Beherrschtwerden*].

(Arendt 2002, 368; my translation)

The slave economy, which had initially made it possible for the free citizens, for the very few, the *oligoi*, to pursue the free ways of life *above* the realm of necessity, was quickly transformed from being a mere precondition of political activity into the very model on the basis on which politics was to be organized.[8] Arendt (2018a, 284) claims that it was "almost immediately after Aristotle" that "rule over others . . . entered the political realm itself and . . . even became its dominating factor." Although this development takes place only after the decay of philosophy itself, Arendt argues that already Plato and Aristotle begin to comprehend the whole realm of human affairs in terms of what the modern age will call *sovereignty*, that is, within the framework of obedience and commands, which is elaborated explicitly only later by Jean Bodin and Thomas Hobbes (Arendt, 1972, 137; see also 2018b, 68). This forms a direct contrast to Ojakangas's (2016, 2) narrative according to which "it is quite likely that sovereignty is a genuinely modern concept."

In her *Denktagebuch*, Arendt describes this prefiguration of sovereignty through a passage from the very end of the *Laws* in which Plato speaks about two fundamental truths, necessary for any citizen to become "god-fearing." On the one hand, Plato asserts, what must be realized is that "the soul [*psychē*] is oldest of all things that partake of generation, and is immortal, and rules over all bodies"; on the other, one must "also grasp that reason which, as we have often affirmed, controls what exists among the stars," that is, the reason that controls the *kosmos* itself, the reason that is reflected in musical and mathematical theory, and the reason that should be applied systematically to ethics and political institutions (*Leg.* 12.967d–e). Arendt argues that instead of seeing the human being itself as the political *archē*, a creature capable of beginning something new in the world, Plato replaces politics as action with a world of necessity and absolute standards:

> It never occurs to Plato that the human being itself might be [a] beginning—and this even though the *archē* is defined as *psychē*. The *archē* that should rule

---

[8] Arendt describes this expansion of necessity from the *oikos* to the realm of politics by noting: "All Greek and Latin words which express some rulership over others, such as *rex, pater, anax, basileus*, refer originally to household relationships and were names the slaves gave to their master" (Arendt 1998, 32n23). Arendt derives this argument from Numa Denis Fustel de Coulanges's book *La cité antique* (1864).

[*herrschen*] is immediately interpreted as a principle. Something rules, not someone. . . . The original identification of ruling [*herrschen*] and beginning that is predetermined in language has the impact that all beginning [*Beginnen*] is already understood as ruling [*Beherrschen*] and that ultimately the element of beginning disappears entirely from the concept of rule [*Herrschaft*]. Therewith the concept of freedom disappears from political philosophy. What remains of it is an empty demand.   (Arendt 2002, 324; my translation)

When Plato replaces the capacity to begin something new and unexpected with transcendent standards and sovereign commands that apply them, "acting is pushed away from the act of beginning" (Arendt 2002, 327; my translation). Reacting to the trauma of Socrates' death, Plato not only effaces the distinction between the *oikos* and the *polis* but simultaneously replaces the relativity of the *doxai* and the inefficiency of rhetorical persuasion within the *polis* with "absolute yardsticks," which can be discovered solely through contemplative introspection, from the inwardness of the human *psychē* (Arendt 2018a, 261). Plato's trauma is reflected in the hope that if Socrates had only "threatened his judges . . . with eternal punishment and shown himself as though he possessed eternal truth, he might have frightened them into acquittal." Plato thus envisions a *polis* that knows no limits between the private and the political and one which would be ruled by a philosopher-king who, in complete distinction to Socrates, could become "capable of forcing them [the judges] as violently through arguments as though he were forcing them through actual violence" (261–2).

3. Transcendent Materialism: Christianity and the Sanctification of Life

For Arendt, the historically important fact was that after Aristotle, later generations would quickly lose the "background of actual political experience" that was still effective in Plato's and Aristotle's political philosophies. By the time Christianity arose, the mere "blurring" of the realms of the *oikos* and the *polis* in Plato and Aristotle would no longer appear as an exception in relation to the earlier Periclean age, but would rather become, as Arendt puts it in *The Human Condition*, "axiomatic to the point of banality" (Arendt 1998, 37). Here, Arendt is using the word "banality" in a similarly critical manner as in her later *Eichmann* book: after Plato and Aristotle the blurring of the *oikos/polis* distinction and the profoundly "materialistic" understanding of politics that this blurring entails become the unquestioned, unthought, and cliché-like presuppositions that will define all of Western political thinking in an axiomatic sense. While Plato's thinking signifies the birth of the Western metaphysics of "man in the singular," for whom politics and action have been relegated to a mere materialistic precondition of contemplation, the rise of Christianity completes this image by conferring "a religious sanction upon the abasement of the *vita activa* to its derivative, secondary position" (16).

It is at this point that Ojakangas's narrative of the Greek origins of biopolitics begins to appear in a radical contrast with Arendt. While Ojakangas (2016, 125–6, 134) argues that after the decline of the city-state, we witness "an essential rupture in the history of Western political discourse" because "biopolitical themes" disappear completely from the works of Christian authors—Augustine's *De civitate Dei* being the decisive historical beacon—Arendt maintains, on the contrary, that this history is defined by a subterranean continuity. For her, it is precisely with Christianity and its notion of God's revelation that "Platonic standards . . . now became fully effective" (Arendt 2018b, 88).[9] Citing Augustine's *Confessions*, Arendt claims that it is precisely in Augustine that the "preestablished harmony" between Plato's theory of forms and the Christian notion of the human being as the image of God comes to the fore: just as Plato had seen all factual beds as equally imperfect at the face of the eternal idea of *the* bed, the Christians now see all humans as equally imperfect images of God, who nevertheless "lives <u>within</u> each of them" as *the* element that makes them human in the proper sense of the word (Arendt 2002, 340; my translations). And, as Arendt (359; my translation) notes, "[f]rom this it consequently follows that the *politikon* is relocated <u>into</u> the human being as a singular creature [*Einzelwesen*]." To the extent that Christianity actually completes Plato's metaphysics of man in the singular, Arendt, in fact, fully agrees with Nietzsche's (1968, 4) famous dictum that Christianity is merely "Platonism for the people" (see Arendt 2018a, 291).

What at first seems like a loss of human animality in favor of human divinity upon closer inspection actually reveals itself as something else: as a subterranean intensification of the animalistic in the human. Arendt offers two reasons for this seemingly paradoxical development. First, she maintains that although life on earth is now only seen as the "first and most miserable stage of eternal life," it is nonetheless also seen, for the first time in history, as

---

[9] Diagnosing this continuity in no way means that Arendt would not recognize the essential differences between the Greek and Christian anthropological paradigms, as for instance Sara Brill (2019, 105–6) argues in her otherwise erudite presentation of Aristotle's "zoological" thinking. Arendt remained fully aware that the Aristotelian definition of the human being as the creature possessing *logos* rested "on the assumption that the human species belongs to and is distinguished by certain characteristics from animal life," which forms a radical contrast to the Christian doctrine of man as a *creatura Dei*, "a being created by God in his own likeness" (Arendt 2018a, 265).

a necessary precondition for the latter. Arendt argues that the Christian vision of otherworldly immortality did not only result in the increase of otherworldliness but rather "in an enormously increased importance of life on earth" (Arendt 1998, 315–16). Second, when Christianity radicalizes the distinction between *ascholia* and contemplation, it also necessarily radicalizes the levelling out of differences within the different articulations of the *vita activa* themselves. Thus, Christianity, in fact, "helped to free the laboring activity ... from some of the contempt in which antiquity had held it." Rather than signaling a loss of human animality, it is "only with the rise of Christianity" that life on earth also becomes "the highest good of man." It is only now that "to stay alive under all circumstances had become a holy duty, and suicide was regarded worse than murder" (316).[10]

It is thus not true that "Foucault is quite alone suggesting that modern governmental technologies ... also have their backdrop in Christian thought and practice" (Ojakangas 2016, 142). Arendt's reflections at the end of *The Human Condition* actually greatly resemble and predate Foucault's much later suggestions according to which one should see the Christian pastorate as the "prelude," "basis," and "background" of modern biopolitics (Foucault 2009, 184, 193, 215). The difference is, of course, that unlike Foucault, Arendt understands the influence of the Christian theology as a reappropriation of the inheritance of Greek philosophy, not as a break from it. In emphasizing the importance of Christianity, Arendt (1994, 436), like Foucault, sees the rise of Christianity and its paradoxical sanctification of human life as the crucial historical instance that gave birth to a new kind of "universal society," and thus as a historical prelude to what she will later term the sphere of "the social."

The difference between Ojakangas's and Arendt's narratives becomes even more evident if we consider one of Arendt's most famous statements in *The Human Condition*. When Arendt (1998, 23, 27) notes that the translation of Aristotle's *zōion politikon* as *animal sociale*—which already occurs in Seneca and becomes the standard translation with Aquinas—is both "an unconscious substitution" and a "profound misunderstanding," what is she actually attempting to say? Commenting on Arendt's seemingly sweeping claim that seems to paint the original Greek experience of politics in a positive light against the degenerated Latin translation, Ojakangas (2016, 138n5), citing the English editor of Aquinas's *De regno*, R. W. Dyson, argues that the Latin

---

[10] On Arendt's account of life as the "highest good" since Christianity, see also chapter 6 by Jussi Backman in this volume.

translation "social animal" actually offers a much better translation of Aristotle's intentions than "political animal."

But is Arendt really arguing that this Latin translation outright distorts Aristotle's definition? Her point is more nuanced. She argues that instead of upholding the ambivalence between Aristotle the historical source influenced by the prephilosophical *polis* and Aristotle the philosopher—the great ambivalence between "eternity" (in philosophy) and "immortality" (in politics) that, according to Arendt (1998, 17–21), characterized Greek thinking in general—the Latin translation now simply opts entirely for the second Aristotle, the philosopher, who, ontologically speaking, already relegated action to the level of labor by seeing all forms of worldly human action as mere *ascholia*. Similarly, when Arendt refers to Aquinas's claim that the life of contemplation is "simply better" than a life of action (318), Aquinas is, according to Arendt, not saying something profoundly anti-Aristotelian, but rather offering a more Aristotelian interpretation of Aristotle than Aristotle himself. In a context in which the prephilosophical *polis* had lost all its influence on Western thinking, Aquinas now fully accepts Aristotle's philosophical critique of Periclean *polis* life. Thus, Ojakangas, once again without realizing it, in fact agrees with Arendt that the vocabularies of the *oikos* and the *polis* were "'mutually contaminated' from the very outset of Western political thought" (Ojakangas 2016, 54). Where they differ is in the evaluation of the nature and relevance of this contamination, whose modern implications I will move on to examine in the concluding section.

4. Conclusion: The Birth of Species-Life and Human Superfluity

Much like Foucault's narrative of the Christian pastorate as a prelude to modern biopolitics, Arendt's account of the victory of *animal laborans* presupposes that "the modern age continued to operate under the assumption that life, and not the world, is the highest good of man" (Arendt 1998, 318). However, in distinction to the immortality of the individual soul in Christianity, the modern era would gradually begin to relocate this immortality into species-life (Arendt 2002, 686). This transformation is signaled most clearly by Karl Marx:

Marx: What happens when you replace the *logon echon* with a "laboring" (=producing) living being [*Lebewesen*]? Marx never doubted the animalistic [*das Animalische*] in the definition *animal rationale*. Through the concept of labor, he tries to connect that which is specifically human [*Menschliche*] directly to the animalistic. This means, mutatis mutandis, to derive [*ableiten*] freedom from necessity [*Notwendigkeit*] . . . Against this the Greeks: they "derive" [*leiten*] freedom from the "rational" or violent domination of necessity [*des Notwendigen*].

(Arendt 2002, 280–1; my translation)

While the Greeks founded their *poleis* by excluding the realm of biological necessity through slavery in order to make freedom beyond *anankē* possible—this was the only way to live well, as Aristotle (*Pol.* 1.1.1252b) emphasized—Marx's thinking took its bearings from the exclusion of everything but the biological. With Marx, speaking in terms of the tradition, freedom now became identical with necessity. As Arendt (2018a, 286) puts it, in terms of the tradition, Marx signals a radical turning away from philosophical "idealism" toward pure "materialism."

Just as Arendt reads the Greek philosophers as representatives of the decline of politics in Greece, she sees in Marx "a mouthpiece of the then still hidden forces of his time" (Arendt 2018a, 299) and a unique "watershed between past and present" (Arendt 2002, 350). Marx was "the greatest of modern labor theorists" (Arendt 1998, 93) and as such, his work disclosed most clearly the way in which the modern world had become "more and more concerned with life (or labor) *per se*" (Arendt 2002, 535) and how life itself had become "the ultimate point of reference" and "the highest good" in the modern age (Arendt 1998, 313). While there had been an "unfolding of glorification of Labor in Locke, Smith, Marx," of these, Marx was "the most radical one" (Arendt 2018a, 441, 443). What Marx, then, signals most clearly is nothing less than a passage to a society in which "men consider all their activities primarily as laboring activities" (289).

For Arendt, Marx signifies what Foucault (1978, 143) termed the "threshold of modernity," the moment "when the life of the species is wagered on its own political strategies," and the moment when the human being is no longer the creature who has an "additional capacity for a political existence," but rather "an animal whose politics places his existence as a living being in question." It is at this point that we can now finally begin to formulate an answer to the question I posed at the beginning of the chapter: Why did Arendt deny being "hostile to life" and why did she insist that life would easily be "whisked away," not when it is seen with contempt but precisely when it is "overestimated," as in the modern age?

It is only when politics has lost all those ideals that the philosophers and theologians still took for granted, only when what Arendt terms as the "weird game of materialism and idealism" that defines all our history comes to an end, that "the materialism inherent in the Western tradition of political thought from its very beginning could now fully assert itself, unchecked by any higher ideal" (Arendt 2018a, 263). This is precisely the moment that Arendt's narrative concerning "the rise of the social" aims to capture: the moment when we are left with nothing else than those activities that were once seen as mere preconditions to a specifically human life and the moment in which politics now becomes equal with "the public organization of the life process itself" (Arendt 1998, 28, 33, 46). From an Arendtian perspective, this is the point after which we may legitimately begin to speak about "biopower."

What so many of Arendt's readers miss is how keenly aware she was of the fact that "the economic sphere of life" had, in fact, always been "a matter of public concern." The crucial thing that made the difference, however, was that up until the modern age, "this [economic] sphere is only to a very small extent the sphere of labor" (Arendt 2018a, 253). To express this differently: When the *oikos/polis* distinction began to blur in Plato and Aristotle, this breakdown happened in the name of *theōria*—not in the name of labor or the species. Economy was indeed "politicized" in Greek philosophy, which itself reflected the reality of the decaying *polis*, but unlike in the modern age, this did not happen for the sake of life itself. Although laboring was always seen as the precondition on the basis of which the specifically human life was made possible, until the modern age, Arendt argues, life was not lived for the sake of laboring.

What Arendt's narrative concerning "the rise of the social" aims to show is that it is only in the modern age that the meaning of politics in its totality of possibilities begins to coincide with economic questions that gain their validity from the underlying reevaluation of the activity of labor; not in the sense that economy now becomes the only political thing per se, but rather the only valuable and meaningful thing within what remains a potentially broader realm of human activity and action. It is only when we understand these complex nuances that we can see why Arendt writes the following words, which summarize her historical genealogy of biological life:

The night-watchman state [*Nachtwächterstaat*], which now only guarantees life and property, is precisely the heir [*Erbe*] of the ancient state, which guaranteed all its citizens livelihood [*Lebensunterhalt*] to allow them *politeuein*. Ever since Plato had essentially replaced the *politeuein* with the *philosophein*, it became the aim of the state to first guarantee the material in order to make the *philosophein* possible; then, without any *philosophein*, to guarantee property [*das Erworbene*] and to make the activity of acquiring [*erwerben*] possible. In the place of the *politeuein* steps the *philosophein*, then acquiring, then (Marx) laboring. Plato, the "idealist," had unleashed the movement of materialization.

(Arendt 2002, 302–3; my translation)

In terms of the tradition, for the *animal laborans*, freedom had begun to signal freedom from politics, and this not for the sake of philosophy or religion, but for the sake of life itself. Arendt always thought that Marx's definition of the human being as *animal laborans* had radically antipolitical consequences and implications: the moment when life itself was seen as the highest good without any form of "idealism" to justify it was precisely the moment when human superfluity was able to emerge. It is in this sense that Arendt writes: "The notion [*Vorstellung*] that human beings are superfluous—parasites who stand in the way of history or nature—emerges when the transformation of society into a society of laborers is finished" (Arendt 2002, 337; my translation). Arendt's warning is that when human existence has been impoverished to a state where nothing else than the biological existence of species-life remains valued, we enter an era where distinctions are now made *within* the sphere of "mere *zōē*," to utilize Arendt's (1998, 97) metaphoric use of Greek terminology. As Arendt writes:

> The social revolution of our times is contained in the one fact that up to not much more than 100 years ago mere laborers had always been denied political rights, whereas we today accept as a matter of course the opinion that a non-laborer may not even have the right to stay alive.   (Arendt 2018a, 290)

These indirect implications of Marx's thinking came clearly to the fore only when "the successors of Marx began to apply his teachings" and "this non-human character of the parasites revealed itself" (Arendt 2018a, 265). It is in this sense that Arendt would claim that "Marxism as an ideology is doubtless the only link which binds the totalitarian form of governments directly to the tradition" (248). In an interesting note to her *Denktagebuch* that reflects on the relationship between human superfluity and totalitarianism, Arendt writes:

> [I]n the totalitarian regimes it becomes evident that human omnipotence corresponds to human superfluity. This is why the praxis of making human beings superfluous, partially through decimation [*Dezimierung*] and generally through the liquidation of human beings as human beings, emanates directly from the belief that everything is possible.   (Arendt 2002, 53; my translation)

While Arendt was always of the opinion that "Nazism owes nothing to any part of the Western tradition, be it German or not, Catholic or Protestant, Christian, Greek, or Roman" (Arendt 1994, 108), she did think that, despite the rather obvious fact that Lenin and Stalin left us with a deformed version of Marxism, it was, to a limited extent, possible to say that in the case of Marxism, it was "the great tradition itself" that had led to totalitarianism (Arendt 2002, 254; see also Arendt 1994, 367). On the contrary, Nazism had "no traditional basis at all" and constituted a "radical negation of any tradition"; it was defined by an "utter emptiness" that was barely disguised "with the smoke-screen of learned interpretations" (Arendt 1994, 108).

However, it is important to emphasize that it would remain Arendt's opinion throughout her life that totalitarianism was something completely unique as a political phenomenon and, rather than being based on any traditions in a causal sense, it formed a radical break in all traditions through a contingent "crystallization" of (mainly modern) political elements—imperialism, racism, the breakdown of the European nation-state system, and widespread individual atomization and loneliness being the most crucial among them (Arendt 1994, 403–5).

And yet, at the same time, Arendt would also sometimes emphasize that perhaps philosophy and our tradition were "not completely innocent." She would also blame the Western tradition for its inability to find a "pure concept of the political," which it was unable to discover precisely because it "spoke of *the* man and dealt with the fact of plurality as a side matter" (Arendt and Jaspers 1993, 203; my translations). If totalitarianism was characterized by the unprecedented organized attempt to "make human beings as human beings superfluous" (*die Überflüssigmachung von Menschen als Menschen*; 202; my translation) then the historical backdrop to this fact was to be found in the following insight: "If Man is the topic of philosophy and Men the subject of politics, then totalitarianism signifies a victory of 'philosophy' over politics—and not the other way around" (Arendt 2002, 43; my translation). Since Plato, there had no longer been "pure philosophy," because "to do philosophy always meant 'doing politics' [*politisieren*], [and it] implied a certain, predetermined disposition [*Ein-Stellung*] toward politics" (495; my translation). Even though there was no direct causal link between the Western tradition and totalitarianism, Arendt's radical critique of the Western tradition is based on the idea that the superfluity of human beings in the plural had been ontologized in the tradition itself from its very beginning.

References

Arendt, Hannah. 1972. *Crises of the Republic*. San Diego, CA: Harcourt.

Arendt, Hannah. 1978. *The Life of the Mind*. Vol. 1, *Thinking*. Edited by Mary McCarthy. San Diego, CA: Harcourt.

Arendt, Hannah. 1994. *Essays in Understanding 1930–1954: Formation, Exile, and Totalitarianism*. Edited by Jerome Kohn. New York: Schocken Books.

Arendt, Hannah. 1998. *The Human Condition*. 2nd ed. Chicago: University of Chicago Press. First published 1958.

Arendt, Hannah. 2002. *Denktagebuch 1950–1973*. 2 vols. Edited by Ingeborg Nordmann and Ursula Ludz. Munich: Piper.

Arendt, Hannah. 2005. *The Promise of Politics*. Edited by Jerome Kohn. New York: Schocken Books.

Arendt, Hannah. 2006. *Between Past and Future: Eight Exercises in Political Thought*. London: Penguin. First published 1961.

Arendt, Hannah. 2007. *Reflections on Literature and Culture*. Edited by Susannah Young-Ah Gottlieb. Stanford, CA: Stanford University Press.

Arendt, Hannah. 2018a. *Kritische Gesamtausgabe*. Vol. 6, *The Modern Challenge to Tradition: Fragmente eines Buchs*. Edited by Barbara Hahn and James McFarland. Göttingen: Wallstein.

Arendt, Hannah. 2018b. *Thinking without a Banister: Essays in Understanding 1953–1975*. Edited by Jerome Kohn. New York: Schocken Books.

Arendt, Hannah, and Karl Jaspers. 1993. *Briefwechsel 1926–1969*. Edited by Hans Saner. Munich: Piper.

Aristotle. 1926. *Nicomachean Ethics*. Translated by Harris Rackham. Cambridge, MA: Harvard University Press.

Aristotle. 1932. *Politics*. Translated by Harris Rackham. Cambridge, MA: Harvard University Press.

Aristotle. 1933. *Metaphysics*. Vol. 1, *Books 1–9*. Translated by Hugh Tredennick. Cambridge, MA: Harvard University Press.

Aristotle. 1935. *Eudemian Ethics*. In *Athenian Constitution, Eudemian Ethics, Virtues and Vices*. Translated by Harris Rackham. Cambridge, MA: Harvard University Press.

Backman, Jussi. 2010. "The End of Action: An Arendtian Critique of Aristotle's Concept of Praxis." In *COLLeGIUM: Studies across Disciplines in the Humanities and Social Sciences*, vol. 8, *Hannah Arendt: Practice, Thought and Judgment*, edited by Mika Ojakangas, 28–47. Helsinki: Helsinki Collegium for Advanced Studies. http://hdl.handle.net/10138/25817.

Blencowe, Claire. 2010. "Foucault's and Arendt's 'Insider View' of Biopolitics: A Critique of Agamben." *History of the Human Sciences* 23: 113–30. https://doi.org/10.1177/0952695110375762.

Braun, Kathrin. 2007. "Biopolitics and Temporality in Arendt and Foucault." *Time & Society* 16: 5–23. https://doi.org/10.1177/0961463X07074099.

Brill, Sara. 2019. "Aristotle's Meta-Zoology: Shared Life and Human Animality in the *Politics*." In *Antiquities beyond Humanism*, edited by Emanuela Bianchi, Sara Brill, and Brooke Holmes, 97–122. Oxford: Oxford University Press. https://doi.org/10.1093/oso/9780198805670.003.0006.

Canovan, Margaret. 1992. *Hannah Arendt: A Reinterpretation of Her Political Thought*. Cambridge: Cambridge University Press.

Castoriadis, Cornelius. 1997. "The Greek and the Modern Political Imaginary." In *World in Fragments: Writings on Politics, Society, Psychoanalysis, and the Imagination*, edited and translated by David Ames Curtis, 84–107. Stanford, CA: Stanford University Press.

Duarte, André. 2005. "Biopolitics and the Dissemination of Violence: The Arendtian Critique of the Present." *HannahArendt.net* 1 (1). http://www.hannaharendt.net/index.php/han/article/view/69/102.

Euben, J. Peter. 2000. "Arendt's Hellenism." In *The Cambridge Companion to Hannah Arendt*, edited by Dana Villa, 151–64. Cambridge: Cambridge University Press. https://doi.org/10.1017/CCOL0521641985.008.

Foucault, Michel. 1978. *The History of Sexuality*. Vol. 1, *An Introduction*. Translated by Robert Hurley. New York: Pantheon.

Foucault, Michel. 2009. *Security, Territory, Population: Lectures at the Collège de France 1977–1978*. Edited by Michel Senellart, translated by Graham Burchell. New York: Picador.

Gündogdu, Ayten. 2015. *Rightlessness in an Age of Rights: Hannah Arendt and the Contemporary Struggles of Migrants*. Oxford: Oxford University Press.

Jaeger, Werner. 1947. *Paideia: The Ideals of Greek Culture*. Vol. 3, *The Conflict of Cultural Ideals in the Age of Plato*. Translated by Gilbert Highet. Oxford: Oxford University Press.

Lemke, Thomas. 2011. *Biopolitics: An Advanced Introduction*. Translated by Eric Frederick Trump. New York: New York University Press.

Nietzsche, Friedrich. 1968. *Kritische Gesamtausgabe*. Vol. 6, bk. 2, *Jenseits von Gut und Böse, Zur Genealogie der Moral*. Edited by Giorgio Colli and Mazzino Montinari. Berlin: Walter de Gruyter.

Ojakangas, Mika. 2016. *On the Greek Origins of Biopolitics: A Reinterpretation of the History of Biopower*. London: Routledge.

Oksala, Johanna. 2010. "Violence and the Biopolitics of Modernity." *Foucault Studies* 10: 23–43. https://doi.org/10.22439/fs.v0i10.3122.

Pitkin, Hanna Fenichel. 1998. *The Attack of the Blob: Hannah Arendt's Concept of the Social*. Chicago: University of Chicago Press.

Plato. 1921. *Theaetetus*. Translated by Harold N. Fowler. In *Plato in Twelve Volumes*, vol. 12. Cambridge, MA: Harvard University Press.

Plato. 1926. *Laws*. Vol. 2, *Books 7–12*. Translated by Robert Gregg Bury. Cambridge, MA: Harvard University Press.

Schaap, Andrew. 2010. "The Politics of Need." In *Power, Judgment and Political Evil: In Conversation with Hannah Arendt*, edited by Andrew Schaap, Danielle Celermaier, and Vrasidas Kalidis, 157–70. Farnham: Ashgate. https://doi.org/10.4324/9781315601854-11.

Schmitt, Carl. 1958. "Staat als ein konkreter, an eine geschichtliche Epoche gebundener Begriff." In *Verfassungsrechtliche Aufsätze aus den Jahren 1924–1954: Materialien zu einer Verfassungslehre*, 372–85. Berlin: Duncker & Humblot.

Suuronen, Ville. 2018. "Resisting Biopolitics: Hannah Arendt as a Thinker of Automation, Social Rights, and Basic Income." *Alternatives* 43 (1): 35–53. https://doi.org/10.1177/0304375418789722.

Suuronen, Ville. 2020. "Mobilizing the Western Tradition for Present Politics: Carl Schmitt's Polemical Uses of Roman Law, 1923–1945." *History of European Ideas* 47 (5): 748–72. https://doi.org/10.1080/01916599.2020.1818115.

Tsao, Roy T. 2002. "Arendt against Athens: Rereading the Human Condition." *Political Theory* 30 (1): 97–123. https://doi.org/10.1177/0090591702030001005.

Vatter, Miguel. 2006. "Natality and Biopolitics in Arendt." *Revista de Ciencia Politica* 26 (2): 137–59. https://doi.org/10.4067/S0718-090X2006000200008.

Villa, Dana. 1996. *Arendt and Heidegger: The Fate of the Political*. Princeton, NJ: Princeton University Press.

Wolin, Richard. 2003. *Heidegger's Children: Hannah Arendt, Karl Löwith, Hans Jonas, and Herbert Marcuse*. Princeton, NJ: Princeton University Press.

8

From Biopolitics to Biopoetics and Back Again

On a Counterintuitive Continuity in Foucault's Thought

Sergei Prozorov

1. Introduction

In the second lecture of his 1980–1 lecture course at the Collège de France, *Subjectivity and Truth*, Michel Foucault discusses various possible designations for the arts of living or techniques of the self, developed in Greek and Latin antiquity, that became the main focus of his research in the 1980s. The manuscript of the lectures features one curious fragment that was not uttered in the lecture itself. In this fragment, Foucault considers the term "biopoetics" as the term covering these numerous arts or techniques:

> Biopoetics would be justified because it is indeed a sort of personal fabrication of one's own life (note that in these arts the question often arises of whether or not an act is beautiful). One could thus follow the problem of sexual conduct: biopoetics where it is a matter of the aesthetic-moral conduct of individual existence; biopolitics where it is a matter of the normalization of sexual conducts according to what is considered politically as the requirement of a population.
>
> (Foucault 2017, 34n)

This note remains the only instance in Foucault's lectures where the concepts of biopoetics and biopolitics figure together, addressing different aspects of sexual conduct. Whereas biopoetics pertains to individual existence taken up in the "aesthetic-moral" aspect, biopolitics pertains to the normalization undertaken on the level of the population. The notion of biopoetics no longer appears in Foucault's texts after this course and has not been addressed in Foucault studies. In the contemporary literature, this notion has been applied

Sergei Prozorov, *From Biopolitics to Biopoetics and Back Again: On a Counterintuitive Continuity in Foucault's Thought* In: *Biopolitics and Ancient Thought*. Edited by: Jussi Backman and Antonio Cimino, Oxford University Press.
© Oxford University Press 2022. DOI: 10.1093/oso/9780192847102.003.0009

primarily in the field of literary theory in two rather different contexts, quite at odds with the focus of Foucault's research. Firstly, biopoetics was advanced as a research program that applies the insights from evolutionary biology to the analysis of literary works (Turner and Cooke 1999). Secondly, it was offered as a synthesis of the problematic of biopolitics with the concerns of literary theory and the refoundation of the latter on an apparently materialist basis (Guyer 2015; see more generally De Boever 2013; Breu 2014).[1] However, none of the studies of biopoetics so far has ventured to explicate Foucault's own account of the relationship between biopoetics and biopolitics.

In this chapter, we explore the meaning and the significance of Foucault's note for our understanding of the relation between his more explicitly political writings and his turn toward the ancient techniques of the self in the 1980s. We argue that Foucault's distinction between biopoetics and biopolitics simultaneously functions as the *articulation* of the otherwise disparate research projects into a meaningful whole. Moreover, even though this articulation is not explicitly pursued in the remainder of the 1980–1 lecture course, its functioning is demonstrated in Foucault's extensive analysis of the transformations in the discourse on marriage in the Hellenistic period, in which biopoetic techniques are presented as the resolution to the problems that, only somewhat anachronistically, could be viewed as biopolitical.

Our reading will go against the more established approach to Foucault's dossier on biopolitics. According to this approach, by 1979 Foucault abandoned not merely the explicit theorization of biopolitics begun in *"Society Must Be Defended"* (Foucault 2003) and the first volume of *The History of Sexuality* (Foucault 1990), but also the wider inquiry into modern European governmentality in which biopolitics was recontextualized in the 1977–8 lectures (see Foucault 2007, 1–11). On a strictly exoteric level, Foucault's discourse on biopolitics expired at the latest with the 1978–9 lectures *The Birth of Biopolitics* (2008), which, as some commentators have correctly noted, were not really about biopolitics either (see Collier 2011, 16–17; Forti 2012, 242–66; Hoffman 2013, 57, 100–2 for alternative readings). Yet, given the abundance of both theoretical and empirical research on biopolitics in the last two decades, in which the concept was expanded and transformed far beyond Foucault's original articulation, sticking to this exoteric level appears to be an overly restrictive methodological choice that is, moreover, entirely contrary to Foucault's well-known vision of his work as a toolkit available for experimental use. In line with this vision, we take Foucault's note on

---

[1] The term has also been used in the context of biosemiotics to interpret the entirety of life as a meaning-making process (see Weber 2016).

biopoetics and biopolitics in *Subjectivity and Truth* as sufficient reason to reject the assumption of a strict discontinuity between the genealogical-governmental phase in Foucault's writings and his turn to the Greeks.

While the resonances between these phases have already been explored elsewhere (see Elden 2016, 2017; Forti 2012; Hoffman 2013), the dominant assumption in the studies of biopolitics remains that Foucault's work on the subject is limited to the first volume of *The History of Sexuality*, "*Society Must Be Defended*," *Security, Territory, Population*, and, perhaps in name only, *The Birth of Biopolitics* (Foucault 1990, 2003, 2007, 2008). On the contrary, we argue that our understanding of Foucault's notion of biopolitics will remain incomplete unless it also takes account of his writings on the biopoetics of antiquity. Our argument in this chapter will proceed in two steps. First, we reconstitute Foucault's analysis of the Stoic discourse on marriage in *Subjectivity and Truth* as a paradigm for the articulation of biopolitics and biopoetics that opens governmental rationalities to various forms of reception, readjustment, or resistance by the subject. We then proceed to Foucault's study of the Cynics in his final lecture course *The Courage of Truth* (Foucault 2011), in which biopoetics is in turn submitted to a politicization that does not take the form of governmental rationality but rather consists in the constitution of a form of life through the confrontation with the existing order of the world. Finally, in the conclusion we address the implications of our reading for contemporary discussions of affirmative biopolitics.

2. Making Government Livable: The Conjunction of Biopolitics and Biopoetics

In the *Subjectivity and Truth* lectures, Foucault analyzes the philosophical discourse on marriage in the Hellenistic period, particularly in such Stoic authors as Musonius Rufus, Hierocles, and Antipater of Tarsus (Foucault 2017, 123–203). The focus of the analysis is the relationship between discourses of truth and the constitution of the subject (see Prozorov 2019 for a detailed discussion). These texts, which prescribe the restriction of sexual relations to the married couple, modified the earlier Greek ethics of *aphrodisia*, which did not privilege any particular type or setting for sexual practices. Instead, the Greeks of the classical period affirmed two principles regulating the "use of pleasures": the principle of activity that discredited any passive position in a sexual relation and the principle of socio-sexual isomorphism that required a proper sexual act to respect the partners' social standing and roles. Without prohibiting any particular type of sexual act, this ethics of *aphrodisia* could nonetheless adjudicate between proper and improper acts (Foucault 2017, 75–93). For instance, a sexual act between a free man and a male slave was proper as long the free man was in the active position and turned improper when he assumed a passive position. On the other hand, a sexual act of a free man with a married woman conformed to the principle of activity but violated the principle of isomorphism insofar as it encroached on the rights of one's neighbor. In contrast to this ethics of activity and isomorphism, the approach to sexuality in the Stoic discourse increasingly privileges the family as the sole legitimate locus of sexual activity, limits sexual relations to the function of procreation, and transforms marriage from an economic relation into an affective bond that goes beyond mere carnal pleasure.

In Foucault's argument, it would be a mistake to view this discourse as an expression of a new moral code arising in the Hellenistic period. Instead, he approaches it as belonging to the genre of "techniques of the self" or, more strictly, techniques of living (*technai peri ton bion*), by which one analyzes, evaluates, and transforms one's existence. These techniques did not produce any break with the existing moral code of the time or the fundamental values of the period, but rather permitted reconciling the emerging Hellenistic code of behavior that valorized marriage with the fundamental values of the Greek ethics of *aphrodisia*. The valorization of marriage as a singular relation distinct from the wider field of social practices appears to exclude the principles of socio-sexual isomorphism and male activity. Nonetheless, the Stoic discourse brought the two together by transforming the relationship to the self at work in sexual practices. Instituting the division between private and public life, making sexual desire the privileged object of the relation to oneself, and linking sexual pleasure with the affective domain, the Stoic philosophers made it possible to continue to affirm male activity and socio-sexual isomorphism while at the same time abiding by the strict rules of conjugal fidelity and the prescription of the affective bond with one's spouse. It was precisely the inequality between husband and wife that now obliged the husband to guide and direct the wife by his own example, thereby proscribing all extramarital sexual relations that this inequality previously allowed and instituting the principle of reciprocity between spouses.

The isolation of conjugal sexuality as a privileged domain permitted to reinscribe the Greek principle of activity and the prescription of self-control it entailed in terms of the idea of self-mastery and the renunciation of extramarital desire (Foucault 2017, 275–6). The valorization of activity exercised on the other was thus converted into an active domination of oneself. Thus, Foucault is able to conclude that the Stoic discourse on sexuality neither reflected nor prescribed a new moral code or a system of values but rather enabled the subject to "[be] transformed in such a way that he can live in this code of conjugality while still maintaining the value of socio-sexual continuity and the principle of activity" (267). In this manner, the old Greek aristocracy could maintain its traditional values in the condition of social and political transformations in the Hellenistic monarchies, marked by the rise of new elites and the weakening of traditional aristocratic privileges: "Philosophical discourse was proposing, was conveying techniques, precisely in order to be able to live, to accept the modes of behavior proposed and imposed from outside, techniques that literally rendered them livable" (275). Foucault's choice of words here is highly important. If we consider the transformations in the modes of governance in the Hellenistic monarchies to be biopolitical insofar as they proposed and imposed modes of behavior, then the discourses on the techniques of living were what made these biopolitical regulations "livable," in the sense of both being tolerable in actual existence and being endowed with some degree of viability, without which they would have remained dead letter. The biopoetic discourse on marriage transformed the subject's relationship to itself, making it possible for him (and never her!) to subjectivize the emerging moral code in a specific manner that would also permit upholding older values that nominally conflicted with it.

This example clearly demonstrates the articulation between biopoetics and biopolitics. While evidently different in many ways, these practices at least unfold on the same level and have ultimately the same object: one's life that could be formed, reformed, transformed, or perhaps deformed in both large-scale regulatory governance of populations and micro-level individual or group exercises that adapted, adjusted, or resisted the rationalities of this governance. Unless this articulation is rendered explicit, the importance of these micro-level exercises for political subjectivation is not appreciated, leading to the familiar interpretation of Foucault's turn to the Greeks as a turn away from politics in any meaningful sense.

Ironically, exactly the same reception appears to meet the work of the author who has arguably done most to popularize the notion of biopolitics since the 1990s, namely, Giorgio Agamben. In the final volume of his *Homo Sacer* series, Agamben performed a similar shift from the studies of sovereign power and economic government toward the quotidian domain of habits, manners, and lifestyles. Just as Foucault's "Greek turn" came as a surprise after decades of focus on European modernity, this new focus of Agamben's work at first glance appears unexpected. Having gained notoriety with hyperbolic claims about states of exception and concentration camps in the early volumes of the *Homo Sacer* series, Agamben has now isolated an almost proverbially banal site of lifestyle, from dating and diet to sadomasochism and shopping, and ultimately including all the acts involving "nutrition, digestion, urination, defecation, sleep, sexuality" that we tend to file under the "private" domain, thereby precluding any understanding of their political significance (Agamben 2016, xx).

This makes all the more important Agamben's theorization of the ontological aspect of these quotidian acts and practices that may help us understand what Foucault intended by designating the techniques of the self as "biopoetic." In Agamben's reading, Foucault's overwhelmingly detailed study of the Greek and early Roman sexual regimen, mnemonic exercises, and techniques of the examination of conscience and truth-telling may have obscured for his readers the ontological question that all those inquiries were meant to elucidate: What is the subject that *is* only the care of its own *self*, whose sole consistency is its own self-fashioning?[2] Agamben's own inquiry into forms of life attempts to show that lifestyle, habits, and taste, which Foucault analyzed under the rubric of "aesthetics of existence" (Foucault 1992, 12, 89–93), are matters far too important to be abandoned to aesthetics: "[A]nyone who practices a *poiesis* and an activity . . . are anonymous living beings who, by always rendering inoperative the works of language, of vision, of bodies, seek to have an experience of themselves and to constitute their life as form-of-life" (Agamben 2016, 247). Thus, rather than treat lifestyle in aesthetic terms, Agamben proposes to reinscribe it in terms of ontology and ethics that, moreover, are found to coincide in it:

> It is necessary to decisively subtract tastes from the aesthetic dimension and rediscover their ontological character, in order to find in them something like a new ethical territory. It is not a matter of attributes or properties of a subject who judges but of the mode in which each person, in losing himself as subject, constitutes himself as form-of-life. The secret of taste is what form of life must solve, has always already solved and displayed. . . . If every body is affected by its form-of-life as by a clinamen or a taste, the ethical subject is that subject that constitutes itself in relation to this clinamen, the subject who bears witness to its tastes, takes responsibility for the mode in which it is affected by its inclinations. Modal ontology, the ontology of the *how*, coincides with an ethics.   (Agamben 2016, 231)

Rather than merely adorn or embellish one's already constituted form of life, tastes, habits, and manners of living constitute both this form and the

---

[2] On this, see Prozorov 2017. On the care of the self and the aesthetics of existence in Foucault, see also chapter 4 by Kalliopi Nikolopoulou in this volume.

subject that takes a stance, bears witness, and assumes responsibility for this constitution. While this question is beyond the scope of the present chapter, the idea of biopoetic subjectivation suggests that it would be fruitful to focus not only on the relation between Foucault's "middle" period and his later turn to the Greeks but also on the relation of biopolitical thinking to Foucault's earlier analyses of the "untamed ontology" of life in *The Order of Things* (Foucault 1970, 282; see also Tarizzo 2011).

Interestingly, this poetic dimension is reserved by Foucault only for these quotidian, micro-level exercises. While all power was endowed with productivity in the methodological prolegomena of the first volume of *The History of Sexuality* (Foucault 1990, 92–102), the actual analysis of the kind undertaken in *Subjectivity and Truth* does not approach macro-level shifts in governmental rationalities as directly productive of transformations in subjectivity. In order to be rendered livable, these shifts required the biopoetic interventions that (re)constituted the subjects' forms of life, which also involved intricate adjustments and shifts of emphasis or focus in these macro-level rationalities of government. Biopolitics, on this reading, needs biopoetics to acquire some hold on the *bios* of the governed, which might come at the cost of substantial modifications in its rationalities that make them livable for the subjects involved.

This perspective suggests that biopoetics and biopolitics do not exclude or succeed one another but may rather be viewed as operating in conjunction in various historical contexts. The perception of a strong discontinuity in Foucault's work between the studies of modern biopolitics and the analyses of Greek and Roman biopoetics thus appears to be at least exaggerated and should rather be rethought as a question of emphasis. While Foucault's analysis of modernity focused on biopolitics and only rarely touched upon biopoetics (for example, in his discussion of counter-conduct, see Foucault 2007, 201–12), his studies of antiquity engage in overwhelming detail with the biopoetic dimension while offering only very general or skeletal formulations about macro-level biopolitical rationalities. This is certainly not because Foucault was unaware of the existence (for example, in ancient Greece) of rationalities of government that we may today easily recognize as biopolitical, be they the upbringing of children in Sparta or the designs of population management in Aristotle's *Politics* (see Ojakangas 2016). The reason that Foucault did not address these rationalities is, in our view, simply and precisely because they are already sufficiently recognizable to us, in contrast to the biopoetic techniques whose significance has declined in the modern era and which require a more detailed elaboration. Rather than suggest that antiquity was biopoetic and modernity biopolitical, Foucault simply focused on what was more distinctive and interesting about each period.

3. The Cynics: Politicizing Biopoetics

Foucault's turn toward biopoetics began with his 1980 course *On the Government of the Living* (2014). Similarly to the lectures of the previous year, *The Birth of Biopolitics*, the course title is deceptive: just as there was nothing about the birth of biopolitics in the 1979 course, the 1980 lectures did not deal with the government of the living in any meaningful way, but from the outset adopted a focus on the subjectivizing aspects of the injunction to truth-telling in early Christianity. The shift of perspective toward biopoetics appears even more pronounced with the turn to the ancient Greece and Rome in the subsequent courses—*Subjectivity and Truth* (1980–1), *The Hermeneutics of the Subject* (1981–2), *The Government of Self and Others* (1982–3)—and volumes two and three of *The History of Sexuality*. However, in his study of the Cynics in his final course *The Courage of Truth* (1983–4), Foucault performs yet another perspectival shift, subjecting biopoetics itself to a kind of politicization that would not be reducible to the government of populations.

This politicization erupts within the very discourse of truth-telling (*parrhēsia*) that primarily preoccupies Foucault in his studies of antiquity. Whereas *On the Government of the Living* concluded by demonstrating how the obligation to tell the truth in Christianity was inextricably tied to one's complete and permanent obedience to the other (Foucault 2014, 265–78, 307–8), the Cynic *parrhēsia* explicitly inverted this relationship: truth-telling is only possible as an act of *disobedience* in the face of all social norms and conventions. In contrast to other forms of *parrhēsia* practiced in ancient Greece, the veridiction of the Cynics was no longer a condition for practicing politics or even an instrument for the attainment of political ends, but rather became itself political in demonstrating how one could live otherwise yet still in accordance with the truth, and thereby pointing to the possibilities of the transformation of the world at large (Foucault 2011, 217–19).

Resonating with Agamben's later inquiries into the "form-of-life," in which *bios* and *zōē* become indistinct, Foucault traced the way the Cynics' true life was constituted through an intricate operation that made life and truth reciprocally conditional: "The Cynics turn life into a vehicle of truth and truth into a vehicle of life, bringing forth a perfect communion between life and truth, such that the body gives form to truth and truth gives form to body" (Lemm 2014, 210). In Foucault's reading, truth in classical Greek philosophy was defined by four attributes: it was something unconcealed, undistorted, straight, and sovereign. Rather than contest any of these four attributes in favor of some new idea of truth, the Cynics appropriated them as inherent in life itself, which evidently altered their conventional meanings. First, the Cynic's life "is without modesty, shame, and human respect. It is a life which does in public, in front of everyone, what only dogs and animals dare to do, and which men usually hide" (Foucault 2011, 243, 252–5). This scandalous behavior that does not recognize social conventions and insists on the complete publicity of all its actions is perhaps the most famous aspect of Cynicism. But this shameless or brazen life is only the literal and consistent application of the principle of unconcealment that defines the Platonic true *logos*. While the Platonic principle of unconcealment sought to secure the conventional and proper forms of life that had nothing to hide precisely because they were fully in accordance with the prevailing codes, the Cynics took this principle to the extreme, arguing that there could be nothing bad in whatever nature had endowed us with.

Second, the idea of true life as unalloyed or undistorted is converted by the Cynics into the principle of a life that is utterly indifferent to its own needs. The Platonic idea of a life purified from all disorder and discord, from all things material and physical, is "revaluated" by the Cynics through the relocation of the ideal of purity toward the very domain of the physical and the bodily that it was supposed to be purified from. In this domain, pure life is a life of poverty, stripped of everything superficial and inessential. For the Cynics, poverty is not an unfortunate accident or even a cultivated indifference to wealth but an active pursuit of ever greater dispossession that seeks to arrive at the absolutely indispensable.

Third, the Platonic principle of a straight life in accordance with the *logos* is converted into a life that accepts no law other than that of nature (Foucault 2011, 262–4). Only what is natural is truly in accordance with the *logos*, hence all social conventions and codes must be abandoned, be it marriage, family, or even the prohibition of incest. This is why the Cynics, in Foucault's reading, adopted the idea of animality as "a reduced, but prescriptive form of life. Animality is not a given; it is a duty. Animality is an exercise. It is a task for oneself and at the same time a scandal for others" (265).

Finally, the Cynics simultaneously apply and reverse the Platonic principle of the immutable and self-contained sovereignty of the true life. The Cynic infamously proclaims himself the true "king," precisely by virtue of his scandalous, dirty, and impoverished life. While in Platonism and Stoicism the philosopher was often *compared* to a king because he was capable of governing both his own soul and the souls of others in accordance with the truth, the Cynic asserts that he is "the only true king. And vis-à-vis the kings of the world, crowned kings sitting on their thrones, he is the anti-king who shows how hollow, illusory and precarious the monarchy of kings is" (Foucault 2011, 275). Yet rather than live a life of contentment and enjoyment, the Cynic king submits his life to tireless tests in order to be able to take care of others, to lead them out of their untruth by his own manifestation of the true life. This care is undertaken in a characteristically confrontational or even "beastly" manner, "with a bark": "[The] Cynic is of service in a very different way than through leading an exemplary life or giving advice. He is useful because he battles, because he bites, because he attacks" (279).

In all these four reversals, the principle of animality remains crucial as a paradoxical *criterion* of truth. The name "Cynic" is of course translated from ancient Greek as "dog-like." While there are various explanations of this comparison, Foucault finds its basis in the destitute, brute, and stripped mode of existence of the Cynics, their "manifestation, in complete naked-ness, of the truth of the world and of life" (Foucault 2011, 183). This mode of existence was not merely an extreme form of self-assertion or self-fashioning but also as the manifestation, the bearing witness to the truth, whereby the body itself became "the visible theatre of the truth" (179–80). Foucault argues that ancient thought generally approached animality as a "point of repulsion" for the constitution of the human being, an "absolute point of differentiation" that, in Agamben's later terminology, was "inclusively excluded" from the human as its negative foundation (Agamben 2004, 18–27). A true life was then the life that successfully excluded, subjected, or dominated one's animal nature. In contrast, the Cynics transform this negative foundation into a pos-itive telos of human existence, whereby animality is not a given to be mas-tered or conquered within oneself but a *model* to be attained in one's existence through courageous practices of truth-telling that break with established ways of living. Yet there is nothing in this model that is not already *given* by nature, which therefore need not be subjected or dominated for this model to be implemented. On the contrary, the constitution of a true *bios* is condi-tioned by the prior grafting of its precepts onto *zōē* itself. Animality is not the other that must be subjected and mastered for a life of truth to be possible but rather the manner in which this life unfolds in the self.

This manner makes all the difference. Despite the fundamental identity between the ideational contents of the truths of the Cynics and their adver-saries, their life remains radically *other* than the life lived by the ostensible proponents of truth:

[T]he Cynic changes the values of the currency and reveals that the true life can only be an other life, in relation to the traditional life of men, including philosophers. . . . [I]t is from the point of view of this other life that the usual life of ordinary people will be revealed as precisely other than the true. I live in an other way, and by the very otherness of my life, I show you that what you are looking for is somewhere other than where you are looking for it, that the path you are taking is other than the one you should be taking.   (Foucault 2011, 314)

We now understand the significance of the final words of Foucault's final lecture course: "[T]here is no establishment of the truth without an essential position of otherness: the truth is never the same; there can be truth only in the form of the other world and the other life" (Foucault 2011, 340). However familiar it is in its nominal content, the truth is made other by its relocation from the domain of discourse toward the realm of life. In the very same movement, life is also made other by the truth, attaining the status of a philosophical life without transcending or negating any of its natural dispositions. By disseminating the truth in its own transformed existence, this life can eventually change the world at large. While both Platonism and Christianity posited, in their own different ways, the existence of *the other world* beyond this one, the Cynics sought to attain another life right here in *this* world and thereby make it *otherwise* that it was. By virtue of their disobedience to all conventional moral codes, the Cynics made every act of veridictive subjectivation a part of the transformation of the wider world: "Through this dissonant irruption of the 'true life' in the midst of the chorus of lies and pretences, of accepted injustice and concealed iniquities, the Cynic makes 'another world' loom up on the horizon, the advent of which would presuppose the transformation of the present world" (Gros 2011, 354). While their orientation toward the transformation of the world renders Cynic *parrhēsia* irreducibly political, their embodiment of the principles governing this transformation in life itself makes it unmistakably *bio*-political.

In his 2010 review of Foucault's two final lecture courses, Michael Hardt briefly addressed the biopolitical significance of the Cynics. Making a distinction between (governmental) biopower and (emancipatory) biopolitics, Hardt argued that while

[biopower] is a form of power in which the life of populations becomes the central object of rule, the militancy of the ancient Cynics is clearly an entirely different politics of life. Biopolitics is the realm in which we have the freedom to make another life for ourselves, and through that life transform the world. Biopolitics is thus not only distinct from biopower but also may be the most effective weapon to combat it.   (Hardt 2010, 159)

In our view, this distinction between biopower and biopolitics is misleading for two reasons. First, it pits politics against power in a manner that is entirely at odds with Foucault's approach, as if there could be a politics without power relations. Secondly, and specifically with respect to the Cynics, their *parrhēsia* is biopolitical precisely and solely to the extent that it brings the power of one's life into play in one's affirmation of truth—it is an *exercise of biopower whose object fully coincides with its subject*. By virtue of this coincidence, biopower is no longer conceived as domination *over* one's life but rather as the power *of* that life itself, which enables the subject to dismantle the effects of domination within one's own existence and thereby open up the possibility of the transformation of the world at large. While Hardt is entirely correct about biopolitics as the realm of freedom for the late Foucault, it can only serve as such by the Cynics' singular operation of the mutual empowerment of truth and life through their very indistinction. Rather than merely resist biopower, the Cynics sought to exercise it in the actual transformation of their lives and the world at large.

Thus, the articulation of biopolitics and biopoetics in Foucault's thought permits us to rethink the problematic of biopolitics rather more broadly than as an episode in the genealogy of modern Western governmentality (or even its ancient prehistory). Life no longer figures solely as the object of politicization in governmental practices but also as the subject of politicization in the course of the confrontation with the world, including its governmental rationalities. While the studies of biopolitics often tend to view its operations as objectifying individuals and populations (and, especially in the Agambenian declension, even exposing them to extermination), Foucault's later work affirms that life is not the eternal victim of power and there is more to biopolitics than "bio-government." The "untamed ontology" of life not only underlies the subjection of living beings to governmental rationalities but also empowers dissensual subjectivities to confront and transform the world in which they dwell.

4. Conclusion

Our account of two patterns of interface between biopolitics and biopoetics in Foucault's late writings highlights the continuity between the two periods of his writings, conventionally seen as focusing respectively on power and ethics. We have demonstrated how these two dimensions have been articulated in the Greek and Roman practices of the self, either through the biopoetic reception and readjustment of governmental rationalities in the Stoic discourse on marriage or through the politicization of biopoetics in Cynic *parrhēsia* that found in the animalistic and confrontational form of life the path toward the wider transformation of the world.

But what are the implications of our argument beyond the exegetical debates in Foucault studies? Both the Stoic emphasis on making governmental practices livable and the Cynic attempt to translate truth into life strongly resonate with the contemporary debates on affirmative biopolitics, which authors such as Agamben (2016) and Esposito (2008) interpret as a politics whose form (*bios*) is derived from *zōē* itself. This leads them to a fascinating (if also paradoxical) quest for a form that would consist in formlessness alone. In order not to negate bare life in the name of its privileged form, the only legitimate form must be somehow based on bare life itself, yet its very bareness evidently makes for a poor basis for the constitution of any form. In contrast, Foucault's reading of the Cynics suggests that a more fruitful alternative to the derivation of *bios* from *zōē* may be the reverse move of bringing the *bios* down to the level of *zōē*, whereby the truths of *bios* are verified as viable in bare life that thereby acquires a form from which it would nonetheless remain indistinct.

Moreover, in contrast to the discourses of affirmative biopolitics that envision it in terms of a radical rupture that lies entirely in the future, Foucault's Cynic version of affirmative biopolitics has the benefit of being based on a well-known historical example. This example was not restricted to antiquity but served as the point of descent of the idea of a militant or revolutionary life that would have enormous influence in the Western tradition. In the lectures on the Cynics, Foucault remarks that militancy was originally not merely a matter of ideological commitments but also a form of life that had to "manifest directly, by its visible form, its constant practice, and its immediate existence, the concrete possibility and the evident value of an *other* life, which is the true life" (Foucault 2011, 184). The radical break with the existing norms, conventions, and habits that the militant ideology promised on the level of the overall social order was to be immediately embodied in the life of the militant. Foucault then proceeded to ridicule the French Left of his time for abandoning this theme of the manifestation of the truth in life or, worse, practicing it in the inverted form of utter conventionalism and conservatism, adopting "all the accepted values, all the most customary forms of behavior, and all the most traditional schemas of conduct" (186). In our view, this criticism remains both timely today and generalizable far beyond France.

While there is no shortage of apparently radical ideas in circulation, there does not seem to be much radicality in the ways of life promoted and practiced by their supporters, which leads to the inevitable suspicion that these ideas were never meant to be lived but only preached. Yet the lesson of Foucault's final lectures is that "another world" may only be reached through an "other life," through making one's life otherwise than it was. Only in this manner may ideas about changing the world gain any kind of vitality.

References

Agamben, Giorgio. 2004. *The Open: Man and Animal*. Translated by Kevin Attell. Stanford, CA: Stanford University Press.

Agamben, Giorgio. 2016. *The Use of Bodies*. Translated by Adam Kotsko. Stanford, CA: Stanford University Press.

Breu, Christopher. 2014. *Insistence of the Material: Literature in the Age of Biopolitics*. Minneapolis: University of Minnesota Press.

Collier, Stephen. 2011. *Post-Soviet Social: Neoliberalism, Social Modernity, Biopolitics*. Princeton, NJ: Princeton University Press.

Cooke, Brett, and Frederick Turner, eds. 1999. *Biopoetics: New Explorations in the Arts*. Saint Paul, MN: Paragon.

De Boever, Arne. 2013. *Narrative Care: Biopolitics and the Novel*. New York: Bloomsbury.

Elden, Stuart. 2016. *Foucault's Last Decade*. London: Polity.

Elden, Stuart. 2017. *Foucault: The Birth of Power*. London: Polity.

Esposito, Roberto. 2008. *Bíos: Biopolitics and Philosophy*. Translated by Timothy Campbell. Minneapolis: University of Minnesota Press.

Forti, Simona. 2012. *New Demons: Rethinking Power and Evil Today*. Translated by Zakiya Hanafi. Stanford, CA: Stanford University Press.

Foucault, Michel. 1970. *The Order of Things: An Archaeology of the Human Sciences*. Translated by Alan Sheridan. London: Tavistock.

Foucault, Michel. 1990. *The History of Sexuality*. Vol. 1, *An Introduction*. Translated by Robert Hurley. New York: Random House.

Foucault, Michel. 1992. *The History of Sexuality*. Vol. 2, *The Use of Pleasure*. Translated by Robert Hurley. London: Penguin.

Foucault, Michel. 2003. *"Society Must be Defended": Lectures at the Collège de France 1975–1976*. Translated by David Macey. London: Picador.

Foucault, Michel. 2007. *Security, Territory, Population: Lectures at the Collège de France 1977–1978*. Translated by Graham Burchell. Basingstoke: Palgrave Macmillan.

Foucault, Michel. 2008. *The Birth of Biopolitics: Lectures at the Collège de France 1978–1979*. Translated by Graham Burchell. Basingstoke: Palgrave Macmillan.

Foucault, Michel. 2010. *The Government of Self and Others: Lectures at the Collège de France 1982–1983*. Translated by Graham Burchell. Basingstoke: Palgrave Macmillan.

Foucault, Michel. 2011. *The Courage of the Truth: Lectures at the Collège de France 1983–1984*. Translated by Graham Burchell. Basingstoke: Palgrave Macmillan.

Foucault, Michel. 2014. *On the Government of the Living: Lectures at the Collège de France 1979–1980*. Translated by Graham Burchell. Basingstoke: Palgrave Macmillan.

Foucault, Michel. 2017. *Subjectivity and Truth: Lectures at the Collège de France 1980–1981*. Translated by Graham Burchell. Basingstoke: Palgrave Macmillan.

Gros, Frédéric. 2011. "Course Context." Translated by Graham Burchell. In Michel Foucault, *The Courage of the Truth: Lectures at the Collège de France 1983–1984*, 343–58. Basingstoke: Palgrave Macmillan.

Guyer, Sara. 2015. *Reading with John Clare: Biopoetics, Sovereignty, Romanticism*. New York: Fordham University Press.

Hardt, Michael. 2010. "Militant Life." *New Left Review* 64: 153–69. https://newleftreview.org/issues/ii64/articles/michael-hardt-militant-life.

Hoffman, Marcelo. 2013. *Foucault and Power: The Influence of Political Engagement on Theories of Power*. London: Bloomsbury.

Lemm, Vanessa. 2014. "The Embodiment of Truth and the Politics of Community: Foucault and the Cynics." In *The Government of Life: Foucault, Biopolitics, and Neoliberalism,* edited by Vanessa Lemm and Miguel Vatter, 208–23. New York: Fordham University Press. https://doi.org/10.1515/9780823256006-014.

Ojakangas, Mika. 2016. *On the Greek Origins of Biopolitics: A Reinterpretation of the History of Biopower*. London: Routledge.

Prozorov, Sergei. 2017. "Living *à la Mode*: Form-of-Life and Democratic Biopolitics in Giorgio Agamben's *The Use of Bodies*." *Philosophy and Social Criticism* 43 (2): 144–63. https://doi.org/10.1177/0191453716662500.

Prozorov, Sergei. 2019. "Why is There Truth? Foucault in the Age of Post-Truth Politics." *Constellations: An International Journal of Critical and Democratic Theory* 26 (1): 18–30. https://doi.org/10.1111/1467-8675.12396.

Tarizzo, Davide. 2011. "The Untamed Ontology." Translated by Alvise Sforza Tarabochia. *Angelaki: Journal of the Theoretical Humanities* 16 (3): 53–61. https://doi.org/10.1080/0969725X.2011.621220.

Weber, Andreas. 2016. *Biopoetics: Towards an Existential Ecology*. New York: Springer.

9

Agamben's Aristotelian Biopolitics

Conceptual and Methodological Problems

Antonio Cimino

1. Introduction

Agamben has played a crucial role in redefining the concept of biopolitics.[1] In his *Homo Sacer* project, he has appropriated the Foucauldian legacy and combined it with key ideas taken from Arendt, Benjamin, Heidegger, and Schmitt. The result is a new, thought-provoking account of biopolitics that has been very influential since the beginning of this century across a wide and diverse range of fields, such as philosophy, cultural studies, sociology, and political theory (see, for example, Mills 2018, 37). Nonetheless, Agamben's views on biopolitics have not gone uncontested. A considerable number of objections have been leveled against both his revision of the concept of biopolitics and the historical accuracy of his analyses (see, for example, Garofalo 2009; Lemke 2011, 59–64; Mills 2018, 37–57; Ojakangas 2016, 17).[2] The aim of this chapter is to contribute to the reassessment of Agamben's account of biopolitics by discussing some conceptual and methodological problems arising from his use of Aristotelian texts. Two issues are crucial in this connection, namely, Agamben's analysis of the difference between "natural life" (Agamben 1995, 3; 1998b, 1), "politically qualified life" (Agamben 1995, 4; 1998b, 2), and "bare life [*la nuda vita*]" (Agamben 1995, 11; 1998b, 8)—in what follows, this differentiation is referred to as "the

---

[1] The *Homo Sacer* series, which has recently been completed, comprises nine books (Agamben 1995, 1998a, 2003, 2009a, 2009b, 2012, 2014, 2015a, 2015b), all of which are now available in a one-volume edition (Agamben 2018). The English translations of the nine books (Agamben 1998b, 1999, 2005, 2010, 2011, 2013a, 2013b, 2015c, 2016) are now collected in a single volume (Agamben 2017). I would like to thank Jussi Backman and Andrew Smith for their insightful comments on earlier drafts of the chapter. Parts of this chapter were presented at a research meeting organized by Professor Christoph Horn (Bonn), whom I thank for his kind invitation.

[2] Criticism has also been raised against the normative claims Agamben has put forward in the last books of the *Homo Sacer* series as well as in other publications that have appeared recently (see, for example, Cimino 2016, 2017).

Antonio Cimino, *Agamben's Aristotelian Biopolitics: Conceptual and Methodological Problems* In: *Biopolitics and Ancient Thought.*
Edited by: Jussi Backman and Antonio Cimino, Oxford University Press. © Oxford University Press 2022.
DOI: 10.1093/oso/9780192847102.003.0010

NPB-scheme"—and his general approach to Aristotelian sources within the framework of his "genealogy" (Agamben 2009a, 2011) or "archaeology" (Agamben 2009b, 2010) of biopolitics.[3] These two issues turn out to be of great importance when we want to understand how Agamben interprets the ancient roots of biopolitics.

Before providing a critical analysis of Agamben's concept of biopolitics, it is appropriate, first of all, to present the essentials of his conception, so as to understand exactly what he means by "biopolitics" and how he conceptualizes the basic characteristics of the relationship between life and the political (section 2). The ensuing reassessment moves in three directions. First, I examine the notion of exception, which Agamben takes from Schmitt and repurposes to account for the NPB-scheme (section 3). Second, I discuss Agamben's use of the NPB-scheme and show the extent to which it is exposed to a number of objections (section 4). Third, I focus on the question of whether the NPB-scheme enables us to capture the nature of power in a consistent and clear way (section 5). The paper will reach three main conclusions. The first conclusion is that the NPB-scheme, which derives from an oversimplifying interpretation of Aristotelian sources, results in an unnecessarily complicated account of biopolitics that fails to provide conceptual clarity. The second conclusion is that Agamben does not justify his use of the NPB-scheme in a persuasive manner, which becomes especially evident in a number of crucial methodological problems that remain unsolved in his genealogy of the NPB-scheme. The third conclusion is that the NPB-scheme is not helpful when it comes to explaining the nature of power.

2. Agamben's Account of Biopolitics

Agamben defines his concept of biopolitics by differentiating between "natural life," "politically qualified life," and "bare life."[4] He outlines this threefold scheme by interpreting the Aristotelian notions of *bios* and *zōē* and introducing "bare life" as an intermediate between "natural life" and political life (Agamben 1995, 3–7; 1998b, 1–4).[5] It is important to explain what these three different notions of life mean according to Agamben. The meaning of

---

[3] References to Agamben's writings include the page numbers of both the original texts and their English translations.

[4] In what follows, I use "political life" as a synonym for Agamben's term "politically qualified life."

[5] Backman (2017) explains in a very persuasive manner why the relationship between *bios* and *zōē* in Aristotle should not be read as a sharp opposition (see also Finlayson 2010; Holmes 2019; Miller 2020). For a detailed analysis of political animality in Aristotle, see Brill 2020 (especially 86–127, 171–98). See also chapter 5 by Adriel M. Trott in this volume.

political life is fairly straightforward. Political life is the life that takes place within a given human community. Agamben seems to suggest that, in this sense, political life is typical of humans. He justifies the correlation between *bios* and political life by emphasizing that *bios* always means "the form or way of living proper to an individual or a group" (Agamben 1995, 3; 1998b, 1). Political life goes beyond the scope of "natural life" because the latter is confined to "the simple fact of living common to all living beings (animals, men, or gods)" (Agamben 1995, 3; 1998b, 1), whereas the former comprises two crucial aspects that are not necessarily inherent in "the simple fact of living," namely language and the quest for the good life (Agamben 1995, 3–16; 1998b, 1–12).

The innovation Agamben introduces into this scheme is the concept of "bare life," which at first sight seems largely coextensive with the notion of "natural life." On closer inspection, however, it is inaccurate to say that Agamben uses "natural life" and "bare life" as synonymous terms. It is certainly true that Agamben uses the two terms interchangeably in the introduction to *Homo Sacer* (for example, Agamben 1995, 6–7; 1998b, 4). Nevertheless, in the course of his analysis, it becomes fairly clear that "bare life" is not the same as the "natural life" he differentiates from political life in his oversimplifying interpretation of the Aristotelian notions of *bios* and *zōē*.

This interpretation of Agamben's notion of "bare life" is confirmed by some of his statements on the issue. When applying the concept of "bare life" or *homo sacer* to contemporary politics, Agamben states that

> [s]acredness is a line of flight still present in contemporary politics, a line that is as such moving into zones increasingly vast and dark, to the point of ultimately coinciding with the biological life itself of citizens. If today there is no longer any one clear figure of the sacred man, it is perhaps because we are all virtually *homines sacri.*   (Agamben 1995, 127; 1998b, 114–15)

This quotation allows us to see very clearly that rather than being equivalent to natural or biological life in general, "bare life" coincides with the natural or biological life that has already been captured in the domain of political power (see also Agamben 1995, 205; 1998b, 183–4). In the phrase "the biological life itself of citizens," the specification "of citizens" is therefore essential. In explaining the notion of "bare life," Agamben also deploys other, more precise terms for "natural life" that distinguish it from both "bare life" and political life. These terms are *"simple natural life"* (Agamben 1995, 98; 1998b, 88) or "natural reproductive life" (Agamben 1995, 121; 1998b, 109).

At this juncture, it is important to understand why Agamben introduces the concept of "bare life." The crucial point here is the specific biopolitical scope of the NPB-scheme. The relevance of this threefold scheme to biopolitics can be explained by considering two points. First, biopolitics emerges at the intersection of "natural life" and political life when the biological (or natural) life of the people (or population) becomes one of the main concerns of political power. Second, Agamben puts forward the thesis that "bare life" is the specific object of sovereign power. This thesis is clearly stated in the introduction to *Homo Sacer*:

> [T]he inclusion of bare life in the political realm constitutes the original—if concealed—nucleus of sovereign power. *It can even be said that the production of a biopolitical body is the original activity of sovereign power.* In this sense, biopolitics is at least as old as the sovereign exception. Placing biological life at the center of its calculations, the modern State therefore does nothing other than bring to light the secret tie uniting power and bare life, thereby reaffirming the bond (derived from a tenacious correspondence between the modern and the archaic which one encounters in the most diverse spheres) between modern power and the most immemorial of the *arcana imperii*.   (Agamben 1995, 9; 1998b, 6)

This account of biopolitics is quite different from that of Foucault. Foucault presents biopolitics and biopower as phenomena typical of European or Western modernity, whereas Agamben argues that the "tie" that connects "bare life" to power is structural and "original," so that—we can draw this conclusion from the passage that has just been quoted—it defines power as such. In other words, Foucault differentiates between sovereign power and biopower, considering the former to be a premodern form of power and viewing the latter as a specific form of power that comes to the fore in modernity (Foucault 1990, 136–8). Agamben complicates this scheme by attaching a structural biopolitical meaning to sovereign power or power in general.

Nonetheless, it would be inaccurate to say that Agamben's concept of biopolitics conflates premodern forms of sovereignty with modern politics so as to produce a general and ahistorical account of power. Indeed, he is quite alive to the distinctions between the various historical forms of biopolitics. It is precisely from this perspective that his statements on the novelty of Nazi biopolitics must be read (see Agamben 1995, 164–5; 1998b, 147–8). Agamben thus outlines a historical evolution of biopolitics, which he does not confine to modernity. It is therefore not correct to say that Agamben's account of biopolitics is based on an "ahistorical" conception of "bare life."[6] Agamben attempts to combine two lines of analysis in order to provide a new understanding of biopolitics, which deviates significantly from Foucault's genealogy of biopower (Agamben 1995, 12; 1998b, 9).[7]

The first line of analysis reworks the Foucauldian thesis concerning the intrinsic link between biopolitics and modernity. On the one hand, Agamben agrees with the thesis that modern biopolitics has peculiar features that cannot be identified in other epochs of Western political history. On the other hand, he disagrees with Foucault about the nature of those features. For Agamben, the main characteristic of modern biopolitics is not the fact that biological life "becomes a principal object of the projections and calculations of State power" (Agamben 1995, 12; 1998b, 9), because the relevance of biological life to political power can already be recognized in antiquity.

The second trajectory of Agamben's analysis draws on the Schmittian account of exception and provides an answer to the question of what exactly characterizes modern biopolitics. The thesis Agamben puts forward is that it is no longer possible to make a sharp differentiation between the exception and the rule, between the domain of "bare life" and the domain of the political. Agamben seems to suggest that the evolution of Western politics coincides with a process that leads to an "irreducible indistinction" (Agamben 1995, 12; 1998b, 9). In sum, Agamben recalibrates the Foucauldian thesis about the emergence of biopolitics by using conceptual resources he borrows from Schmitt. At this juncture, it is appropriate to explain in more detail how Agamben uses Schmitt's concept of exception when articulating the relation between "natural life," political life, and "bare life."

3. Life and Exception: Reconceptualizing Biopolitics

Agamben understands the concept of exception in terms of "an inclusive exclusion" (Agamben 1995, 11; 1998b, 8). He uses this concept to reinterpret the notions of *bios* and *zōē* in a manner that hardly remains true to their

---

[6] This critique against Agamben is formulated, for example, by Lemke (2011, 62–3).

[7] Lemke differentiates very persuasively between three main accounts of biopolitics in Foucault's work (see Lemke 2011, 33–52). Each of these three accounts suggests an intrinsic relationship between biopolitics and modernity. First, "biopolitics [in Foucault, A.C.] stands for a historical rupture in political thinking and practice that is characterized by a rearticulation of sovereign power" (34). This "rearticulation," which takes place in modernity, consists in the transition from sovereign power—that is, power understood in terms of "seizure" or "deduction" (Foucault 1990, 136)—to biopower, which is believed to "*foster* life" (138) by managing the population and disciplining bodies. The second meaning links biopolitics with the emergence of nineteenth- and twentieth-century racism. The third account concerns the relationship between biopolitics and liberalism.

Aristotelian sources. The concept of "inclusive exclusion" can be explained by analyzing two passages in which Agamben elaborates on his interpretation of Schmitt. In the first passage, Agamben explains:

> The exception is a kind of exclusion. What is excluded from the general rule is an individual case. But the most proper characteristic of the exception is that what is excluded in it is not, on account of being excluded, absolutely without relation to the rule. On the contrary, what is excluded in the exception maintains itself in relation to the rule in the form of the rule's suspension.
>
> (Agamben 1995, 21–2; 1998b, 17–18)

It must be noted, first of all, that this paraphrase of Schmitt's concept of exception concentrates on its juridical meaning, which becomes conspicuous when it comes to defining the nature of the sovereign as the one "who decides on the exception" (Schmitt 2005, 5; see also Agamben 1995, 15; 1998b, 11). Agamben draws attention to the crucial fact that exception must be understood as a peculiar type of exclusion, whereby what is excluded is still related to that from which it is excluded. It is for this reason that Agamben rephrases Schmitt's account, thereby defining exception as "inclusive exclusion."

Agamben, however, goes beyond the purely juridical meaning of exception, so as to formulate a more general and formal account of it. In the second passage, we read that "[w]e shall give the name *relation of exception* to the extreme form of relation by which something is included solely through its exclusion" (Agamben 1995, 22; 1998b, 18). Agamben uses this account of exception in various ways. It is worth realizing that he does not abandon the juridical (or Schmittian) meaning of exception (that is, exception as the state of exception). The juridical meaning still plays a crucial role in his more historico-empirical account of modern biopolitics, that is, when he analyzes the manner in which the state of exception is inherent in twentieth-century political and juridical systems (Agamben 2003, 2005).

Nonetheless, Agamben does not confine himself to accepting Schmitt's notion of exception and his "juridico-institutional" (Agamben 1995, 9; 1998b, 6) approach to power. He deems it necessary to combine it with Foucault's biopolitical approach. This combination leads Agamben to widen the scope of the concept of exception to such an extent that the very relation between sovereign power and life is now conceptualized in terms of exception, that is, as "inclusive exclusion." It is "*the original activity of sovereign power*"—that is, "*the production of a biopolitical body*"—that has to be seen as exception, which implies an inclusion of "bare life" into the domain of sovereign power "by means of an exclusion" (Agamben 1995, 9–10; 1998b, 6–7). In this sense, the exception no longer means (only) the emergence of the state of exception but the specific manner in which sovereign power is connected to life. In other words, "the exception is the structure of sovereignty" (Agamben 1995, 34; 1998b, 28), so that the state of exception, on which the sovereign decides, ends up being only one aspect of a more fundamental structure that defines the nature of sovereignty itself.

In section 5, I will raise the question of whether this definition of (sovereign) power is plausible and convincing. At this juncture, I want to draw attention to how Agamben uses the notion of exception to explain both the relationship between (sovereign) power and (bare) life, and the relationship between "natural life," political life, and "bare life." To this end, it is appropriate to elaborate on the passage that has just been quoted. Not only does Agamben consider the exception to be "the structure of sovereignty," thereby claiming to identify *the* essential aspect of sovereign power in general. He also argues that the relation of exception has an explanatory function when we want to describe both the historical origin and the development of Western politics. This is how we have to understand his thesis that "biopolitics is at least as old as the sovereign exception" (Agamben 1995, 9; 1998b, 6). He thereby rejects the Foucauldian thesis concerning the modern origin of biopolitics and suggests that politics and biopolitics coincide: "The structure of the exception…appears from this perspective to be consubstantial with Western politics" (Agamben 1995, 10; 1998b, 7). Agamben thus portrays the birth of Western politics as the emergence of the relation of exception between sovereignty and life. He goes so far as to describe the history of Western politics as the history of the various ways in which such a relation of exception has unfolded. This allows him to reformulate the Foucauldian thesis about modern biopolitics. From this perspective, it is true that according to Agamben, biopolitics is not typical of Western modernity. It is nonetheless possible to identify a specific characteristic of modern biopolitics, that is, the fact that "the realm of bare life—which is originally situated at the margins of the political order—gradually begins to coincide with the political realm" (Agamben 1995, 12; 1998b, 9).

In other words, the boundaries between "natural life," political life, and "bare life" are subject to historical development. Agamben therefore asks us to pay attention to how this blurred boundary ("indistinction") between "natural life," political life, and "bare life" manifests itself in a different manner in each epoch of Western political history. It must also be noted that there are passages of *Homo Sacer* in which Agamben takes his reformulation of the concept of exception to extremes, in such a way that he argues that the role of language in the emergence of politics can also be explained in terms of exception (Agamben 1995, 11; 1998b, 7–8). With such statements, Agamben seems to suggest that the relation of exception defines not only the history of Western politics but also the history of humankind in general.

After examining the manner in which Agamben uses, or rather abuses, the concept of exception, the most intuitive question that arises is whether the overextension of this notion prevents us from conceptualizing the scope of sovereign power in a fruitful way. A number of objections can be leveled against Agamben in this regard.

First, Agamben suggests that the relation of exception is the privileged way of analyzing sovereign power. He does not, however, provide compelling evidence that alternative notions do not supply us with conceptual tools that are similarly useful when it comes to analyzing the nature of power. He does not even test the concept of exception by comparing it with other theoretical models. Agamben confines himself to postulating that the structure of sovereignty is a relation of exception. When he argues that *"the original activity of sovereign power"* is *"the production of a biopolitical body"* (Agamben 1995, 9; 1998b, 6), he ultimately means that "bare life" is in essence life that is exposed to death and violence (see section 5). Nevertheless, the structure of the exception is by no means necessary to arrive at this conclusion.

Second, the concept of exception could at best explain *how* sovereign power deals with "bare life," but it does not illuminate the specific reasons *why* sovereign power is supposed to include life by excluding it. We can also ask why we must insist on the primacy of such an "inclusive exclusion" as if this were the prominent activity of sovereign power. Agamben seems to consider the relation of exception to be *the* a priori structure specific to power. We can certainly concede that spatial relationships of inclusion and exclusion—be they literal or figurative—are intrinsic to power, but we have no evidence that spatial relationships are the only a priori structures that make the nature of power intelligible.

Third, critical questions can also be raised with regard to Agamben's use of the relation of exception when it is introduced to elucidate the intricate relationship between "natural life," political life, and "bare life." It is not self-evident that the concept of "inclusive exclusion" is the most appropriate way to describe how "natural life" (*zōē*) and political life (*bios*) intersect in humans. As Agamben himself reminds us, it goes without saying that the most obvious—and traditional—way to interpret the Aristotelian definition of man as a political animal is to say that "political" is "a specific difference that determines the genus *zōon*" (Agamben 1995, 5; 1998b, 2). It is not clear why we should give up this reading in favor of the alternative interpretation based on the concept of exception. Further considerations lead us to challenge the way Agamben interprets the Aristotelian notions of *bios* and *zōē* through the lens of the exception.

4. Agamben's Use of the NPB-scheme: Objections and Open Questions

I have so far shown the extent to which Agamben's rethinking of biopolitics in terms of the NPB-scheme is exposed to a number of objections. Agamben introduces the notion of "bare life" to reconceptualize the intersection of *bios* and *zōē*. I have argued that this account of biopolitics is not satisfactory, however, because it is based on the unwarranted overextension of the Schmittian notion of exception, which does not allow us to account for the relationship between "natural life," political life, and "bare life" in a persuasive manner. Agamben's differentiation between "natural life," political life, and "bare life" does not seem very convincing for the numerous reasons I have discussed in the preceding section. He initially appears to emphasize the difference between "natural life" and political life, but afterwards he introduces the notion of "bare life" as "a zone of indistinction" (Agamben 1995, 121; 1998b, 109). The question therefore arises as to why we initially need to differentiate elements or aspects that eventually end up being conflated with one another. The aim of this section is to elaborate on Agamben's use of the NPB-scheme and to show that it leaves a considerable number of crucial questions open.

4.1 Nature, Politics, and Culture

The first issue that comes to the fore in this connection is that Agamben seems to use the NPB-scheme to conceptualize the nature-culture relationship as well. Agamben's differentiation between "natural life" and political life seems to parallel the differentiation between nature and culture, and "bare life" serves as an intermediate element both between "natural life" and political life, and between nature and culture.[8] The following quote provides evidence of such an overlap: "[T]his life is not simply natural reproductive

---

[8] For the purposes of my analysis, I adopt Edward Burnett Tylor's definition of culture as "that complex whole which includes knowledge, belief, art, morals, law, custom, and any other capabilities and habits acquired by man as a member of society" (Tylor 1958, 1).

life, the *zoē* of the Greeks, nor *bios*, a qualified form of life. It is, rather, the bare life of *homo sacer* and the *wargus*, a zone of indistinction and continuous transition between man and beast, nature and culture" (Agamben 1995, 121; 1998b, 109).

The scheme can also be made more complicated by noting that the traditional definition of the human as a political animal goes hand in hand with the definition of the human as the animal equipped with *logos*. This point, which is explicitly discussed by Agamben (see Agamben 1995, 11; 1998b, 7–8), is quite crucial when it comes to clarifying the connection between the two parallels just mentioned—that is, the parallel between nature and politics and the one between nature and culture. These two parallels seem to overlap and even coincide to an extent that Agamben does not, however, clarify. This overlap or coincidence is clearly attested to by the way in which Agamben recapitulates the meaning of the concept of "bare life" in the conclusion of *Homo Sacer*. Agamben states: "The fundamental activity of sovereign power is the production of bare life as originary political element and as threshold of articulation between nature and culture, *zoē* and *bios*" (Agamben 1995, 202; 1998b, 181). This phrasing leads me to formulate a number of questions that Agamben's account of biopolitics leaves unanswered. I would like to draw particular attention to three problems.

1. The first problem concerns the relationship between politics and culture. It is not clear whether Agamben thinks politics and culture coincide, and, if they do, to what extent such coincidence can be ascertained. We can certainly say that politics is cultural, since we cannot imagine political phenomena without assuming the structural relationship between politics and language. This is precisely the crucial point that Agamben wants to emphasize when he concentrates his attention on the role of the law. The formulation of laws and norms is inconceivable without language.[9] The same applies to all rituals and practices that constitute the domain of the political and involve forms of linguistic performativity.[10] We can therefore certainly agree with Agamben on the fact that the two traditional definitions of human being (that is, the human as a political animal and as an animal equipped with *logos*) cannot be separated. Nevertheless, the question arises as to whether we may also maintain that culture as such is political, and, if so, to what

---

[9] For the essential link between language, politics, and law, see especially *The Sacrament of Language* (Agamben 2009b, 2010).

[10] Agamben's major investigation into this subject is certainly the comprehensive study *The Kingdom and the Glory* (Agamben 2009a, 2011).

extent. Agamben does not seem to provide any clear answer to this question.

2. If the domains of politics and culture do not coincide, then a second problem emerges, that is, whether we have to rearticulate the NPB-scheme by introducing a fourth element—that is, culture. If we subscribe to Agamben's scheme, culture seems to overlap with both political life and "bare life" because political life and "bare life" both involve language, rituals, and political practices. If culture is conceptually and in reality different from both "bare life" and political life, it is plausible to introduce a fourth component and name it "cultural life" or simply "culture." If this is the case, it is not clear how we should rearticulate the nature-culture divide. This leads to the third problem.

3. If we assume for the sake of argument that the nature-politics intersection and the nature-culture intersection coincide, the question then arises as to whether it is appropriate to present the differentiation between nature and culture in terms of exception. We must then explain in what sense "natural life" is an exception (in the technical sense put forward by Agamben) in relation to culture. Agamben does not seem to provide an answer to this question either.

4.2 Methodological Issues

The precise scope of Agamben's differentiation between and conflation of "natural life," political life, and "bare life" is not clear. It may indeed be interpreted in conceptual, ontological, or historical terms.

If we interpret the NPB-scheme in *conceptual* terms, we imply that the scope of Agamben's investigations only includes the way philosophy has traditionally conceptualized the nature of power, so that this question is not necessarily relevant to the actual political practices of Western history.

If we interpret the NPB-scheme in *ontological* terms—that is, if we assume that the NPB-scheme reflects differentiations and intersections that are factually given in reality—then Agamben would have to clarify the way in which philosophical conceptualization and actual practices are linked to one another. Does philosophical conceptualization confine itself to reflecting actual practices? And if so, how accurately? Or does philosophical conceptualization have an impact on actual practices? What is the nature of this effect?

If we interpret the NPB-scheme in *historical* terms, we imply that the threefold differentiation is not a natural given but is subject to historical evolution, so that, for instance, what is—or is understood as—"natural life" in antiquity does not necessarily coincide with what is—or is understood as—"natural life" in our age. It goes without saying that historical evolution can be relevant to the NPB-scheme when we interpret it in conceptual or in ontological terms. This also means that the three possible interpretations of the NPB-scheme can be combined. The problem here is not that we must choose one of these possible interpretations. We may certainly accept one, two, or all of them. The issue here is rather the fact that Agamben does not elucidate the nature of the NPB-scheme.

An example can help me to clarify this important point. If we assume that the NPB-scheme must be interpreted in conceptual terms, then the question arises as to how we must interpret Agamben's use of the Aristotelian notions of *bios* and *zōē*. We can point out a number of methodological issues that come into play if we raise this question.

1. Agamben seems to imply that the Aristotelian differentiation between *bios* and *zōē* is much more than one philosophical conceptualization among others.[11] He clearly takes for granted that the *zōē*/*bios* distinction is representative of "the classical world" (Agamben 1995, 3; 1998b, 1). As a result, Agamben's use of this distinction relies on three unquestioned assumptions. The first assumption is that Aristotle's writings are not just one philosophical source among many others but rather privileged philosophical texts. The origin of this assumption can be located with a reasonable degree of certainty in the work of Heidegger and Arendt, who are known to be crucial sources of inspiration for Agamben's philosophical work.[12] The second assumption is that philosophical texts are not just one source among many others (literary, historical, juridical, medical, epigraphic, and other texts) but rather privileged texts in general. The third assumption is that Aristotle is representative of "the classical world" as such. This assumption is far from being self-evident for the simple reason that antiquity is much more differentiated and fragmented than Agamben seems to suggest.

2. We can concede for the sake of argument that Aristotle's writings are privileged sources among both philosophical and nonphilosophical texts, and are representative of the way "the classical world" articulates the differentiation between *bios* and *zōē* when the specific nature of political community must be defined. However, it is not clear to what

---

[11] In what follows, when I speak of "the Aristotelian differentiation between *bios* and *zōē*" or "the Aristotelian account of the relation between *bios* and *zōē*," I actually mean Agamben's interpretation of that differentiation or account.

[12] For a well-articulated critique of Heidegger's idealization of the Greeks, see Most 2002.

extent the Aristotelian account of the relation between *bios* and *zōē* can also provide us with reliable information about the actual social and political practices of "the classical world." The fact that a thinker or an intellectual describes social and political phenomena in a certain way does not necessarily mean that his or her description is an accurate report of actual states of affairs. In other words, philosophical discourse and actual political practice do not necessarily go hand in hand with one another. This statement applies to the terms bilaterally. This means philosophical discourse does not necessarily reflect actual social and political practices. At the same time, philosophical discourse does not necessarily translate into social and political practices.

3. We can again concede for the sake of argument not only that Aristotle's writings are privileged sources among both philosophical and nonphilosophical texts but also that they are an accurate description of social and political practices in Athens in the fourth century BCE, in the other Greek cities, and in general in "the classical world." And we can also concede that Aristotle's texts reflect actual social and political practices to a high degree. It remains unclear, however, what this tells us about social and political practices in the other epochs of Western history. It is not at all self-evident that the Aristotelian account of the relation between *bios* and *zōē* has remained the fundamental frame of reference in subsequent epochs. A considerable number of ruptures and discontinuities in both the history of philosophical thought and the history of social and political institutions and practices can be noted (see Ojakangas 2017). Agamben himself outlines an evolution of biopolitics (see, for example, Agamben 1995, 123; 1998b, 111), but he does not clarify whether such an evolution affects philosophical discourse only or political discourses and practices as well—nor, indeed, how it does so.

5. The NPB-scheme and the Nature of Power

In the preceding sections, I have explained how Agamben deploys the Schmittian notion of exception in order to provide a new interpretation of the Aristotelian notions of *bios* and *zōē*, which results in the NPB-scheme. I have argued that Agamben's interpretation causes a number of conceptual and methodological difficulties. In this last section, I very briefly discuss the extent to which the structure of the exception and the NPB-scheme are the best ways to capture the nature of power. First of all, it is important to look at how Agamben defines sovereign power by using the concept of exception and arguing that power itself—not only life and its articulations (that is, "natural life," political life, and "bare life")—is also structurally linked to the logic of the exception in multiple ways.

The first thing to notice is that when Agamben elaborates on the exceptional nature of sovereign power, he does not confine himself to applying the Schmittian definition of the sovereign as the one "who decides on the exception." He refines this definition by pointing out other specific ways in which sovereign power is exceptional. I would like to draw special attention to two peculiar ways in which the exceptional nature of power becomes apparent. They are both discussed by Agamben in *Homo Sacer* (Agamben 1995, 114–15; 1998b, 102–3).

The first exceptional characteristic of the sovereign is that "the killing of the sovereign" is never "classified simply as an act of homicide" (Agamben 1995, 114; 1998b, 102). It is a special crime, which is not comparable to regular homicide and therefore deserves special judicial treatment. The second exceptional characteristic of the sovereign is that he or she may not be subject to "an ordinary legal trial" (Agamben 1995, 115; 1998b, 103)— as is the case, for instance, with the procedure of impeachment. The point that Agamben wants to put forward when discussing the exceptional nature of the sovereign is the following: not only is the object of power, that is, "bare life," characterized by the relation of "exception" (Agamben 1995, 21–2; 1998b, 17–18) in the various intricate ways that we have already pointed out, the bearer of power, too, has an exceptional nature because frequently those who hold such an office are not subject to the law in the same way and to the same extent as citizens. It is also worth noting that the intrinsic relationship between sovereign power and exception is not only structural. It is also the historical evolution of power that is described by Agamben as a development of the exceptional nature of "bare life." According to him, the various ways in which the exception of "bare life" takes shape correspond to different forms of (bio)political power.

The question arises as to whether using the structure of the exception is the best way to capture the nature of power. When appropriating the Schmittian definition of the sovereign as the one "who decides on the exception," Agamben clearly chooses to give priority to the concept of exception and to pay scant attention to the concept of decision. It is clear that Agamben insists on the primacy of the exception when he wants to identify "[t]he original political relation" (Agamben 1995, 202; 1998b, 181), whereas decision seems to play an ancillary role in this connection. In other words, decision is considered to be the decision *of* the exception in the sense of both a *genitivus subiectivus* and a *genitivus obiectivus*. It is the decision made by sovereign power, which is entitled to such a decision because of its exceptional nature. At the same time, it is also the decision about the inclusion and exclusion of "bare life." I am not arguing that the importance of the concept of exception is not justified. It does indeed go without saying that it is a matter of choice, and there are no doubt many different reasons to prioritize one or the other of the two concepts. We should rather ask ourselves which of the two concepts is more appropriate for a general definition of power. I am convinced that the concept of exception makes things unnecessarily complicated. The structure of exception is not the only conceptual resource which would allow us to draw the conclusion that, as Agamben puts it, "*the production of a bio-political body is the original activity of sovereign power*" (Agamben 1995, 9; 1998b, 6) or that "*life exposed to death (bare life or sacred life) is the originary political element*" (Agamben 1995, 98; 1998b, 88).

Even if we accept these two definitions, the question then arises whether the structure of exception is actually more fundamental than the concept of decision when it comes to defining power. If we want to adhere to these two formulations, nothing prevents us from using the concept of decision to reconceptualize power and to say, for instance, that the sovereign is the one who decides on the life or death of those who are subject to him or her. Moreover, if "*life exposed to death (bare life or sacred life) is the originary political element*" (Agamben 1995, 98; 1998b, 88) that defines the nature of sovereign power, it is not clear why the life of nonhuman animals, which is naturally exposed to death and violence, may not be considered to be an "*originary political element*" to the same extent. We face the same problems that already arose in our discussion of both the boundaries between nature, politics, and culture, and the boundaries between "natural life," political life, and "bare life": Agamben introduces differentiations that do not help us gain real conceptual clarity and end up causing more problems than they can actually solve. The nature of power seems more diverse and intricate than Agamben appears to suggest when he links sovereign power with "bare life" and introduces the NPB-scheme. Thus, it would seem that Agamben's Schmittian reading of the Aristotelian notions of *bios* and *zōē* proves neither persuasive nor compelling.

Despite these primarily negative conclusions about Agamben's approach to both Aristotle and the history of biopower in general, I am convinced that his *Homo Sacer* project can provide us with a number of fruitful suggestions and intuitions, which should be refined and developed in a different manner. I think Agamben is fundamentally right in arguing that Foucault's understanding of the history of biopower must be corrected. In this regard, I am inclined to agree with Agamben, against Foucault, that biopower does not emerge only in modernity but is coextensive with power as such. Agamben's exhortations to investigate the origin of biopower in antiquity are therefore worth taking seriously. They rightly challenge optimistic and simplistic assumptions about modernity, which very often turns out to be less modern than is usually believed. From this point of view, Agamben seems to head in the right direction when he challenges Foucault's distinction between sovereign power and biopower and points out the various ways in which sovereign violence still defines modern democracies.[13]

Having said that, this chapter has tried to show the extent to which Agamben's account of biopolitics, which is largely based on the reformulation of Schmitt's notion of exception, is undermined by important shortcomings that challenge his version of the history of biopower, in particular his approach to Aristotle. The application of the Schmittian notion of exception to ancient Greek and Roman sources risks losing sight of the multiple and intricate forms of biopower and biopolitics that come to the fore in Western history and philosophy. While we certainly need to correct Foucault's narrative and reconsider the history of biopower, we also need to scrutinize the extent to which Agamben's alternative story is philosophically convincing and historically accurate.

References

Agamben, Giorgio. 1995. *Homo sacer: Il potere sovrano e la nuda vita*. Turin: Einaudi.

Agamben, Giorgio. 1998a. *Quel che resta di Auschwitz: L'archivio e il testimone*. Turin: Bollati Boringhieri.

Agamben, Giorgio. 1998b. *Homo Sacer: Sovereign Power and Bare Life*. Translated by Daniel Heller-Roazen. Stanford, CA: Stanford University Press.

Agamben, Giorgio. 1999. *Remnants of Auschwitz: The Witness and the Archive*. Translated by Daniel Heller-Roazen. New York: Zone Books.

Agamben, Giorgio. 2003. *Stato di eccezione*. Turin: Bollati Boringhieri.

Agamben, Giorgio. 2005. *State of Exception*. Translated by Kevin Attell. Chicago: University of Chicago Press.

Agamben, Giorgio. 2008. *Signatura rerum: Sul metodo*. Turin: Bollati Boringhieri.

---

[13] This different approach to the history of biopower is compatible with Foucault's idea of "a historical ontology of ourselves" (Foucault 1984, 45). Even if biopower is coextensive with power as such and has therefore always existed, it has also changed historically; accordingly, a historical investigation into the different forms of biopower remains relevant to an "archaeological" and "genealogical" analysis of modern governmentality. On genealogy and archaeology, see Foucault 1984, 45–6; Agamben 2008, 2009c.

Agamben, Giorgio. 2009a. *Il Regno e la Gloria: Per una genealogia teologica dell'economia e del governo*. Turin: Bollati Boringhieri.

Agamben, Giorgio. 2009b. *Il sacramento del linguaggio: Archeologia del giuramento*. 2nd ed. Rome: Laterza.

Agamben, Giorgio. 2009c. *The Signature of All Things: On Method*. Translated by Luca D'Isanto with Kevin Attell. New York: Zone Books.

Agamben, Giorgio. 2010. *The Sacrament of Language: An Archaeology of the Oath*. Translated by Adam Kotsko. Stanford, CA: Stanford University Press.

Agamben, Giorgio. 2011. *The Kingdom and the Glory: For a Theological Genealogy of Economy and Government*. Translated by Lorenzo Chiesa with Matteo Mandarini. Stanford, CA: Stanford University Press.

Agamben, Giorgio. 2012. *Opus Dei: Archeologia dell'ufficio*. Turin: Bollati Boringhieri.

Agamben, Giorgio. 2013a. *The Highest Poverty: Monastic Rules and Form-of-Life*. Translated by Adam Kotsko. Stanford, CA: Stanford University Press.

Agamben, Giorgio. 2013b. *Opus Dei: An Archaeology of Duty*. Translated by Adam Kotsko. Stanford, CA: Stanford University Press.

Agamben, Giorgio. 2014. *L'uso dei corpi*. Vicenza: Neri Pozza Editore.

Agamben, Giorgio. 2015a. *Altissima povertà: Regole monastiche e forma di vita*. 5th ed. Vicenza: Neri Pozza Editore.

Agamben, Giorgio. 2015b. *Stasis: La guerra civile come paradigma politico*. Turin: Bollati Boringhieri.

Agamben, Giorgio. 2015c. *Stasis: Civil War as a Political Paradigm*. Translated by Nicholas Heron. Stanford, CA: Stanford University Press.

Agamben, Giorgio. 2016. *The Use of Bodies*. Translated by Adam Kotsko. Stanford, CA: Stanford University Press.

Agamben, Giorgio. 2017. *The Omnibus Homo Sacer*. Stanford, CA: Stanford University Press.

Agamben, Giorgio. 2018. *Homo sacer: Edizione integrale 1995–2015*. Macerata: Quodlibet.

Backman, Jussi. 2017. "Aristotle." In *Agamben's Philosophical Lineage*, edited by Adam Kotsko and Carlo Salzani, 15–26. Edinburgh: Edinburgh University Press. https://doi.org/10.3366/edinburgh/9781474423632.003.0002.

Brill, Sara. 2020. *Aristotle on the Concept of Shared Life*. Oxford: Oxford University Press.

Cimino, Antonio. 2016. "Agamben's Political Messianism in 'The Time That Remains.'" *International Journal of Philosophy and Theology* 77 (3): 102–18. https://doi.org/10.1080/21692327.2016.1226934.

Cimino, Antonio. 2017. "Europe and Paul of Tarsus: Giorgio Agamben on the Overcoming of Europe's Crisis." In *Saint Paul and Philosophy: The Consonance of Ancient and Modern Thought*, edited by Gert-Jan van der Heiden, George van

Kooten, and Antonio Cimino, 297–308. Berlin: De Gruyter. https://doi.org/10.1515/9783110547467-017.

Finlayson, James Gordon. 2010. "'Bare Life' and Politics in Agamben's Reading of Aristotle." *The Review of Politics* 72 (1): 97–126. https://doi.org/10.1017/S0034670509990982.

Foucault, Michel. 1984. *The Foucault Reader.* Edited by Paul Rabinow. New York: Pantheon.

Foucault, Michel. 1990. *The History of Sexuality.* Vol. 1, *An Introduction.* Translated by Robert Hurley. New York: Vintage Books.

Garofalo, Luigi. 2009. *Biopolitica e diritto romano.* Naples: Jovene.

Holmes, Brooke. 2019. "Bios." *Political Concepts: A Critical Lexicon,* no. 5. Accessed September 26, 2019. https://www.politicalconcepts.org/bios-brooke-holmes.

Lemke, Thomas. 2011. *Biopolitics: An Advanced Introduction.* Translated by Eric Frederick Trump. New York: New York University Press.

Miller, Paul Allen. 2020. "Against Agamben: Or Living Your Life, *Zōē* versus *Bios* in the Late Foucault." In *Biotheory: Life and Death under Capitalism*, edited by Jeffrey R. Di Leo and Peter Hitchcock, 23–41. New York: Routledge. https://doi.org/10.4324/9781003021506-3.

Mills, Catherine. 2018. *Biopolitics.* London: Routledge.

Most, Glenn W. 2002. "Heidegger's Greeks." *Arion: A Journal of Humanities and the Classics* 10 (1): 83–98.

Ojakangas, Mika. 2016. *On the Greek Origins of Biopolitics: A Reinterpretation of the History of Biopower.* London: Routledge.

Ojakangas, Mika. 2017. "Biopolitics in the Political Thought of Classical Greece." In *The Routledge Handbook of Biopolitics*, edited by Sergei Prozorov and Simona Rentea, 23–35. London: Routledge. https://doi.org/10.4324/9781315612751-2.

Schmitt, Carl. 2005. *Political Theology: Four Chapters on the Concept of Sovereignty.* Translated by George Schwab. Chicago: University of Chicago Press.

Tylor, Edward Burnett. 1958. *The Origins of Culture.* New York: Harper & Brothers.

Index